CELEBRITY HUMANITARIANISM AND NORTH–SOUTH RELATIONS

Discussion over celebrity engagement is often limited to theoretical critique or normative name-calling, without much grounded research into what it is that celebrities are doing, the same or differently throughout the world. Crucially, little attention has been paid to the Global South, either as a place where celebrities intervene into existing politics and social processes, or as the generator of Southern celebrities engaged in 'do-gooding'. This book examines what the diverse roster of celebrity humanitarians are actually doing in and across North and South contexts. Celebrity humanitarianism is an effective lens for viewing the multiple and diverse relationships that constitute the links between North and South. New empirical findings on celebrity humanitarianism on the ground in Thailand, Malawi, Bangladesh, South Africa, China, Haiti, Congo, US, Denmark and Australia illustrate the impact of celebrity humanitarianism in the Global South and celebritization, participation and democratization in the donor North. By investigating one of the most mediatized and distant representations of humanitarianism (the celebrity intervention) from a perspective of contextualization, the book underscores the importance of context in international development.

This book will be of interest to students and researchers in the fields of development studies, celebrity studies, anthropology, political science, geography, and related disciplines. It is also of great relevance to development practitioners, humanitarian NGOs, and professionals in business (CSR, fair trade) who work in the increasingly celebritized field.

Lisa Ann Richey is Professor of International Development Studies in the Department of Society and Globalisation, Roskilde University, Denmark.

CELEBRITY HUMANITARIANISM AND NORTH–SOUTH RELATIONS

Politics, place and power

Edited by Lisa Ann Richey

Routledge
Taylor & Francis Group

LONDON AND NEW YORK

First published 2016
by Routledge
2 Park Square, Milton Park, Abingdon, Oxon OX14 4RN

and by Routledge
711 Third Avenue, New York, NY 10017

Routledge is an imprint of the Taylor & Francis Group, an informa business

2016 selection and editorial matter, Lisa Ann Richey; individual chapters, the contributors

British Library Cataloguing-in-Publication Data
A catalogue record for this book is available from the British Library

Library of Congress Cataloging-in-Publication Data
Celebrity humanitarianism and North–South relations : politics, place and power / edited by Lisa Ann Richey.
pages cm
Includes bibliographical references and index.
1. Humanitarianism—Developing countries—Case studies.
2. Celebrities—Political activity—Case studies. I Richey, Lisa Ann.
BJ1475.3.C45 2016
361.7'4—dc23
2015009677

ISBN: 978-1-138-85427-7 (hbk)
ISBN: 978-1-138-85428-4 (pbk)
ISBN: 978-1-315-72118-7 (ebk)

Typeset in Bembo
by Swales & Willis Ltd, Exeter, Devon, UK

Dedicated to Sandra Ann Richey,
who might just have a copy of *The Star* lying around near her chair

CONTENTS

FIGURES

CONTRIBUTORS

Dan Brockington is a Professor of Conservation and Development at the School of Environment, Education and Development, University of Manchester, UK. His research covers diverse aspects of development, with much attention on the dynamics of long-term livelihood change (especially in Tanzania) and the social consequences of conservation policy (globally). His interest in celebrity stems from exploring the role of celebrity in environmental affairs, and this has led to an examination of its role in development more broadly. This means his research spans remote village locations to plush fundraising events, which can be confusing. His books include: *Fortress Conservation* (2002), *Nature Unbound* (with Rosaleen Duffy and Jim Igoe, 2008), *Celebrity and the Environment* (2009) and *Celebrity Advocacy and International Development* (2014).

Lene Bull Christiansen is an Associate Professor at the Department of Culture and Identity at Roskilde University, Denmark. She holds a PhD in International Development Studies from the same institution and holds a post-doctoral research grant from the Danish Council for Independent Research. Her research focuses on Danish celebrity involvement in development aid campaigning. She organizes the Roskilde University-based research cluster Celebrities as New Global Actors, and is a Core Researcher of the Research Network on Celebrity and North–South Relations.

Alexandra Cosima Budabin is a Center for Human Rights Research Fellow and Adjunct Professor at the University of Dayton, USA. She holds a PhD in Politics from the New School for Social Research (USA). Her work focuses on non-state actors in human rights, humanitarianism, genocide, and conflict resolution. A Core Researcher of the Network on Celebrity and North–South Relations, Alexandra has written about Mia Farrow and Ben Affleck.

Johanna Hood is an Assistant Professor of International Development Studies at Roskilde University, Denmark. She received her PhD from the University of

Technology, Sydney, in International Studies. Beyond examining alternative forms of celebrity, Johanna's research interests include the impacts of race and ethnicity on media and public health campaigns, welfare in China, and China's plasma economies. She is the author of *HIV/AIDS, Health and the Media in China: Imagined Immunity through Racialized Disease* (2011). Johanna is a Core Researcher of the Research Network on Celebrity and North–South Relations.

Mary Mostafanezhad is an Assistant Professor in the Department of Geography at the University of Hawai'i at Manoa. Mary's current research is situated at the intersection of critical geopolitics and cultural and development studies and explores popular humanitarianism in several contexts including tourism, fair trade, celebrity humanitarianism and corporate social responsibility. Mary is the author of *Volunteer Tourism: Popular Humanitarianism in Neoliberal Times* (2014) and co-editor of *At Home and in the Field: Ethnographic Encounters in Asia and the Pacific Islands* (2015) and *Moral Encounters in Tourism* (2014). She is also a board member for the Association of American Geographers Recreation, Tourism and Sport Specialty Group, the co-founder of the American Anthropological Association Anthropology of Tourism Interest Group as well as the Critical Tourism Studies Asia-Pacific Consortium, an affiliated faculty member in the Thai Studies Department at the University of Hawai'i at Manoa and an affiliated researcher in the Research Network on Celebrity and North–South Relations.

Danai Mupotsa is a Lecturer in the School of Literature, Language and Media at the University of the Witwatersrand, South Africa. She received her PhD in African Literature from the same institution. Areas of interest include performance studies, queer theory, gender, sexualities and feminist theory, affect theory, new materialisms, visual analysis, critical race theory, popular culture, psychoanalysis, and Southern African, North American and Caribbean literatures.

Mette Fog Olwig is an Assistant Professor in International Development Studies at the Department of Society and Globalisation at Roskilde University, Denmark. Her research has included projects on ethical production, investments and consumption, and the social dimensions of climate change and development in Ghana, Tanzania and Vietnam. She received her PhD in Geography from the University of Copenhagen. Mette is a Core Researcher of the Research Network on Celebrity and North–South Relations.

Louise Mubanda Rasmussen is an Assistant Professor in International Development Studies at the Department of Society and Globalisation, Roskilde University, Denmark. She holds a PhD in African Studies from the University of Copenhagen. Her work focuses on the interrelations between representations of development and local practices of development, with an emphasis on HIV/AIDS interventions implemented by local NGOs and faith-based organizations. She is currently working on a post-doctoral research project entitled "Madonna's Malawi: celebritization and the NGO economy" funded by the Danish Research Council for the Social Sciences. Louise is a Core Researcher of the Research Network on Celebrity and North–South Relations.

Lisa Ann Richey is Professor of International Development Studies and Director of the Doctoral School of Society and Globalisation at Roskilde University, Denmark. She also serves as Vice-President of the Global South Caucus of the International Studies Association (ISA). She is the author of the books *Brand Aid: Shopping Well to Save the World* with Stefano Ponte (2011), *Population Politics and Development: From the Policies to the Clinics* (2008), and the co-editor with Stefano Ponte of *New Actors and Alliances in Development* (2014). She works on new actors in international aid, citizenship and body politics, and gender and the global South. She leads the Research Network on Celebrity and North–South Relations: https://celebnorthsouth.wordpress.com/

Annika Bergman Rosamond is Senior Lecturer in International Relations at the Department of Political Science, Lund University, Sweden. She is also the director of a faculty-wide MA programme in Global Studies. Her key research interests include celebrity activism and international relations, gender, feminism and international relations as well as broad debates in cosmopolitan theory and security studies. She is the editor of *War, Ethics and Justice: New Perspectives on a Post-9/11 World* (with Mark Phythian 2012). Annika is a Core Researcher of the Research Network on Celebrity and North–South Relations.

Anke Schwittay is a Senior Lecturer in the Anthropology and Development Studies at the University of Sussex, UK. She earned her PhD in Anthropology from the University of California at Berkeley. Anke is the author of *New Media and International Development: Representation and Affect in Microfinance* (2014).

Robert van Krieken is Professor of Sociology at the University of Sydney and Visiting Professor at University College Dublin. His research interests include the sociology of law, criminology, the sociology of childhood, processes of civilization and decivilization, cultural genocide, and the history and sociology of celebrity, as well as contributing to the theoretical debates around the work of Elias, Foucault, Luhmann and Latour. Previous books include *Norbert Elias* (1998), *Celebrity and the Law* (2010, co-authored) *Celebrity Society* (2012) and *Sociology*, 5th edition (2014, co-authored).

ACKNOWLEDGEMENTS

This collection has benefited from the support of the Global Dynamics Research Priority Initiative at Roskilde University, the Danish Independent Research Council, the Sustainability Platform at the Copenhagen Business School, and the Department of Sociology and Social Research at the University of Trento. We would also like to thank Jessica Lerche for her copy-editing and Khanam Virjee and Helen Bell, our editorial team at Routledge, for their work with us. We are grateful for the input from three anonymous reviewers and also colleagues who read the proposal and chapters in various stages and gave useful comments to improve the collection – in particular, Mike Goodman, Ilan Kapoor, and Stefano Ponte. It has been a pleasure to work with such a diverse team of dedicated authors from around the globe and around the disciplines who respected, critiqued, appreciated, and improved each other's work. Any remaining shortcomings in the collection should be attributed to the editor.

INTRODUCTION

Celebrity humanitarianism and North–South relations – politics, place and power

Lisa Ann Richey

As I wrote this book introduction, North–South relations were pessimistically characterized by a tone of humanitarian crisis over how to respond to the worst outbreak of the Ebola virus in history. During this time, I was receiving social media updates from a former student I taught in South Africa, whose profession as written on visa forms is "humanitarian." He was working as the first emergency response team director treating Ebola in Liberia. He lamented the lack of attention and resources that had been committed to fight the disease. Ebola became a symbol of "the moral bankruptcy of capitalism" as coined by John Ashton, the president of the UK Faculty of Public Health.[1] The US had promised to send troops, and the Cubans had pledged to send doctors, but in the early stages of the Ebola crisis, no one offered to send celebrities.[2]

Then, as reported by *The Independent* newspaper in the UK, Sir Bob Geldof received a call from the UN that the Ebola virus was "getting out of control" so he decided to re-record the Band Aid single from 30 years before to "just stop Ebola."[3] *Do They Know it's Christmas?* was re-released and immediately became the number one ranked song in 63 countries. The internet was awash with a wide spectrum of reactions to the new Band Aid, creating what optimists might consider a global public sphere for debating the role of celebrities in humanitarianism, the appropriate place of African artists in solidarity movements for Africa and whether or not the damage done by the outdated lyrics: "Well tonight thank God it's them instead of you" could be repaired with the hurried change to "Well tonight we're reaching out and touching you." While all the intrigue of which stars were in and which were out of Bob Geldof's passion play pervaded the global popular media, the public remained uninformed about even the most basic aspects of the initiative: where would the money raised by the single actually go?[4]

We know from nearly a decade of attention paid to global humanitarianism of the photogenic variety that "offering support for global charities has become practically part of the contemporary celebrity job description and a hallmark of the established star" (Littler 2008, p. 237). Selling products to "help" distant others, be it Band Aid or "brand aid," has linked celebrities and corporations to global humanitarian causes in unprecedented ways (Richey & Ponte 2011). Correspondingly, the development sector and the celebrity industry have increasingly formalized relationships, based on a cadre of full-time celebrity liaison officers in non-governmental organizations (NGOs), and specialized talent agencies linking performers to philanthropic causes (Brockington 2014). Geldof's spectacle was only the tip of the iceberg of celebrity humanitarianism for Ebola. There was also a scaled-up global health response from philanthropist George Soros and the "aid celebrity" Dr. Paul Farmer (Richey & Ponte 2011);[5] "the Ebola Fighters" were named *Time* Magazine's Person of the Year for 2014;[6] a total of $1.5 billion was eventually committed by public and private donors;[7] and my former student's co-worker was invited to the White House to participate in the US's State of the Union Address on behalf of "thousands of Ebola health care workers."[8]

When celebrities become involved in North–South relations money is pledged, individual and institutional networks are mobilized, and attention is drawn toward

FIGURE 0.1 Dr. Pranav Shetty, shown here in the field, was invited to sit with US First Lady Michelle Obama for the 2015 State of the Union Address. Born in India, raised in Trinidad, trained in the US, an humanitarian volunteer, he is the Global Health Emergency Coordinator for International Medical Corps. Photograph by International Medical Corps.

particular crises, and away from others. What are the specific configurations of power that take place when celebrities engage in humanitarianism? Does celebrity engagement provoke similar responses in different places across the globe? And what does this mean for humanitarian politics? This book aims to better understand the relationships of politics, place and power in grounded studies of celebrity humanitarianism.

Ebola, like the Ethiopian famine of the mid-1980s and its Band Aid response, provides the perfect catalyst for contemporary celebrity humanitarianism. As explained by Müller: "A disaster like a major famine makes it easier to uphold the fantasy that, in alleviating concrete suffering or preventing starvation, we contribute to justice; it should thus come as no surprise that a famine gave birth to Band Aid 'common-sense humanitarianism'" (Müller 2013, p. 481). The cutting edge of contemporary scholarship on celebrity engagement with humanitarian interventions suggests that populist celebrity advocacy marks a disengagement between the public and politics across North and South. Celebrity humanitarianism and development advocacy, argues Brockington (2014), is the terrain of elites in the North, in spite of popular misconceptions that celebrities are successful because of their appeal to "the people." Critics like Littler (2008) and Kapoor (2013) argue that celebrities actually appeal to "the people" by playing with the humanitarian needs of "others" – effectively selling the poor for profit in global capitalist relations – and making celebrity humanitarianism inherently destructive for the South. In contrast, supporters like Cooper (2008) suggest that celebrities can be an innovative, positive force in "changing the world" by forging new diplomatic links across contexts. Yet social theorists like van Krieken (2012) chart convincingly that celebrity politics is nothing new, and that the history of celebrity humanitarianism runs alongside "development" and the drive toward "modernity." Thus, we might assume that celebrity and North–South relations are intertwined, perhaps even in ways that we did not imagine.

Academic discussion over celebrity engagement is often limited to theoretical critique or normative name-calling between "the skeptics" and "the optimists" (Chouliaraki 2013, ch. 4), without much grounded research into what it is that celebrities are doing, the same or differently – in different or even the same places – throughout the world. This book provides a critical investigation into what celebrity humanitarianism in North–South relations suggests for contemporary configurations of *politics, place and power*. We examine *politics* to understand how values are linked with authority in global constellations of humanitarian helping, and in local recipient environments. We investigate the importance of *place* and context, and each chapter presents new empirical findings on celebrity humanitarianism on the ground in Thailand, Malawi, Bangladesh, South Africa, China, Haiti, Congo, US, Denmark and Australia. Celebrity interventions provide an empirical focus point for studying the relations of *power* that may be reproduced or disputed from one context to another. We gaze through the keyhole of "celebrity" in order to investigate fundamental concepts such as accountability, agency, authenticity, brand, development, mediation, humanity, inequality, pity, public engagement and representation.

Why is it important to understand celebrity humanitarianism?

Celebrity engagement in humanitarian causes and development interventions has raised the interest levels of numerous publics in both North and South. It has sparked a growing academic debate across disciplines and has been the subject of heated popular debate as well. Scholars, students and the general public are quick to support some celebritized causes and to condemn others. The terrain of intervention in development and humanitarian causes is changing rapidly with the engagement of new actors, relations and alliances across geographical, financial and political distances. But these changes come into a context of historical familiarity (see Littler forthcoming), and alongside long-established socioeconomic and political power relations, as reactions to Ebola clearly show.

We have scholarship that suggests that celebrity involvement changes humanitarianism in important ways. For example, celebrity humanitarianism has been held responsible for reproducing "neoliberal subjectivity" (Biccum 2007), and for "establishing a hegemonic culture of humanitarianism in which moral responsibility . . . is based on pity rather than the demand for justice" (Müller 2013, p. 470; Boltanski 1999). Thus, celebrities need to be understood in their function as new actors in North–South relations. In her engaging book documenting changes in humanitarian communication over the past four decades, Chouliaraki argues that we have moved into the "post-humanitarian" age, in which solidarity is driven by neoliberal logics of consumption and where utilitarianism and doing good for "others" depends on doing well for yourself. As Chouliaraki describes, celebrity humanitarians are at the forefront of this societal shift:

> The tearful celebrity, the rock concert, the Twitter hype and the graphic attention are . . . prototypical performances of post-humanitarianism which limit our resources for reflecting upon human vulnerability as a political problem of injustice and minimizes our capacity of empathy with vulnerable others as others with their own humanity.
>
> *(Chouliaraki 2013, p. 187)*

Celebrity humanitarianism can be read as a performance between the celebrity as benefactor and the public for whom the celebrity functions as a proxy philanthropist. As Duncombe has illustrated, "The 'humble roots and common tastes' celebrity stories not only make this contemporary Pantheon of Gods acceptable to a democratic audience . . . they also hold out the promise that this can happen to you" (2007, p. 108). The popular attraction to celebrity fantasies is linked to a life without consequences, an escape into activities with no agency (ibid.). Thus, celebrity humanitarianism provides the possibility to vicariously participate in the caring activities of our favorite celebrities, while disengaging from the consequential activity of what "really" happens in international development or humanitarianism on the ground.

Questions of power, accountability, and who actually constitutes "the public" of North–South relations need academic investigation. Chouliaraki also emphasizes that humanitarian communication in the new media favors partial, personal read-ings as opposed to more objective, shared interpretations of humanitarian problems, and thus is less effective at integrating audiences and providing a shared founda-tion for collective action (ibid). Therefore, critical scholarship must question the "optimists" who lead us to believe that globalization and mediatization are perme-ating all corners of the globe and "networking" everyone, while leaving isolation, misunderstanding and callousness as part of a "pre-humanitarian" past (for a useful overview, see Robertson 2015). Crucially, little scholarly attention has been paid to the Global South, either as a place where celebrities intervene in existing politics and social processes, or as the generator of Southern celebrities engaged in "do-gooding" (Littler 2008). This edited book is about what a diverse roster of celebrity humanitarians are actually doing in and across Northern and Southern contexts.

Situating celebrity humanitarianism within contemporary academic debates

Celebrities are now an increasingly studied topic on their own terms, with a his-tory of critical concern for the relationship between celebrities and politics that Wheeler dates back to the German sociologist Leo Lowenthal's (1944) critique of the replacement of "idols of production" such as politicians with "idols of consump-tion" such as film stars (Wheeler 2013, p. 1). Contradicting some fundamentalist academic presumptions that scholarship on celebrity would be a purely cultural, fun and dumbed-down area of inquiry, the introduction to the first volume of the flagship journal *Celebrity Studies* could be productively confused with describing the goals of social science inquiry, or perhaps the discipline of anthropology. In the journal introduction Holmes and Redmond specify that the aims of celebrity studies are "to defamiliarise the everyday, and to make apparent the cultural politics and power relations which sit at the center of the 'taken for granted'" (2010, p. 3).

This book takes up this call to "defamiliarise" celebrity humanitarians with whom many Western media consumers have become saturated – such as the pop singer Madonna or the actress Angelina Jolie – while also making apparent the poli-tics and power relations constituting important interactions in less visible "celebrity societies" (van Krieken 2012) such as those in Bangladesh, South Africa or China. We know that celebrity engagement in humanitarianism has become increasingly prominent and the subject of debate in academia and the popular media, yet we are lacking when it comes to a grounded understanding of the importance of context and the differences of politics, place and power in shaping celebrity engagements in North–South relations. This leads us to consider a series of questions: Which publics are engaged, through which celebritized means and what does this mean for politics and how development and humanitarianism are "done"?

Wilson (2011) argues that celebrities represent a form of global governmen-tality that brings Western audiences into alignment with international programs. Celebrity advocacy is assumed to preserve stereotypes, particularly about the Western Self and the "Other," which fit conveniently into the wider discourse of assumptions about the natural order of world politics (Repo & Yrjölä 2011). When celebrities have taken on humanitarian causes, acting as "aid celebrities" (Richey & Ponte 2011) to promote international development or as celebrity diplomats (Cooper 2008) across North–South contexts, they have typically received academic criticism.

This book speaks to three relevant literatures for the study of celebrity humanitarianism: (1) *the interdisciplinary literature on aid celebrities* (primarily from the fields of international development studies and geography); (2) *the literature on celebrities and representation of "Others"* (particularly from media and communications studies, cultural studies and anthropology); and (3) *the emerging literature on new actors and alliances in North–South relations* (drawing on international relations and global studies). Scholarship on celebrity do-gooding in transnational contexts of humanitarianism, development and diplomacy has been blossoming in diverse specialist and interdisciplinary journals within these three research categories (Brockington 2014; Chouliaraki 2012; Dieter & Kumar 2008; Goodman & Barnes 2011; Huliaras & Tzifakis 2010; Littler 2011; Müller 2013; Repo & Yrjölä 2011; Scott 2014; and Wheeler 2011).

Celebrity humanitarianism can be best understood through the consideration of key books which have been published over the past couple of years analyzing the multifaceted nature of celebrity humanitarianism from a rigorous academic perspective. From *the interdisciplinary literature on aid celebrities*, two different and critical books have taken on celebrity interventions in North–South relations. The most significant book in the field of empirically-grounded work on celebrity and development (Brockington 2014) focuses exclusively on celebrity advocacy and lobbying in international development, examining its history, relationships, consequences, wider contexts and implications. Brockington argues that celebrity advocacy signals a new aspect of elite rule. From an in-depth analysis of actual celebrity advocacy in Britain, and drawing on some comparative material from the US, we understand how corporations, politicians and the NGO community have begun to orient around the aura of celebrity. A pragmatic conclusion suggests that if development is to work better, it must negotiate within this new terrain of celebritized relationships. A significant theoretical critique of celebrity humanitarianism is provided in the book by Kapoor (2013) on celebrity humanitarianism. Kapoor claims that celebrity legitimates and promotes neoliberal capitalism and global inequality. This polemic engages an ideological critique, drawing heavily on the theories of Žižek, to argue that celebrity humanitarianism is a moral spectacle that entwines frenetic development NGOs, big business and sexy stars. Kapoor illustrates how celebrities' involvement in international development advances the celebrity brand and contributes to a "post-democratic" political landscape managed by unaccountable elites.

From *the literature on celebrities and representation of "Others,"* a seminal text has been published by Chouliaraki (2013) arguing that contemporary humanitarianism is under pressure from economic, political and technological transformations which have significantly altered the possibilities for global solidarity. She shows how international development aid has become instrumentalized as international organizations and NGOs compete for market share and donor funding, while the scholars focus on administrative policy rather than critical, normative theory. Simultaneously, argues Chouliaraki, the grand narratives of solidarity have been replaced by individualist projects. This is linked to changes in technology and new media forms where audiences in the North have become both producers and consumers of a public communication that obfuscates the distant "Others." Coming from media and communication studies, the book considers solidarity as "a problem of communication," and analyzes humanitarianism as performance, providing a convincing argument for scholars of humanitarianism that communication matters: words and images perform and significantly shape social reality across North–South relations.

Third, from *the emerging literature on new actors and alliances in North–South relations,* Mark Wheeler's (2013) monograph, *Celebrity Politics,* looks specifically at the engagement of celebrities in "traditional" politics. Drawing on the foundational work of John Street (Street 2004, 2010, 2012) for understanding celebrities doing politics and politicians performing as celebrities, Wheeler makes the case that "traditional civic duties are being replaced by alternative forms of virtuous participation" and that celebrities are actually engaging the public in politics (2013, p. 2). While the book's scope includes both national and global politics, the specific claims about celebrity transnational activism are based on the workings of celebrity diplomats (drawing on the classic Cooper 2008) and global activists (from the first book to examine this: Tsaliki, Frangonikolopoulos & Huliaras 2011). Wheeler offers a taxonomy of celebrity politics that can provide a macro-level, sense-making framework for understanding a variety of celebrity engagements in diverse places.

All of these books and the articles mentioned at the beginning of this section have created knowledge about what Driessens (2013, p. 546) terms "the celebrity apparatus," which consists of the celebrity, the media, the public and the celebrity industry. However, the existing literatures still lack, for the most part, any empirical grounding from the side of the recipients of humanitarian "help." The chapters in this book begin to build up the research corpus necessary to develop an understanding of celebrity humanitarianism that moves between Northern and Southern perspectives, and to test existing theories of celebritized intervention for "fit."

The next section will provide an introduction to the critical concepts in understanding celebrity to be grounded in the following chapters in this book, starting with the concept at the core of our common enterprise, "celebrity."

Defining the concepts: "celebrity," "North–South relations" and "humanitarianism"

How do we make "celebrity" a theoretical concept that helps us to understand something about the constitution of our social world in the contemporary period of North–South relations? Our book focuses on the conceptualization of celebrity humanitarianism in order to stress the modality of interaction, and we are not engaging in the debates over what a "real" celebrity is, whether limited to the Hollywood A-list or expanded to include anyone with more than a handful of followers on social media. Celebrity constitutes an intellectual space where questions of authenticity, accessibility, popularity and brand can also be interrogated. However, it is important to clarify that this conceptualization is functionalist in its intentions: the point of this collection is not to understand celebrities as humanitarian actors in order to better understand the nature, function or relevance of celebrities. We argue instead that it is necessary to understand how celebrities function as new actors, to better understand contemporary processes of North–South relations of humanitarianism, development and, following Brockington (2014), of elite rule in post-democracy. One need not buy into a historically deterministic grand theory of representation and democracy to recognize that there are new alliances and competitive spaces that shape the ways that North–South relations are conceived, and celebrities have become increasingly visible as part of the "development" brand (Richey & Ponte 2014).

Celebrity

Since the purpose of this book is to use "celebrity" as an instrumental concept, and other recent work has reviewed the literature on its various definitions in scholarship (Driessens 2013), here I will discuss only briefly how this book engages with the celebrity concept and why the findings in the following chapters suggest that "celebrity" is a concept in need of further development. Driessens (2013) presents a "tentative mapping of celebrity definitions" that is organized along the components of the "celebrity apparatus" (celebrity, the media, the public and the celebrity industry). In our approach to celebrity humanitarianism, we focus primarily on two of these components: the celebrity and the public. Thus, theoretically, we considered defining celebrity as put forth in Boltanski and Thévenot (1991). They define "celebrity" as a state of superiority in a world where opinion is the defining instrument for measuring different orders of "greatness." In their approach, being a celebrity is characterized by having a widespread reputation, being recognized in public, being visible, having success, being distinguished, and having opinion leaders, journalists and the media as your testimonials (ibid. pp. 222–30). The test of celebrity is the judgment of the public – but who are the celebrity public in the context of North–South relations? The chapters in this book demonstrate how celebrity humanitarians are constituting "caring" publics and particular politics. For example, in chapter 4, Mupotsa introduces us to the celebrity philanthropy of Sophie Ndaba, whose spectacular orphan benefit/wedding event became a way for South Africa's newly rich "Black Diamonds" to "give back" to needy "others" who are not constituted by the expected distances of race, geography or culture. Chapter 8 challenges us to consider how celebrities costumed as genitalia for a development fundraising show in Denmark can amalgamate popular opinion in favor of international aid, while offending both the "others" of the aid itself and many others in the donor North.

Instead of focusing analytically on celebrities as actors, the authors in this collection engage celebrity actions, the processes of making an intervention in North–South relations, as a celebrity humanitarian. When considering how to reconcile analytically such diverse examples of celebrity humanitarians as Angelina Jolie, the A-list Hollywood actress (featured in chapter 1) with Mohammed Yunus, the Bangladeshi founder of the Grameen Bank (featured in chapter 3), we draw foundationally on Brockington's definition of "celebrity":

> Celebrity describes sustained public appearances that are materially beneficial, and where the benefits are at least partially enjoyed by people other than the celebrity themselves, by stakeholders whose job it is to manage the appearance of that celebrity. According to this definition, members of the public interviewed by roving reporters would not be celebrities. Academics promoting their books in the media would qualify if those media opportunities were provided by an agent promoting their book.
>
> *(2014, p. xxi)*

This definition is useful for orienting contextually grounded studies because it focuses on the materiality of celebrity as performance for profit. It is also a functionalist argument: celebrities are such because they function as such – there is no ontology in celebrity per se. This allows for significant flexibility in the concept: to include non-film stars and those who claim to be anything but celebrities. The celebrities under study in this book are both individuals from the entertainment industry who cross over into fields of humanitarianism and international development, as well as experts (intellectuals, politicians, professionals) who are reconfigured as celebrities vis-à-vis the mediatization of their persona.

Just as celebrity itself is an unstable category (see Driessens 2013, p. 557), celebrity humanitarian may be a category that can change over time or with place. For example, chapter 7 suggests that the actor Sean Penn may be considered a celebrity humanitarian of considerably more standing in Haiti than in the US.

Humanitarian celebrities provoke questions about mediatization, representation and aspirational distance. When celebrities are "narrowcasting" representations of the relationship between North and South (images of global inequality, of transnational need, etc.) what is their context? Which audiences are being targeted? Which audiences are reached? What are the geographical and cultural boundaries of the celebrity engagement? What are the identities and practices represented to these audiences? Is there any possibility for interrogating these representations of North–South relations? If so, who does that and from which standpoint do they claim to speak?

North–South relations

To define the scope of celebrity action across these texts a term is borrowed from international relations and development studies – "North–South relations." The traditional meaning of this term is drawn from political science descriptions of the relationships that emerged at the end of World War II and decolonization. Its common usage dates back to the 1970s when the North was the "wealthy, industrialized nations of the non-communist world," aligned diplomatically against the "countries of the so-called developing world" in the South.[9] While remaining a contested term, North–South relations came to be used commonly in describing trade relations, security policy, diplomacy, development aid, capital flows, or economic integration between states or groups of states. Yet, in the postcolonial era of trade and aid regimes characterized more strongly by global transnational governance and less by negotiations between states, North–South has come to take on a different scope of understanding. Today, it is used to capture differences at multiple levels (from global flows to local communities) and to highlight relationships that are neither spatial nor geographical. There is no "North" as an empirical place, but rather "North" as a position in a hierarchy between North and South, across levels and geographies.

In this book, our conceptual context is described as "North–South relations" meant to encompass both international development and humanitarian interventions. "Development" is typically understood as those aid relationships aiming to combat poverty and/or and reduce economic inequality. In contrast, "humanitarian" interventions are viewed as short-term responses to unanticipated crises, typically caused by war, and environmental or "natural" disasters.[10] Brockington explains that the "fundamental difference between the two is that development is something that you, or your community, can do to yourself or itself. But humanitarianism requires a needy other. The history of humanitarianism begins with the recognition of the humanity of distant strangers" (2014, p. xxii).

In spite of the potential distinctions in conceptualization and practices, our book merges "international development" and "humanitarianism" under the marker of "North–South relations." This is a deliberate choice to both connect the past forms of North–South linkage, from slavery and empire to 1970s development as modernization (in the classical Rostowian "stages of economic growth" sense). It is also to open up the field of scrutiny to include the many other, increasingly relevant, terms of engagement between North and South that fall outside of traditional international development assistance – corporate social responsibility, remittances, consumption-based humanitarianism or "brand aid," and investment. North–South relations suggest a flow, a mobility and a necessarily transnational character to the object of our study.

Celebrity actors operate within and across North and South, with consequences for development and humanitarianism. In the South they perform site visits, establish development organizations, serve international governmental organizations, and behave as "disaster tourists." In the North, they act as witnesses, ambassadors, fundraisers and activists. The diverse sites of engagement offer varying opportunities and constraints. A comparison of contexts reveals the underlying dynamics of power of celebrity humanitarians. Celebrities gain power based on their ability to reach audiences – building authority, legitimacy and influence – and impacting local and global processes of governance. Thus, there is a pressing need to examine celebrities and the role of context in the power relations that constitute North–South relations.

Humanitarianism

Humanitarianism, with or without celebrities, is being conceptually debated, understood, and reworked through a large and diverse academic literature that, for the most part, we will not cover in this book (for a selected overview, see books by Barnett 2011; Fassin 2012; Waters 2001). International relations scholars use "humanitarianism" with a specific historical reference to the 1864 Geneva Convention's recognition in international law of humanitarian principles to govern the moral practice of war. The expansion of humanitarian space from the governance of war to more nebulous interventions on behalf of an assumed shared humanity dates back to the 1970s crisis in Biafra (see Vestergaard forthcoming for an in-depth review). As suggested by its title, "The problems with humanitarianism," Belloni (2007) argues that intervention in the domestic affairs within states on the grounds of a shared humanity, as humanitarianism is currently practiced in North–South relations, serves to support the interests of powerful elites and undermine the moral basis of human rights on which this intervention is predicated. One of the unanswered questions addressed in this book is the following: to what extent are the problems with celebrity humanitarianism actually indicative of, or derived from, ongoing problems of humanitarian intervention in general? Our empirical cases expand beyond the Western international relations scope of humanitarianism – with Bangladesh, South Africa and China in chapters 3, 4 and 5 – and thus suggest that more work is needed on the contemporary trajectory that is taken by the concept "humanitarianism" to move it from post-Westphalian notions of international versus state and into the realm of global governance of North–South relations.

However, as part of our pragmatic analytical framework, we have chosen to retain the term "humanitarianism" to signify the practices of the celebrities described in the following chapters. Kapoor notes that the terms "charity," "philanthropy" and "humanitarianism" are often used interchangeably, but that "charity" carries an explicitly Christian genealogy, while "philanthropy" is used for secular, and typically corporate interventions (2013, p. 4). Littler used the term "do-gooding" to describe a particular type of response to suffering at a distance – one that "generates a lot of hype and PR but is relatively insignificant in relation to international and governmental policy" (2008, p. 240). This is a useful catchall concept that works across the public–private and the religious spectrum, but our empirical examples suggest that celebrity "do-gooding" actually interacts in interesting ways with international policy and how it is understood (for example, Angelina Jolie's work for UNHCR with Burmese refugees in chapter 1) and also with governmental policy (for example, the use of Madonna's projects in Malawian political debates in chapter 2).

"Humanitarianism" for the authors in this book signifies the "do-gooding" response to distant suffering, whether this distance is actually geographical or geo-political (historically-derived inequalities characterized by an economic disparity), that includes an explicit or implicit claim for the moral basis of its good-doing. In chapter 9, van Krieken, acknowledging that humanitarianism arises when the devout worry about the moral character of society, points out that "establishing the moral character of society takes on a life of its own, overshadowing the sorts of social, economic and political issues underpinning the problems being addressed" (van Krieken, chapter 9). Celebrities play important roles in representing, embody-ing and also in shaping the meanings of what is considered to be "moral" through the management of affect, or feelings, between audiences of donors and recipi-ents. Thus, traditional understandings of humanitarianism help us to grasp why this realm is fertile for interventions by celebrities:

> "The humanitarian imperative" is in this sense a vague, moral goal. What is the "dependent variable"? . . . The basic problem, then, is that the "prod-uct" of humanitarian organizations' activities is mushy . . . the product is measured in terms of what are in effect needs and "good feelings" of a dis-tant constituency, political advantages of distant countries, and so forth. This is why publicity is so important in the manner in which relief programs are administered. The point is not the good feelings of clients, the refugees, but those on the other end of the mercy calculation, the feelings of the donors.
> *(Waters 2001, pp. 41–2)*

Even authors who are deeply critical of the "actually existing practices of humani-tarianism" do not neglect the moral imperatives that it, however imperfectly, attempts to manifest in the world. In his classic book on famine, De Waal argues that his critique is "not to abandon humanitarianism, which can again be a force for ethical progress. But a humanitarianism that sets itself against or above poli-tics is futile" (1997, p. 6). Our chapters demonstrate the kinds of politics, both global and local, that are actually taking place around celebrity interventions, and the epilogue makes a strong case for how these politics can and should be taken seriously.

Organization of the book

Methodology and research questions across the chapters

This book is based on the contributions of scholars of geography, development studies, anthropology, cultural studies, political science, and sociology. Thus, our common analytical approach is pragmatic and aims to clearly situate each of the empirical case studies within the most relevant literatures for understanding the research puzzle of the chapter. Similarly, there is no single, "best" methodo-logical approach to the study of celebrity humanitarianism. The chapters in this book, however, do deviate from much of the work on media and culture in that they consider both the material and the representational sides of the celebrity intervention. Studying celebrities "up close" is a difficult task, of course, and much of the conceptual debate about the production of authenticity around the personae of celebrities applies to issues of data collection as well. Therefore, the chapters present a fuller picture of celebrity humanitarianism when the frame of reference is expanded beyond the mainstream media coverage of the celebrity's "good deed."

The chapters in this book use grounded empirical cases to answer the following questions:

How do celebrities mediate elite politics between North and South? Particularly in chapters 3 (Schwittay), 6 (Budabin), 7 (Rosamond) and 8 (Olwig & Christiansen).

Which publics are engaged in diverse places, through which celebritized means and what does this mean for politics? Particularly in chapters 7 (Rosamond), 8 (Olwig & Christansen) and 9 (van Krieken).

How do celebritized interventions impact local politics of development that take place in the South? Particularly in chapters 1 (Mostafanezhad), 2 (Rasmussen), 4 (Mupotsa), and 5 (Hood).

How can the perspective of Southern celebrities shape our understanding of development practices? Particularly in chapters 3 (Schwittay), 4 (Mupotsa), and 5 (Hood).

How do humanitarian representations of power (concepts of "need" and agency) change in different places as celebrities try to "sell" a particular cause to a particular audience? Particularly in chapters 1 (Mostafanezhad), 3 (Schwittay), 4 (Mupotsa), 6 (Budabin), 7 (Rosamond) and 9 (van Krieken).

These research questions are addressed by thematically organized chapters divided across two themes: *(1) What impact do celebrities have in the global South?* And *(2) What does celebrity engagement mean in the donor North?* The use of the term "North–South relations" has been outlined above as describing the scope of analysis in each chapter's case studies, but further clarification is necessary to explain why the book is organized according to what our critics might argue is an artificial divide between North and South, or clinging to unhelpful typology between geopolitical spheres of "oppressor" and "oppressed."

First, we begin by highlighting the contribution that this book makes toward analysis that begins and ends with the global South. This is a purposive choice in tracing the trajectory of contemporary celebrity humanitarianism back to its "noble" historical roots in universal human rights and emancipating individuals from the oppressive powers of their states, but also back to its "dishonorable" roots in slavery, colonialism and ongoing forms of exploitation. The "South" in this book is a relative position in a power structure that has historically and geographically specific roots and takes culturally specific forms. Our chapters demonstrate how the "South" can produce different kinds of celebrity humanitarians (for example, Pu Cunxin in China or Sofie Ndaba in South Africa). The chapters also show how celebrities can produce different kinds of "South" or intended recipients of humanitarian do-gooding (comparing Haiti and New Orleans in chapter 7, or Washington and Kinshasa in chapter 6). Using the perspective of "celebrity impact in the global South" allows us to unpack these variations across politics, place and power in each of the different chapters.

Second, we explore what the processes of celebritization suggest for participatory democracy and for the "donor North." Here again we are not embracing an archaic notion that only Western OECD countries are "donors" or humanitarian actors, but we are exploring empirically the theories outlined above that suggest that the entry of celebrities into the realm of humanitarianism has produced changes in what is considered possible and actually practiced. When celebrities signify "the public" or the agents of humanitarianism, who is their audience and which public are they actually constituting? The chapters in this section all subject the donor North to critical examination, both in its relation to the recipient South and in the relationship constituted amongst the "helpers" themselves, be that problematically elitist as argued in chapter 6 or problematically democratic as argued in chapter 8. These sections can be read independently, but should be considered together to understand why celebrity humanitarianism is an effective lens for viewing the multiple and diverse relationships that constitute the links between North and South.

Part I Celebrity impact in the global South

The first five chapters examine the celebrity impact in the global South. Mary Mostafanezhad's chapter 1, entitled, "Angelina Jolie and the everyday geopolitics of celebrity humanitarianism in a Thailand–Burma border town," is an ethnographic account of the geopolitics of Jolie's work in Burmese refugee camps. In February 2009 United Nations High Commissioner for Refugees (UNHCR) Goodwill Ambassador Angelina Jolie visited Mae La refugee camp in the Thai–Burma border zone to help draw attention to ongoing human rights abuses in Burma as well as to the 147,000 refugees that live in nine camps along the border. Her day-long visit was successful in attracting international media coverage and was applauded by UNHCR for the worldwide response it elicited. Mostafanezhad draws on ethnographic research among Burmese refugees and human rights activists in the border area, to examine the sentimental geopolitics of Jolie's visit in popular media as well as the everyday geopolitics of hope that gossip about her visit engendered in the camps.

This chapter demonstrates how the widespread gossip – both in the actual refugee camps and in the media – privileged the re-presentation of Jolie's sentimental encounter with Burmese exiles rather than drawing attention to the continued human rights atrocities in Burma. As a result, Angelina's experience of humanitarian travel as an international celebrity perpetuated a geopolitics of hope that foregrounded sentimental rather than political concern. In addition to the depoliticizing effects of her visit to the camp, the geopolitics of hope that emerged in the media obscured the widespread geopolitics of fear that consumes Burmese exiles in the border zone. Drawing on emerging theories in critical geography about "everyday geopolitics," the chapter addresses how this visit was interpreted in the media as well the phenomenology, or lived experience, of those most affected.

In addition to theorizing the implications of Jolie's intervention in this case, the chapter also identifies its practical consequences and its potential and limitations for celebrity humanitarianism in the Global South.

Chapter 2 moves to another continent and female superstar, with Louise Mubanda Rasmussen's work entitled "Madonna in Malawi: celebritized interventions and local politics of development in the South." This chapter uses Madonna's humanitarian work in Malawi to examine how celebritized development may interact with local politics of development in the country. Madonna's efforts to support local orphan care and education projects have become highly controversial, both globally and locally. Some Malawians interpret Madonna as a person who cynically exploits poor Africans to promote her own brand, and who makes grand promises that never materialize. Yet, for others, she is seen as a worthy humanitarian who is at least doing something, in contrast to local elites who are viewed as even more corrupt and self-serving than the global superstar.

Based on six months' ethnographic research in Malawi, this chapter analyzes how Madonna's humanitarian work has been received in Malawi. Data include a mixture of participant observation, informal conversations, Malawian newspaper articles and online commentary, as well as formal interviews with NGO officials working in the field of Madonna's interventions for "orphans and vulnerable children." The chapter situates Madonna's local humanitarianism within the wider context of Malawi's recent political history of a democratic transition and a massive growth of NGOs. Madonna's interventions are interpreted by Malawians against a backdrop of suspicion towards the motivations of foreign development actors, an experience of international and local NGOs lacking transparency and accountability, and a government equally unaccountable for development. In this context, there are multiple "local" interpretations of Madonna's humanitarian work. While the middle class and the elite debate Madonna's authenticity as a humanitarian as either genuine or a matter of cynical branding, the rural poor are more concerned with their everyday survival and the limited extent to which they can influence how – and indeed whether – this humanitarianism will benefit them. Madonna's interventions become coupled with an experience of politics as being confined to an elite, far removed from the concerns of everyday Malawians, and very much concerned with the politicians' own enrichment and promotion. The chapter concludes that a personified celebrity intervention may illuminate the contradictions between how development is represented in the North and how it is experienced in the South, and it may also trigger local debates around development, elitism and corruption. In this way, a controversial celebrity intervention may open up a contentious debate around the local politics of development. However, in a country like Malawi these debates tend to ignore the voices of the most marginalized and fail to fundamentally question entrenched inequalities.

Chapter 3, "Muhammad Yunus: a Bangladeshi aid celebrity," examines the subject of another quite different type of celebrity humanitarian than Madonna. Anke Schwittay analyzes the Nobel Peace Prize winner and founder of the Grameen Bank, whose work and persona are intertwined with a personal geographical location and political platform for his microcredit revolution. Remaining firmly rooted in the developmental shadow state of Bangladesh and its poor female clients, while at the same time lobbying at the highest international levels as a tireless advocate for the poor, allows Yunus to constitute himself as an authentic aid celebrity from the Global South.

This chapter relies on data from the genre of (auto)biographical writings read against the large body of academic literature on microfinance and its complex gender relations. Schwittay illustrates how Yunus' success has been reliant on the creation of an affect-charged persona of the charismatic and inspiring leader of the microcredit movement, transforming lives of poor Bangladeshi women. Furthermore, she analyzes Yunus' work as a contentious development expert, highly critical of Northern interventions, notably those of the World Bank. The chapter concludes that gender plays a central role in Yunus' constitution as an aid celebrity, and while his authenticity at representing poor women in the Global South is a strength, the prescriptions and practices of the development interventions he advocates have also been subject to significant criticism. Yunus remains disengaged from more critical accounts of the ways in which microfinance operates within a Bangladeshi economy of shame that works through peer pressure, notions of purdah, and the dispossession of poor women. One of the reasons why microfinance continues to be popular in the face of such criticism is precisely the way in which it, and Yunus, capitalize on the affect generated by images and stories of poor women. This case holds important lessons for the limitations of authenticity in celebrity humanitarian representations and the potential for conflict and convergence between global and local gender norms.

In chapter 4 Danai Mupotsa explores a South African celebrity humanitarian, Sophie Ndaba, and her work in post-apartheid neoliberal relations of consumption. In the chapter, entitled "Sophie's special secret: public feeling, consumption and celebrity activism in post-apartheid South Africa," Mupotsa explores the relationship between distance and aspiration in a reading of the race, class and gender relations of celebrity humanitarianism. Sofie Ndaba came to the attention of the South African public as a much-loved single woman in the popular soap opera *Generations*. The television show has garnered scholarly attention as signaling the aspirations of an emergent black consumer middle class through the use of a dramatic romantic narrative plot that constantly seduces and disappoints its audience. Through this celebrity, like many of her contemporaries, Ndaba has propelled herself into a narrative similar to the fictional plot of the show, becoming an entrepreneur and public speaker on charity-related matters. Ndaba's 2012 wedding ended up as a dramatic public sham marriage, yet the wedding scene is compelling because of the ways it draws together a range of logics tied to the work of celebrity, public memory, intimacy and citizenship in South Africa.

In this example of a popular soap opera star from a disadvantaged background who becomes a popular philanthropist in South Africa, there is a project of storytelling that attends to self-work and social uplift. Images of black women as celebrity models of inclusion become objects of circulation not simply as ideal consumers, but consumable themselves. Mupotsa demonstrates how black women as celebrities, in the space of global celebrity humanitarianism, contaminate powerful readings of activism that depend on distance from the abject others to be acted upon in building the self. The charity–celebrity–brand of Sophie Ndaba teaches us new ways to think about the impact of celebrity humanitarianism in the Global South, and problematizes theorization of "celebrity" as a contextual entity.

The final chapter in the section devoted to the Global South examines one of the most interesting and powerful sites for celebrity philanthropy – China. Johanna Hood analyzes local celebrity mechanisms in China's public health realm in chapter 5, entitled "Celebrity philanthropy in China: the political critique of Pu Cunxin's AIDS heroism." The text first gives a thorough introduction to the context of the emergence of celebrity activism on health issues in the international arena and the controversial and problematic state management of HIV/AIDS in China. Hood then turns to the rise of "HIV/AIDS Heroes" as a particular kind of aid celebrities in the People's Republic of China with a case study of the actor Pu Cunxin.

Hood's analysis rests on data from over 300 recent articles written in English and Chinese on Pu, together with participant observation conducted during fieldwork in China in 2003–8, to explore the emergence and significance of his fame within its local context. The chapter examines Pu as both an aid celebrity and an AIDS hero. Analyzing Pu Cunxin's media identity reveals some unique features of the operation of the Chinese "aid celebrity." Pu's efficacy as a contemporary Chinese aid celebrity does not rely solely on his status as an actor or popular cultural figure – social positions which, until this past century, were often poorly regarded in China. In fact, an examination of his case suggests that the power or impact of an "aid celebrity" cannot be measured strictly with reference to the realm of pop culture and popular perception. Pu Cunxin's uniqueness derives from his conformity with state visions of celebrity involvement in the promotion of public health, while simultaneously raising tacit social criticism of state inadequacy in the same arena. He also gains popularity by evoking centuries-old notions of the kinds of heroism and civility that can be expected from the cultivated classes. The chapter demonstrates how, together with a tightly controlled performance directed by the Chinese state, Pu has coupled this with a very subtle critique of an inadequate, however improving, party-state. When considering the impact of celebrity humanitarianism in the Global South, chapter 5 reminds us to pay attention to the special role of the state as part of the institutional framework that underpins celebrity interventions.

Part II Celebritization, participatory democracy, and the donor North

The next four chapters address the donor North with particular interest in the process of celebritization and its effects on participatory democracy in North–South relations. In chapter 6, Alexandra Cosima Budabin analyzes the American film star

Ben Affleck's work on behalf of the Democratic Republic of Congo (DRC) in "Ben Affleck goes to Washington: celebrity advocacy, access and influence." The data for chapter 6 come from a close reading of ECI's organizational materials, US Congressional records, mainstream media reporting, US tax returns, financial disclosure sites, and Affleck's writings. Affleck's case demonstrates the complex linkages that construct the "relationship" of North–South relations.

With the founding of the Eastern Congo Initiative (ECI) in 2010, Affleck entered the field of celebrity humanitarianism to spur social and economic development. ECI's objectives are split between the US and DRC. In the North, Affleck raises funds from elite circles and lobbies political spheres in the US to shape foreign aid practices. In the South, ECI distributes grants to local partners, with a focus on civil society. This partly reflects the ECI's negative assessment of the capacity for governance in a dysfunctional Congo. Budabin finds that there are strategic logics behind straddling contexts in both North and South in order to build credibility for a celebrity actor within elite circles. The chapter offers findings on the working of post-democratic politics of a celebrity-led NGO. Budabin concludes that the celebrity humanitarian may enjoy additional opportunities in the North, but offers less transparency and accountability for development interventions. Overall, a celebrity-led NGO distorts development processes by coalescing political and financial elite support for a celebrity figure, rather than following a path of public consultation and evaluation.

The next chapter, entitled "Humanitarian relief worker Sean Penn: a contextual story," presents an online ethnography of one of Hollywood's most famous "bad boys." Sean Penn has become known for acting as a loud critic of global and domestic injustices and for his opposition to military intervention, voicing opposition to the US involvement in the Second Iraqi War and posing moral questions over the lawfulness of the UK's presence in the Falklands Islands in 2012. Annika Bergman Rosamond analyzes media representations of Sean Penn's financial and hands-on efforts to assist the victims of Hurricane Katrina in New Orleans in 2005 and also his support for the victims of the 2010 Haitian earthquake.

Comparing Penn's humanitarian work in two different contexts reveals the commonalities of the moral imperative of cosmopolitanism that undergirds the bulk of celebrity humanitarianism in North–South relations. This cosmopolitanism, as explained in chapter 7, assumes that individuals are part of a shared moral order with responsibilities that extend beyond political boundaries – in other words, that celebrities, like the rest of us, have a moral obligation to "help." This cosmopolitanism becomes predictably complicated by context, and Bergmann Rosamond's chapter helps us to begin unpacking the important elements of race, gender and nationalism that are at stake in Penn's interventions in Haiti and New Orleans. Patriotism and male privilege become entangled with cosmopolitan, "other-regarding" acts by an individual. Chapter 7 argues that authenticity in celebrity humanitarianism need not be without self-interest; in fact, loudly voicing unpopular political opinions and engaging in messy hands-on work may be in the mutual interest of celebrity humanitarians and the recipients of their help.

Chapter 8 explores the meanings of celebrity-led benefit events within the context of Scandinavia. In contrast to most cases of celebrity humanitarianism which rely on constructions of the authentic, caring, celebrity do-gooder, Danish celebrity events play heavily on irony and politically incorrect representations of the humanitarian "other." In "Irony and politically incorrect humanitarianism: Danish celebrity-led benefit events," Mette Fog Olwig and Lene Bull Christiansen conduct case studies of the country's largest NGO, media and celebrity event – "Danmarks Indsamling" (Denmark's Fundraiser) and the smaller, non-commercial Fairtrade music festival, Fairtrade Concert. The authors examine how the role of celebrities in these events regulates the political circulation of meanings ascribed to the imagined connection between the Danish public and "Africa." They describe the overall format of the Danish events as shaped by a global tendency towards a depoliticization and celebritization of development aid, but that the popular events remain nonetheless in line with local Danish cultural norms by being inclusive and *folkelig* (for and of the people), often through an ostensibly politically incorrect, unassuming and underplayed, irony.

The fundraising performances to support international development among the Danish public include white celebrities pretending to be "African" while dancing in coconut bra and straw skirt costumes, and a sketch of celebrities costumed as a penis, anus and testicles. By skillfully analyzing celebrity humanitarianism performances within a deep cultural reading of national identity and transnational "help," chapter 8 argues that what may be otherwise interpreted as absurd and anomalous examples are, in fact, effective ways of democratizing North–South relations for the Danish public. This reliance on irony, however, is dangerous as it excludes the very participatory possibilities of those with something at stake in colonial and racist structural inequalities.

While the previous chapter has made important claims for the localizing tendencies in the globalization of celebrity humanitarianism, chapter 9, the final chapter in this section, explores the historical links between celebrity humanitarianism and colonialism. Robert van Krieken analyzes how the logic of humanitarianism, or, using Hannah Arendt's (1963) turn of phrase, "the passion for compassion," has always been an essential and contested element of the colonial project.

In what might be a surprising resemblance to chapter 7's description of Sean Penn in Haiti, chapter 9, "Celebrity, humanitarianism and settler-colonialism: G.A. Robinson and the Aborigines of Van Diemen's Land," charts the work of G.A. Robinson, a "hard-working and public-spirited" colonizer who went to Australia "to live among savages for £50 a year." In an explicitly detailed chapter, van Krieken unearths the relationships of power around the "humanitarian experiment" of 1824. Celebrity explorers and missionaries were key to the spread of empire, with "good-doing" and issues of economic inequality the object of intense public interest over the course of the nearly two hundred years of colonial expansion. The power politics of elite global humanitarian networks of the 19th century are charted in this chapter and van Krieken makes a strong case for considering contemporary celebrity humanitarianism in a historical perspective deeply rooted in colonialism and "modernity." He documents the disconnect between intentions and outcomes in humanitarianism, concluding that: "As an exercise in humanitarian intervention, Robinson's removal of the Aborigines of Van Diemen's Land to Flinders Island was a failure that could hardly have been more spectacular, perfectly fine except for the fact that everybody died."

The book concludes with an epilogue by Dan Brockington on "The politics of celebrity humanitarianism." Drawing on the traditional use of the term, "epilogue" to refer to the final scene of a play that comments on, or summarizes, the main action, spoken from inside the story by one of the actors, Brockington takes up the play of politics. Reflecting on the material from the previous chapters, he asks a fundamental normative question: What politics do we want from celebrity humanitarianism?

The epilogue reviews the book's contribution to understanding the diversity of Southern politics of celebrity humanitarianism, and to the different manifestations of the celebrity industry in diverse cultural contexts. Brockington also traces how the preceding chapters have contributed to our understanding of the tensions between structure and agency in the work of celebrity humanitarians. He concludes with reflections on the dilemmas of post-democracy (Crouch 2004), the increasingly limited distribution of the benefits of capitalism and the dangers of using privilege to combat privilege through celebrity humanitarianism. The epilogue concludes with both a normative call and a research agenda derived from the previous chapters: "understanding the actually existing politics of celebrity humanitarianism, in all its diversity, actually creates more room for normative agendas which can place such high demands on it."

Conclusion: politics, place and power

As complexity in North–South relations intensifies and democratic face-to-face accountability becomes increasingly impossible, back talk is incomprehensible, and culture is confusing, there are openings for celebrities as mediators of this global social distance. This sort of complexity is at the very foundation of North–South relations exemplified by contemporary humanitarian and development realities, such as the Ebola anecdote that began this introduction. Yet, as celebrities (and corporations) become increasingly involved in shaping the meanings of humanitarianism, the field itself will be increasingly shifted toward the elite, the profitable and the photogenic. It would be naïve to imagine a time when "development" was more "authentically" concerned with mitigating the negative effects of poverty and inequality. If anything, as chapter 9 clearly demonstrates, at the heart of the humanitarian impulse is the push for modernity that we see in both colonialism and development. It would be intellectually arrogant and culturally Anglocentric to assume that global celebrity cultures of iconic suffering are unilaterally shaping "local" celebrity cultures across the globe. Chapter 8 suggests the impervious nature of a local culture more ironic than iconic. However, to understand their relationships, linkages, misconnections and transnational flows, we need far more attention to the actual practices of elite leadership in comparative contexts. Thus, this book's conclusions, not its premises, are critical. Nine substantive chapters focusing on the impact of celebrity humanitarianism in the Global South and celebritization, participation and democratization in the donor North illustrate the social structuring of celebrity through institutional forms of life, or, in other words, the staging of inequality.

Notes

1 *Independent on Sunday* newspaper from August 3, 2014, referenced in "Give me the money, now! But what will happen tomorrow? Ebola as a symbol for the 'moral bankruptcy of capitalism'. " aspiration&revolution blog by Tanja R. Müller, October 14, 2014, at https://tanjarmueller.wordpress.com/2014/11/21/band-aid-thirty-the-imf-and-the-call-to-trust-the-doctor/ [accessed January 20, 2015].
2 Although it should be noted that the Nigeriafilms.com reported that film writer Tunde Kelani "disclosed that he plans to converge Nollywood celebrities to help create an awareness campaign on the dreaded Ebola virus." http://www.nigeriafilms.com/news/28313/16/ebola-virus-celebrities-needed.html [accessed October 3, 2014].
3 "Band Aid 30: Bob Geldof rewrites classic lyrics for Ebola-fighting 30th anniversary release," *The Independent*, January 12, 2014, http://www.independent.co.uk/arts-entertainment/music/news/band-aid-30-bob-geldof-rewrites-classic-lyrics-for-ebolafighting-30th-anniversary-release-9852301.html [accessed January 12, 2015].
4 "Band Aid 30: 'Buy the song. Stop the virus'. Just don't ask how." Róisín Read on Manchester Calling blog at http://www.blog.hcri.ac.uk/band-aid-30-just-dont-ask-how/ [accessed January 20, 2015].
5 "Does Paul Farmer have the Ebola Solution? George Soros is Spending $4 Million to Find Out." *Forbes*, September 16, 2014. http://www.forbes.com/sites/randalllane/2014/09/16/does-paul-farmer-have-the-ebola-solution-george-soros-is-spending-4-million-to-find-out/ [accessed January 20, 2015].
6 http://time.com/time-person-of-the-year-ebola-fighters-choice/ [accessed January 20, 2015].
7 The largest donors were the US government and the World Bank, followed by the UK, the African Development Bank and the International Monetary Fund. The Gates Foundation, Mark Zuckerberg and the Paul G. Allen Family Foundation also gave donations to fight Ebola. "UN Ebola chief calls for final funding push to defeat virus in West Africa," *The Guardian*, January 9, 2015, http://www.theguardian.com/world/2015/jan/20/un-ebola-chief-calls-for-final-funding-push-to-defeat-virus-in-west-africa [accessed January 20, 2015].
8 http://www.whitehouse.gov/blog/2015/01/18/meet-dr-pranav-shetty-guest-first-lady-state-union [accessed January 20, 2015].
9 "North–South Policy – What's the Problem?," *Foreign Affairs*, January 30, 2015, http://www.foreignaffairs.com/articles/33958/roger-d-hansen/north-south-policy-whats-the-problem [accessed January 30, 2015].
10 There is a significant gap between the portrayal of the causes of humanitarian disasters as "emergencies" and considerations of their historical and political roots, and these differences shape both conflict itself and institutional resilience, as argued by Roberto Belloni (2007).

References

Arendt, H. 1963. *On Revolution*. London: Faber.

Barnett, Michael. 2011. *Empire of Humanity: A History of Humanitarianism*. Ithaca: Cornell University Press.

Belloni, Roberto. 2007. The trouble with humanitarianism. *Review of International Studies*, 33 (3), 451–74.

Biccum, A. 2007. Marketing development: Live 8 and the production of the global citizen. *Development and Change*, 38 (6), 1111–26.

Boltanski, L. 1999. *Distant Suffering: Morality, Media and Politics*. Cambridge: Cambridge University Press.

Boltanski, L. & Thévenot, L. 1991. *De la justification*. Paris: Gallimard.

Brockington, D. 2014. *Celebrity Advocacy and International Development*. London and New York: Routledge.

Chouliaraki, L. 2012. The theatricality of humanitarianism: a critique of celebrity advocacy. *Communication and Critical/Cultural Studies*, 9 (1), 1–21.

Chouliaraki, L. 2013. *The Ironic Spectator: Solidarity in the Age of Post-Humanitarianism*. Cambridge: Polity.

Cooper, A.F. 2008. *Celebrity Diplomacy*. Boulder: Paradigm Publishers.

Crouch, Colin. 2004. *Post-Democracy*. Cambridge: Polity.

De Waal, Alexander. 1997. *Famine Crimes: Politics and the Disaster Relief Industry in Africa*. Oxford: James Currey.

Dieter, H. & Kumar, R. 2008. The downside of celebrity diplomacy: the neglected complexity of development. *Global Governance*, 14, 259–64.

Driessens, Oliver. 2013. Celebrity capital: redefining celebrity using field theory. *Theory and Society*, 42, 543–60.

Duncombe, Stephen. 2007. *Dream: Re-Imagining Progressive Politics in an Age of Fantasy*. New York: The New Press.

Fassin, Didier. 2012. *Humanitarian Reason: A Moral History of the Present*. Berkeley, CA: University of California Press.

Goodman, M.K. & Barnes, C., 2011. Star/poverty space: the making of the "development celebrity." *Celebrity Studies*, 2 (1), 69–85.

Holmes, Su & Redmond, Sean, 2010. Editorial: a journal in celebrity studies. *Celebrity Studies*, 1 (1), 1–10.

Huliaras, A. & Tzifakis, N. 2010. Celebrity activism in international relations: in search of a framework for analysis. *Global Society*, 24 (2), 255–74.

Kapoor, I. 2013. *Celebrity Humanitarianism: Ideology of Global Charity*. New York: Routledge.

van Krieken, R., 2012. *Celebrity Society*. London & New York: Routledge.

Littler, J. 2008. "I feel your pain:" cosmopolitan charity and the public fashioning of the celebrity soul. *Social Semiotics*, 18 (2), 237–51.

Littler, J. 2011. Introduction: celebrity and the transnational. *Interpreting* (March 2012), 37–41.

Lowenthal, Leo. 1944. The Triumph of Mass Idols. In: *Literature, Popular Culture and Society*. Palo Alto, CA: Pacific Books.

Müller, Tanja R. 2013. The long shadow of Band Aid humanitarianism: revisiting the dynamics between famine and celebrity. *Third World Quarterly*, 34 (3), 470–84.

Repo, J. & Yrjölä, R. 2011. The gender politics of celebrity humanitarianism in Africa. *International Feminist Journal of Politics*, 13 (1), 44–62.

Richey, L.A. & Ponte, S. 2011. *Brand Aid: Shopping Well to Save the World*. Minneapolis: University of Minnesota Press.

Richey, L.A. & Ponte, S. 2014. New actors and alliances in development. *Third World Quarterly*, 35 (1), 1–21.

Robertson, Alexa, 2015. *Media and Politics in a Globalizing World*. Cambridge, UK: Polity.

Scott, Martin, 2014. The role of celebrities in mediating distant suffering. *International Journal of Cultural Studies*, 14 (4), 1–18.

Street, J. 2004. Celebrity politicians: popular culture and political representation. *British Journal of Politics and International Relations*, 6 (4), 435–52.

Street, J. 2012. Do celebrity politics and celebrity politicians matter? *British Journal of Politics and International Relations*, 14 (3), 346–56.

Street, John. 2010. *Mass Media, Politics and Democracy*. Basingstoke: Palgrave Macmillan.

Tsaliki, L., Frangonikolopoulos, C.A. & Huliaras, A. (eds). 2011. *Transnational Celebrity Activism in Global Politics*. Chicago: Intellect.

Vestergaard, M. forthcoming. Humanitarian categorization of victimhood – the case of the International Committee of the Red Cross' Engagement in the Nigeria–Biafra Conflict, 1967–70. PhD Dissertation, Dept. of Society and Globalisation, Roskilde University, Denmark.

Waters, T. 2001. *Bureaucratizing the Good Samaritan: The Limitations of Humanitarian Relief Operations*. Boulder, CO: Westview Press.

Wheeler, M. 2011. Celebrity diplomacy: United Nations' Goodwill Ambassadors and Messengers of Peace. *Celebrity Studies*, 2 (1), 6–18.

Wheeler, M. 2013. *Celebrity Politics*. Cambridge: Polity.

Wilson, Julie A. 2011. A new kind of star is born: Audrey Hepburn and the global governmentalisation of female stardom. *Celebrity Studies*, 2 (1), 56–68.

PART I
Celebrity impact in the global South

1

ANGELINA JOLIE AND THE EVERYDAY GEOPOLITICS OF CELEBRITY HUMANITARIANISM IN A THAILAND–BURMA BORDER TOWN

Mary Mostafanezhad

Introduction

I meet Dara, a 44-year-old Burmese[1] exile and former political prisoner, in Mae Sot, a Thai–Burmese[2] border town known as "Little Burma" because it is home to more than 200,000 Burmese residents (Arnold 2013). We sit at the hand-carved table in front of a colorful guesthouse that is well known among the many non-governmental organization (NGO) practitioners. I was introduced to Dara through a friend who works for an NGO in Chiang Mai city, located approximately 357 km northeast of Mae Sot. As Dara tells me about his experience working with numerous local NGOs, we are interrupted by the sound of chanting monks in the temple across the road. Dara smiles and it seems the chanting comforts him. He raises his voice slightly to compensate for the noise as he explains to me how he would like others to know more about the continued struggles of exiled Burmese. Dara has an aura of calm intellectualism about him; for more than 20 years he has engaged with the myriad political, economic and social challenges of Burmese exiles. I explain to Dara that I am interested in how Burmese exiles perceive Angelina Jolie's visits to the refugee camps. At first Dara looks puzzled, perhaps because of the strange nature of my request. To clarify that he knows what I am talking about, I ask him, "Have you heard of Angelina Jolie?" He chuckles as his eyes light up and replies, "Oh, Angelina Jolie! Of course I know her. And did you know she adopted one of the refugee children?"

Drawing on conversations with Burmese residents of northern Thailand, in this chapter I examine the everyday geopolitics of Jolie's humanitarian interventions and the implications of the "moral support" that she engendered among Burmese exiles. Investigations of "the communicative cultural flows circulating between the celebrity, their impoverished 'Others' and the non-destitute, non-celebrity 'ordinary' subject can tell us something both about how such power relationships are maintained and how the possibilities of change to global injustices are imagined or disavowed" (Littler 2008, p. 237). Through an examination of these linked discursive circuits, I argue that instead of drawing attention to the continued human rights atrocities in Burma, widespread moral, rather than political support, materialized among many Burmese exiles. As a result, Jolie's experience as a celebrity humanitarian perpetuated a popular geopolitical discourse of North–South relations that foregrounded aestheticized cosmopolitan celebrity care over place-based political concern for Burmese exiles.

As I continued my conversations with Burmese exiles, I found that many were often emotionally invested in the idea that Jolie was now raising a Burmese child. When asked what they knew about this rumor, many smiled as they imagined how exciting it might have been to be chosen as Angelina's child. Kyine, for example, a middle-aged mother of two, believed that Jolie had adopted not one, but two children: "I've heard that [Jolie] adopted two kids. It means she saved their lives. People like her must have a soul filled with compassion to save all refugees." As Kyine's comment highlights, Jolie is quite well known among Burmese in the Thai–Burmese border area, both for her role in popular movies such as *Lara Croft: Tomb Raider* and *Mr. and Mrs. Smith,* as well as for rumors that she had adopted a Burmese child from one of the nine refugee camps that line the Thailand–Burma border.

Indeed, as a United Nations High Commissioner for Refugees (UNHCR) Goodwill Ambassador, Jolie has visited the refugee camps along the Thailand–Burma border four times since 2002. Her recurrent trips are indicative of her concern for one of the most protracted displacement situations in the world. Her most recent visit to mark World Refugee Day in June of 2014 was widely publicized through images and short documentaries.[3] Her one-day visits were meant to draw attention to ongoing human rights abuses in Burma, as well as to the plight of the approximately 147,000 refugees that live in the nine camps along the border (UNHCR 2014). Jolie's sojourns were successful in attracting international media coverage and were applauded by UNHCR for the worldwide attention they drew to the camps, which had first been established in 1983.

Today Jolie is perhaps the single most well-known international female celebrity humanitarian. In a recent article, entitled "Angelina Jolie Died for Our Sins," *Esquire* magazine explains how:

> One could make the argument that she is the most famous woman in the world. Why not, then, just go ahead and make the argument that she is the best woman in the world, in terms of her generosity, her dedication, and her courage? The two arguments would seem hopelessly disconnected — the first being an objective assessment, or at least amenable to fact; the second being subjective and sentimental — but in truth they have become inextricable.[4]

Jolie developed an interest in humanitarian issues in 2003 while filming the Hollywood blockbuster, *Tomb Raider*, in Cambodia.[5] Since then, she has personally donated more than US$5 million to UNHCR and visited more than 40 refugee sites to speak out against prolonged refugee crises around the world (UNHCR 2014). She was the first to receive the Citizen of the World Award from the United Nations Correspondents Association in 2003 and in 2005 she was granted the United Nations Association of the US Global Humanitarian Award (UNHCR 2014). With an active role in more than 29 international charities and foundations such as UNICEF, UNHCR, Médecins Sans Frontières, as well as her founding of the Maddox Jolie-Pitt Foundation in 2006 (an environment and food security NGO in Cambodia created with her husband, movie star Brad Pitt), Jolie's humanitarian commitments are wide-ranging. In terms of her growth as an actress, Littler observes how "if a wild-child role in *Girl Interrupted* seemed just the right [movie] outlet for Jolie in her twenties, a project like *A Mighty Heart*, about geopolitics and real love, seems perfect for her now" (Littler 2008, p. 237). Indeed, representations of Jolie stem from her mixed reputation as a rebellious teenager, to a home wrecker, to a happy homemaker with "an ever-expanding globe trotting brood, which includes a mix of Pitt-Jolie progeny and international orphans" (Wilson 2010, p. 28).

It is important to note that the relationship between UNHCR and Burmese exiles is highly political. In 2005 UNHCR concluded its registration of refugees along the border despite the continued violence in Burma and ongoing displacement of Burmese exiles into Thailand. Today, more than 60,000 Burmese living along the Thailand–Burma border are not officially classified as refugees despite the precarious nature of their situation (Tan & McClellan 2014). It is within this complex geopolitical context that, as an ambassador of UNHCR, Jolie's humanitarian missions in the Thailand–Burma border have taken place. I focus on perspectives from Burmese residents in a Thai–Burmese border town, in part, to illustrate how communicative cultural flows resist simplistic utopian or dystopian views of celebrity humanitarian interventions. Critical geopolitics is a subfield in political geography that examines how political power and discourse mediate geographical imaginations of the "North" and "South". In this way, it highlights how humanitarian practice is shaped through geopolitical discourse. Thus, I engage with recent work on how popular media and lived experience articulate everyday geopolitical outcomes through a "grounded but translocal" perspective of celebrity interventions in the Thai–Burmese border area (Katz 2001).

This chapter is organized as follows. First, I identify linkages between emerging literature on everyday geopolitics and celebrity humanitarianism. I also examine how this work intersects with recent research on the role of celebrity humanitarianism in humanitarian interventions. I then examine what I call the "celebrity cosmopolitan aesthetic" or the widespread shift towards cosmopolitan and aestheticized humanitarian concern, rather than place-based politics of concern. Expanding on existing studies in everyday geopolitics, I then examine the affective experience of Burmese exiles' interpretations of the event as an act of moral support and social solidarity. Far-reaching support of Jolie among Burmese exiles, I argue in the following section, is simultaneously coupled with widespread critiques of the UN and its perceived lack of political-economic backing. Finally, I theorize how the everyday geopolitics of Jolie's intervention – albeit inadvertently – served to depoliticize the refugee crisis along the Thailand–Burma border.

The everyday geopolitics of celebrity humanitarianism

While Jolie may be the most popular female celebrity to partake in humanitarian work, she is not the first. Early examples included Audrey Hepburn's work with UNICEF and also Jane Fonda's protests against the Vietnam war (Littler 2008; Benwell et al. 2012). Yet it is significant that popular attention to celebrities and their causes has intensified rapidly over the past two decades and charity work is now seen as an essential part of being a celebrity. The growth of celebrity humanitarianism exists within broader shifts of the post-Fordist cultural turn, which set the stage for cosmopolitan celebrity charity and widespread support of the poor in the Global South as a way for celebrities to reframe themselves as caring, compassionate and borderline religious beings (Littler 2008, p. 237). It is perhaps no wonder, then, that celebrity humanitarianism is, for the most part, positively received by major development institutions such as the UN and the World Economic Forum (Repo & Yrjölä, 2011, p. 45).

Yet, despite widespread support of Jolie's humanitarian efforts by popular media, academic attention to celebrity humanitarianism has tended to be more critical than popular media would suggest (Barron 2009; Biccum 2011; Boykoff & Goodman 2009; Brockington 2014; Goodman 2011; Kapoor 2012; Kellner 2010). Over the last decade, academic interest in celebrity advocacy has grown in leaps and bounds (van Krieken 2012; Cooper 2009; Littler 2007; Kapoor 2012; Ponte & Richey 2011; Richey & Ponte 2008). Post-colonial critiques of Western development practitioners that use celebrities to promote First World agendas are commonly addressed in the literature (Lousley 2013, p. 7). Repo and Yrjölä highlight how celebrity humanitarianism is intensely gendered in the way that male and female celebrities select their causes and strategies of involvement (2011). Academic investigations are often focused on questions around the credibility of celebrities in politics (Street 2004). These questions of legitimacy are central to celebrity humanitarianism. Thus, celebrities matter, but perhaps not in ways we might have predicted (Scott 2014, p. 16).

Despite this academic critique, Jolie's popularity as a Hollywood superstar-cum-humanitarian continues to expand in *both* the North and the South. Transnational celebrities such as Jolie are indicative of what Littler describes as communicative cultural flows that circulate between the celebrity, their impoverished others and the ordinary or "neutral" subject:

> Three key figures are often present in discussion around this issue: the celebrity (mainly belonging to the global West/North); their impoverished

Others (often belonging to either "the rest" of the world, or to the zones Manuel Castells terms "fourth worlds"); and the "neutral" position of the non-destitute, non-celebrity "ordinary" subject."

(2008, p. 246)

These communicative flows are primarily examined from the perspectives of the celebrities and their representations in popular media. Yet perspectives from the "impoverished others" are curiously absent from the literature. While the cultural politics of celebrity humanitarianism have been a notable topic of academic inquiry over the past decade, the role of everyday geopolitics in celebrity interventions is relatively absent from academic critique (Benwell et al. 2012, p. 405). I argue that celebrity humanitarians now play a key role in geopolitical discourses of North–South relations.

Traditionally, the term "geopolitics" has referred to the impact of geography on politics. Today, geopolitics incorporates a much broader range of connotations that are inclusive of everyday experience and encounters. In human geography it is used to examine how space is constructed through various discursive, material and power relations. Critical geopolitics – now mainstream geopolitics in human geography – emerged in the early 1990s to include, for example, textual and discourse analysis (Dittmer & Gray 2010). In this way, critical geopolitics offers more nuanced understandings of political practices. Critical geopolitical scholars now consider people such as NGO practitioners, journalists, bloggers and activists as political subjects. Thus, the "critical turn" in geopolitics includes everyday geopolitics.

This theoretical shift facilitates the inclusion of the study of celebrity humanitarianism, which represents an undertheorized gap in the literature as the role of celebrities in contemporary society calls "into question any sharp distinction between elite and popular geopolitical discourses and practices including what has been termed alter-geopolitics (Koopman 2011), anti-geopolitics (Routledge 2003), banal geopolitics (Sidaway 2008), feminist geopolitics (Dowler & Sharp 2001) and subaltern geopolitics (Sharp 2011)" (Benwell et al. 2012, p. 405). Here, celebrity humanitarianism disrupts categories in geopolitical research where "[T]he world of celebrity geopolitics would appear to connect the national parliament/congress with the popular/everyday and the 'celebrity' with the 'politician' (and the citizen) in interesting ways" (Benwell et al. 2012, p. 406). The separation of the elite and the mundane is increasingly blurred through celebrity humanitarianism where celebrity engagement with the poor in the Global South complicates geopolitical thought. This distinction is especially nuanced by the ways celebrities and politicians, for example, communicate with their publics through Facebook and Twitter and how "the distinction between elite and popular political communication breaks down" (Benwell et al. 2012, p. 406). Feminist geopolitical scholars have been particularly influential in challenging binaries such as public/private and public/political and demonstrating how the private is also political (Dittmer & Gray 2010, 1666). As a result, there is an emergent interest in the

everyday, mundane and popular sphere of human experience. This work emphasizes "the topologies of power that connect the phenomena often described as
scales – body, locality, regional, national, global (Sharp 2007)" (Dittmer & Gray
2010, 1666).

Celebrity humanitarianism is also gendered. We may also, for example, consider how Jolie's representations are reflective of stereotypes around ideal Western
womanhood. Cultural categories such as race, class, gender and ethnicity mediate how Jolie's work is both received and imitated in the North. For example,
her experience on the border to demonstrate her concern for Burmese refugees
shapes powerful, political and gendered discourses about appropriate *female* celebrity humanitarian engagement. While it is beyond the scope of this chapter to
elaborate, it is also important to point out that traditional gender roles in Burmese
society inherently mediate Burmese exiles' interpretations of Jolie's role with
UNHCR. For example, women in Burmese society who fulfill their traditional
role in managing the household tend to be idealized. Yet, these gender norms may
be challenged by international gender practices such as Jolie's travel without her
husband and children to the camps. Thus, "Rather than conceiving of these as
scales, with the sense of analytical division that comes with that concept, scholars in
feminist geopolitics tend to conceive of politics as 'grounded but translocal' (Katz
2001, p. 1231) in a way that refuses to ghettoize gender as a local phenomenon (to
be juxtaposed with purportedly gender-neutral – and thus masculinity normed –
macro-accounts of political processes" (Dittmer & Gray 2010, 1666).

Methodology

Drawing from critical phenomenological perspectives, I focus on everyday conversations among Burmese exiles and their interpretations of Jolie's humanitarian
work. These are "everyday experiences of space and geopolitics that are neither
scripted nor found embedded in celluloid or print" (Dittmer & Gray 2010, 1667).
Critical phenomenology links the phenomenal with the political (Good 1994) and
attends "to the many, and often highly charged political, social, and discursive
forces that contribute to life in particular settings" (Desjarlais & Jason Throop
2011, p. 93). While phenomenological studies emerged in human geography in
the 1970s (e.g. Tuan 1974), phenomenological research was only recently recognized as a useful methodology in geopolitical research (Dittmer & Gray 2010).
Critical phenomenological ethnography in particular is a framework that facilitates
the examination of linkages between popular discourses on celebrity humanitarianism and the corollary everyday geopolitics of Burmese exiles. This framework
"recognizes the macro structural dimensions of our social existence (the way discursive regimes are embodied and played out in everyday social practice)" while
also "foreground[ing] the personal, intimate, singular, and eventful qualities of
social life" (Mattingly 2010, p. 7). Combined with an ethnographic lens, critical
phenomenology facilitates the examination of the implications of celebrity humanitarianism as a social practice in the Global South.

This chapter is based on participant observation and conversations with Burmese exiles, NGO practitioners and activists in northern Thailand. Conversations in Burmese were translated by my Burmese friend, Dara. Conversations that could be conducted in English or Thai were carried out by myself, as I am a native English speaker and am proficient in Thai. Conversations with NGO practitioners were conducted in English. Conversations typically lasted between 30 and 50 minutes and took place in people's homes, hospitals, offices in NGOs and teashops. All names of informants and places are pseudonyms.

The celebrity cosmopolitan aesthetic

As a Goodwill Ambassador for UNHCR, Jolie's primary role is to "give a voice to refugees and internally displaced people. She undertakes advocacy on their behalf, representing UNHCR and the High Commissioner at the diplomatic level and engaging with others on global displacement issues" (UNHCR 2014). With Brad Pitt and her six children in tow, Jolie is often represented in the popular media as a globetrotting mother with a predilection for war and disaster-torn areas, as her recent missions to Lebanon, Iraq and Afghanistan indicate (Krever 2014). Jolie's interest in displacement issues and her generosity as well as the attention she has brought to humanitarian crises have been well received by the general public in the North. Her image continues to adorn covers of publications ranging from *Rolling Stone* to *Marie Claire* to *People Magazine*. She is depicted in multifarious images as, for example, a celebrity, humanitarian, mother and partner (now wife) of Brad Pitt. When shown in her humanitarian role, she tends to be surrounded by groups of children, huddled in a refugee tent with a small family or bending over an elderly couple as if to bless them with her saintly presence. These kinds of aesthetically sophisticated photographs signify her intimate connection with refugees from around the world and are key signifiers of her humanitarian spirit.

Along with other high-profile celebrity humanitarians, Jolie now plays a key role in geopolitical discourses of North–South relations. This role is maintained in part through the celebrity cosmopolitan aesthetic – defined by celebrities' widespread privileging of the aesthetics of global poverty over a place-based politics of concern. It is notable that celebrity care most frequently transpires in "transnational terrain" (Littler 2008, p. 239). For Jolie, the transnational nature of her humanitarian, as well as her motherly endeavors, plays into her image as a caring cosmopolitan celebrity. Her visits to refugees in more than 40 countries since 2001 are illustrative of her unbound geography of care. She highlights some of her adventures in her travel memoir, *Notes from My Travels: Visits with Refugees in Africa, Cambodia, Pakistan and Ecuador,* which depicts her experience in refugee camps on three continents (Jolie 2003). In addition to her book written for popular audiences, she also publishes diaries from her UNHCR excursions on the official UNHCR website (Jolie 2004).

Jolie's transnational scope of care demonstrates "a globalised sensibility and a cosmopolitan caring, an effect augmented by Jolie's high-profile Benetton-style

adoption of a range of differently shaded children from a variety of countries. And
her engagement with politically sensitive subjects such as refugees, environmen-
talism and Darfur marks her as a very modern breed of American liberal" (Littler
2008, p. 238). In the context of Africa, Browning has similarly critiqued how AIDS
articulates with multiculturalism in ways that aestheticize race through Benetton's
clothing advertisements (Browning 2013, p. 143). Browning's work illustrates how
the highly racialized, gendered and popularized development culture represented
through Jolie is not limited to Jolie. Indeed, the tastefully photographed images of
Jolie's round-the-world missions that often depict her surrounded by a predictable
entourage of adoring children and the elderly are also widespread among other
female celebrities (Chouliaraki 2006). These images are part of the broader celebrity cosmopolitan aesthetic which takes on new discursive forms in popular culture
in the North. For example, Jolie's cosmopolitan care is echoed in what Goodman
refers to as "iCare capitalism," or "the overt creation of economic, brand, and self-
value out of lives saved and death staved," which is now in full swing (Goodman
2013, p. 105). The entanglement of capitalism, celebrity care and cosmopolitanism
shapes geopolitical discourses of North–South relations in ways that simultaneously
empathize and aestheticize the poor in the South while contributing to an increasingly cosmopolitan celebrity-consumer culture in the North.

These aestheticized experiences are represented by Jolie's one-day site visits to
the refugee camps along the Thailand–Burma border. Jolie describes her experience as one of beauty and raw emotion. In an interview after her 2009 visit to Ban
Mai Nai Soi refugee camp, Jolie explained: "I was saddened to meet a 21-year-
old woman who was born in a refugee camp, who has never even been out of
the camp and is now raising her own child in a camp" (McKinsey 2009). This
sentiment appears again in her official UNHCR refugee diary where she empa-
thetically writes about life in the refugee camp during her 2004 visit. She describes
her experience entering the camp: "We drive into the camp. A vast bamboo city
(since 1993). Right away you can see a difference on the faces. There is sadness,
heaviness in the air." This passage is juxtaposed with the following sentence which
aestheticizes her emotional experience: "The children are beautiful and shy. Many
of them born here. Stateless. I meet a woman washing clothes . . . " (Jolie 2004).

The simultaneous focus on the caring and the aesthetic aspects of her experience
are recurrent in her UNHCR refugee diary. She continues to write:

> We step up on a hill and suddenly I am overwhelmed with a view of the
> camp from above. It's beautiful and sad; I am overwhelmed by a mix of emo-
> tions. It is a city full of special people. Survivors. Remarkable families. It is
> also a prison . . . Down the path we hear singing and follow it. We find one of
> the teachers playing an old guitar and teaching the kids a new song. It's more
> than just a song. It is a way of keeping a language and culture alive when liv-
> ing in another country. We spent a while there. It was wonderful. A moment
> of smiles and peace. They laughed at me because I didn't know if I should
> clap or stomp . . . We get out and walk around. They are such a beautiful and

gracious people. It makes me imagine how Myanmar could be. The sun is going down and women are bathing their children outside. Peaceful.

(Jolie 2004)

Jolie's UNHCR diary is written as a travel memoir of her experiences in the refugee camps. Jolie's diary is critical to her broader celebrity cosmopolitan aesthetic which overshadows the political–economic–social differences between Jolie and the refugees that she cares for. As Littler explains, "in terms that mobilise the language of justice which can acknowledge the structural inequalities in global social systems whilst simultaneously denying the material implications of the wealth of the star and how they contribute to the spaces where suffering takes place. In either way, the intimacy, the confession of truly caring, the performance of a celebrity 'soul', attempts to present itself as plugging the gap" (Littler 2008, p. 248).

Thus, while there is little doubt that Jolie's one-day site visits to the refugee camps along the Thailand–Burma border have brought increased attention to the ongoing refugee crisis among popular audiences in the North, this attention is strategically situated in ways that obscure the political–economic relationship between herself and the Burmese exiles she shows compassion for. This is because her intended audience in the North is asked, not what political–economic

FIGURE 1.1 As a part of a special envoy of the United Nations High Commissioner for Refugees (UNHCR), Angelina Jolie visits Burmese refugees in a camp along the Thai–Burma border for World Refugee Day in June 2014. Photograph from UNHCR/R. Arnold.

relationships facilitated this refugee crisis, but rather what to think about Jolie's compassionate concern.

Jolie's cosmopolitan celebrity care extends into her personal life as well. Repo and Yrjölä explain how, "[a]s a sort of 'mother-without-borders,' Jolie constructed a model of what became referred to as the 'rainbow family' (*Telegraph*, 29 October 2005). The projection of the rainbow family metaphor onto the international system promoted the vision of a harmonious interracial and multicultural world community, but at the same time the parallel depended on racial and economic differentiation through beliefs attached to biological parenthood" (Repo & Yrjölä 2011, 50). Jolie's cosmopolitan sensibility as both a humanitarian and mother, work to discursively shift our understanding of development and inequality from the historically situated and place-based to a less grounded cosmopolitan care. In this way, a particular kind of geopolitical discourse of North–South relations is constructed through Jolie's concern for exiles "everywhere." This concern is also aestheticized in ways that render the often-unidentified refugee an object of, as well as an aestheticized recipient of care.

"Love operates within political limits"

While riding the red *songthaew* or covered hatchback truck with two benches in the back where passengers sit, a small woman with enormous bags of fruit and vegetables sat next to me. I decided to ask her if she knew of Jolie. She explained that she did know Jolie and that she was waiting to see her someday. I then asked her if she knew what she did in the camps along the border. She explained: "She [Jolie] is a rich and famous actress; she has an ability to help us . . . her visit could make us feel happy at least." In a different context, Muang, a Burmese reporter and former political prisoner, sat down at the plastic table in the large kitchen at a local NGO. Muang was a tall, dark-haired man with khaki pants, a T-shirt from an NGO and black glasses. When I asked him what he thought of Jolie's visits to the camps, he replied with a wide grin on his face, "refugee camps, most of the refugees know the artists . . . they want to meet and see, not just Angelina Jolie but other actors and actresses. They would become happy." He further explained:

> She is not only a celebrity for one country; she is a celebrity for the whole world. Many people, millions of people, they know her. They love her a lot. At the time when Angelina Jolie visited the Burmese refugee camp I was still in prison. At that time, I wasn't present. I just heard about Angelina's visit in jail. I was in prison but I heard about her on the radio. We secretly had a radio. That's where we heard it. We are happy that she came to the camps. We were so happy. Anyhow, that's it. She is one of the huge supporters, she emotionally supports the people and that is good . . . Her emotional support is good. That's why many refugees felt so happy to see Angelina Jolie because she is a very famous girl. It's good.

While sitting around a wooden table at a local restaurant dedicated to providing space for the sale of Burmese handicrafts and art to tourists, Aye, a former political prisoner and journalist described his thoughts on Jolie's visit to the camps:

> I thank her very much, because she's an actress. She is not the kind of actress that goes to nightclubs or other places like that . . . She comes here to the refugees and wants to support and honor them. I am thankful to her. There should be more actors, actresses and famous people like Jolie; there should be more. Not only in Burma but also in other refugee camps . . . All around the world. [The celebrities] should go and meet and donate . . . There should be more support because there is more need.

The sentiment of moral support was invariably echoed by other Burmese exiles as Jolie's visits were largely interpreted to be a positive indication of her commitment.

Kywe, a young mother of three, the youngest of which was strapped to her chest in patchwork sling, explained that she believed Jolie could help the refugees "because she is interested in us and our issues, so she may help us. She is the one supporting us all the way." The social solidarity that Kywe describes is similarly articulated by Kyine who explained: "what I heard is that she visited there as an ambassador for UNHCR. I think she can help people; I feel so cheerful as well because she came here . . . [celebrities] can [help] because they are the public figures. Let's take Jolie. She is famous, attractive and a hard worker. That is why she became an ambassador . . . "

While the moral support and sense of social solidarity that Jolie engendered among Burmese exiles is clearly present, the material–political effects of Jolie's flying visits are less well understood. Moe, an NGO practitioner, medical assistant and human rights activist, explained that he didn't see Jolie himself but that gossip quickly spread around the camps of her visit: "When I got to the camp it was 2009. So I just heard what others were talking about . . . I heard that her visit brought a lot more help for refugees, she also organized some activities for the refugees and so on . . . " When I asked him what she specifically did for people living in the camps he stated: "I just heard that she donated or gave some support for us. But I just don't know what exactly she did." Khin, a reporter for a Burmese magazine, explained that she knew Jolie had visited the camp but she didn't realize that she was a donor. She explained: "we didn't know she was one of the donors for us at that time. We found out later about it and I like her so much now . . . I am so proud of her." When asked how Jolie might benefit people in the camps, Khin replied: "well, they didn't get any material support from it. But she can share what she witnessed with the world . . . I feel so glad that she went there. As a very famous and rich woman like her, coming to a place like this is so amazing." Kywe similarly explained: "I just heard that she visited there . . . It makes me realize that they care about us, they acknowledge us and motivate us too." In this instance, "they" seems to imply celebrities, and perhaps people in the North more generally.

These comments also seem to indicate Burmese exiles' faith in the power of celebrities to transmit their plight to a global audience.

The moral support that Jolie incited in the camps is not unlike the moral support of the US Peace Corps. For example, the second director of the US Peace Corps, Jack Vaughan, noted how the Peace Corps was about love, "but love operated within political limits and the emotional social activism often did more for the helpers than for the helped" (Hoffman 1998, p. 9). In this way, Burmese exiles' experience of Jolie is complicated by the inherent "bumpiness of mediation" (Dittmer & Gray 2010, 1673) where the emotional and political responses to the refugee crisis along the border are entangled in complicated geopolitical discourses that situate the Global North as giver and the Global South as receiver of aid. Indeed, as Goodman notes "before those ever accompanying choruses of 'at least they (that is, so-called caring celebrities, and corporations) are doing something' become even louder, our job is surely, first and foremost, to be doggedly engaged with, and critical about, what that 'something' is, where it has come from, how it is done, and what its impacts are" (Goodman 2013, 104). It is to the aftermath of Jolie's visits and the politics of her role as a representative of UNHCR along the Thailand–Burma border that I turn next.

"United Nothing"

Among Burmese exiles in northern Thailand the acronym UN is widely understood to stand for "United Nothing." Indeed, it was explained to me that most people believe the UN cannot do anything for the border situation. Additionally Dara, who is well informed about Burmese and Thai politics as well as international relations, explained that the UN needs to be seen as apolitical in order to get along with the complicated network of states, NGOs and other political actors. To enforce his point, Dara smiled as he pulled out his smartphone and looked up the website http://www.unitednothing.org/. This website, he explained, was evidence that the UN is not going to do anything for their ongoing predicament. The relationship between UNHCR and Burmese exiles in Thailand is complicated. While it is beyond the scope of this chapter to describe the details of this relationship, it is important to reiterate that the UN stopped registering refugees in 2005, despite clear evidence that ongoing violence and persecution in Burma continues to push people out of the country to seek asylum in Thailand or a third country (Couldrey et al. 2008; Horstmann 2014). Additionally, the UN refers to the nine camps along the border as "temporary shelters" rather than refugee camps. This is despite the fact that many of the camps have been in operation for more than 30 years, and many families have seen multiple generations grow up in the camps (Naing 2014b, 2014c, 2014a). Interestingly, this critique does not seem to be directed at Jolie, though she is a known representative of UNHCR.

There is a history to UNHCR's use of celebrities to realize its humanitarian goals. Yrjölä points out how the UN's use of "goodwill ambassadors was inaugurated in the 1950s with Danny Kaye and Audrey Hepburn. Like Jolie, Kaye and Hepburn were described as 'messengers of peace' and were meant to advocate the universal validity of the liberal values of openness, responsibility and democratic peace in order to create a more peaceful, prosperous and just world" (Yrjölä 2011). Jolie is widely seen as one of the most legitimate celebrity humanitarians to date (Clarke 2009). Wheeler highlights how "her links with UNHCR were established over several years in which she 'auditioned' to become a Goodwill Ambassador . . . Since assuming her position as UNHCR's 'poster star', Jolie has appealed to a young and marginalized audience. Her photogenic qualities have meant that she has attracted the attention of the world press and UNHCR has sought to place similarly 'attractive' refugees in the camera frame next to her to provide an iconographic representation of displacement" (Wheeler 2011, p. 56). Indeed, Jolie seems to have been handpicked by UNHCR for her ability to address issues of displacement while remaining remarkably eloquent and apolitical to the structural causes of displacement as well as UNHCR's sometimes contested role in the refugee sites. Indeed, in some cases, celebrities have become critical of the UN, which has contributed to more strict guidelines regarding the role of celebrities with institutions such as UNHCR. For example, in 2003 the UN developed "Guidelines for the Designation of Goodwill Ambassadors and Messengers of Peace" in order to thwart such "internal" critique of the institution.

Jolie's influence in popular culture extends well beyond her work with refugees. Her work contributes to the broader reconfiguration of popular humanitarianism in the West. She is credited with raising the bar for celebrity humanitarian rivals, expanding the volunteer tourism market – now the fastest-growing niche tourism market in the world (Mostafanezhad 2014; Vasquez 2010), and popularizing international celebrity adoptions. Yet, despite the far-flung positive response to Jolie's visits, her activities on behalf of the camps are not well known. Rumors of her visits to the camp schools as well as walking through the camps with a production crew were widespread, and indeed imply that she was witnessed. It is noted on the UNHCR website that each of her visits to the camps were day trips, so it is not surprising that the full extent of her activities in the camps are not altogether clear. For example, I was at a local teashop with Maung, a 29-year-old man from Yangon. Maung had lived in northern Thailand for more than ten years and was well connected with the Burmese and NGO community. He taught English to Burmese exiles and was personally invested in Burmese politics. Despite the fact that Maung was highly critical of the UN, he strongly believed that Jolie, by her expression of concern for Burmese exiles, had helped the refugees. Maung explained:

> Even by just visiting they are happy . . . Even by caring for the people, it is good. She adopted a baby in the camp. I think she tried to adopt one of the refugee boy babies. She tried it. I don't know if it worked though . . . She definitely tried. That's good. She's the ambassador of the UN.

When I asked Hla, a former political prisoner and NGO practitioner, what she thought about Jolie's visit, she explained: "I just know about Angelina Jolie from my friends. I didn't know Jolie's plan. I have no idea what she did at the camps . . . " Similarly, Kyine, explained: "I didn't see her but I heard of her visit. I could only watch the short documentary film that she made . . . I wish I could meet her." She further explained how she had read about her visit in a magazine and that while she didn't know anyone who met her, "it would be good if we could talk to some people who worked together with the crew for her documentary film. I am not really sure where they were though." The recurrent commentary about the moral support that Jolie's visits engendered among Burmese exiles in the border was coupled with the equally invariable uncertainty about the material implications of her visit. Rather, the effects of her visits as described by Burmese exiles were limited to the oft-stated and somewhat elusive idea that Jolie drew attention to their issues.

Popular humanitarian (in)action

Observations among Burmese exiles dovetail with UNHCR and Jolie's self-identified mission to bring attention and respect to the lives of the refugees. Indeed, Look to the Stars, a popular website that highlights the humanitarian work of celebrities, explains how Jolie's primary role with UNHCR is "to help educate the public not only about the plight of refugees, but also about the perseverance and courage they show in overcoming all odds to rebuild their lives."[6] When asked what she hoped to accomplish meeting with refugees and internally displaced persons, Jolie answered, "Awareness of the plight of these people. I think they should be commended for what they have survived, not looked down upon."[7] Jolie's intentions are consistently articulated as "expanding awareness" of humanitarian issues, yet it is rarely made clear what her audiences should be aware of. This seemingly deliberate apolitical commentary helps limit critique of her interventions. Yet this goal of "bringing attention to the crises" has not had the kinds of political–material implications that one may have hoped, given the widespread attention paid to her visits. Perhaps this is not surprising; in an audience study of the effects of celebrity humanitarianism on the public, Scott concludes that it is "clear is that celebrities are generally ineffective in cultivating a cosmopolitan engagement with distant suffering" (Scott 2014, p. 1). This relationship is not without precedent. The UN's initial use of celebrities to support their initiatives can be traced to UNICEF's attempt to work with Marlon Brando in 1966 to raise money for starving children in India affected by the famine (Wheeler 2011). Wheeler highlights "how the UN and its agencies have developed their celebrity relations from ad-hoc to fully fledged systems of political campaigning" (Wheeler 2011, p. 48). Additionally, Chouliaraki similarly describes how Audrey Hepburn's role with UNICEF illustrates a key aspect of celebrity humanitarianism – its dependence on spectacle and a politics of pity, which she argues, "prioritizes the moral plea to alleviate distant suffering over the re-distribution of global resources as a means for changing the conditions of suffering" (Chouliaraki 2011, p. 2).

Thus, the rise of celebrity humanitarian interventions like Jolie's are part and parcel of the broader expansion of the popular humanitarian gaze, or the "the geopolitical assemblage of institutions, cultural practices and actors (e.g. celebrity humanitarians, alternative consumers and volunteer tourists) that play a critical role in the privatization and depoliticization of popular humanitarian interventions" (Mostafanezhad 2014, p. 111). The critique is not so much that the intentions of celebrity humanitarians are misguided, but rather that their intentions reframe the plight of refugees along the border in ways that conjure an apolitical response. Littler points out how celebrity charity is often framed in ways that suggest that luck, rather than politics, is the cause of social and political injustices. This reframed focus on luck allows for what Boltanski refers as the "politics of pity" whereby the relationship between those who suffer and those who do not suffer is separated, and the suffering itself is turned into a spectacle (Boltanski 1999). Building on Boltanski's notion of the politics of pity, one could consider how pity is used to redirect our attention away from the socio-political–economic disparities between Jolie and the refugees she cares about.

Littler, for example, explains how "Pity is often used as a discursive mode to mediate between celebrity and suffering: the extremities involved foreground the starkness of the opposition between fabulous celebrity wealth and grinding poverty. The fantasy that these things are not connected, sustained by the wish not to have to wish away privilege, often works through the register of pity rather than engagement with political questions of cause, effect and social justice" (Littler 2008, p. 247). Yet it is also true that during her visit to the camps in 2009, "Jolie called on the Thai government to grant Myanmar refugees in northern Thailand greater freedom of movement, after spending a day listening to refugees tell of the difficulties they have faced in two decades of living in closed camps" (McKinsey 2009). Jolie's refugee journal posted on the UNHCR website and her commentary to media reporters are the most obvious ways in which she made this call (Jolie 2004). The response of NGO practitioners who work in the region is mixed. For example, an Australian NGO practitioner explained:

I hope they know their role, and the limits of their knowledge and capacities. I don't believe celebrities should do politics, but given the state of personality politics in particular, I think we should be realistic and use this situation wisely, somehow. I mean, people don't really know about policies that party candidates stand for, people want to know about the personality of those who they can vote for. So taking this notion further, yes I think celebs can help, but only to a certain extent. I worry about a future when George Clooney or Angelina Jolie tell us what to do in Africa or Burma, and not the Africans or Burmans themselves.

Thus, while Jolie "has become a credible international figure and has sought to use her star power to pressurize recalcitrant states to accord with agreements they have made in the General Assembly . . . her influence may prove counter-productive as her leading role in UNHCR's campaigns may reflect an overestimation of her powers to effect lasting change" (Wheeler 2011, p. 59).

As a UNHCR Goodwill Ambassador, footage from her 2009 visit to the camps remains on the website and is used to inform viewers of the continued refugee crisis along the border. Jolie's visits to the camps occurred as a representative for UNHCR, which in Thailand does not operate under the International Convention of Refugees, the key international treaty that shapes the rights of refugees. The fact that it never signed the 1951 UN Refugee Convention which would require Thailand to adhere to international standards in its treatment of asylum seekers, severely limits what UNHCR can do along the border. As Kyle, a Canadian reporter with more than a decade of experience working on Burmese issues in Thailand explained to me:

> When Angelina Jolie comes with the UNHCR, you assume that UNHCR is a force for good and there's no critique of what UNHCR policies are. Obviously, I know UNHCR is limited. There are a lot of restrictions on what they can do. It's difficult. They have to work through official channels. They have a hard time . . . You hear all these ridiculous horror stories about the things the UNHCR has done because their policy is basically to try to get along with everyone and then help the refugees at the same time. You can't always do that.

UNHCR's interest in maintaining a perceptively apolitical stance on refugee registration is illustrated by Jolie and her representation of Burmese exiles. UNHCR explains how Jolie's "work helps to facilitate lasting solutions for people displaced by conflict and has inspired others to take a more active role" (UNHCR 2014). Yet apolitical participation in the refugee crisis along the border is clearly an impossible goal that may do more harm than good. UNHCR, like the celebrities that represent the institution, tends to lean towards less political framings of highly contested human rights agendas. Littler explains how this leaning "tends to focus on symptoms rather than core problems, providing, for example, tools for illiteracy rather than addressing the problem of core funding in schools or economic inequality (Littler 2008, p. 243). Yet, celebrity, and perhaps academic expectations around the power of celebrity to ameliorate longstanding structural violence may reflect naiveté around the politics of diplomacy where it seems that "a gulf exists between celebrity and political expectations in which popular political 'narratives' uncomfortably clash with the realist policies that have defined international power" (Wheeler 2011, p. 58).

While reception of Jolie's visits among Burmese exiles seem to be primarily positive, the limitations of Jolie's visits were noted by a young man, Khin, who explained how, "All other organizations should work together with her. Not just a person can help." Indeed, Khin's comment highlights the larger issues at stake in Jolie's humanitarian interventions. For example, the focus on Jolie's individual sojourn on the Thailand–Burma border and her compassionate concern for refugees in Thailand and beyond may inspire people to identify with Jolie's sentimentality as well as to become aware of the issues that are the focus of her attention. Yet this focus on individual compassion falls short of the broader structural violence that is the cause of her concern. This observation is not just a theoretical one; it is also a practical one that Jolie's strategists seem to have tuned into. Ironically, at times it seems that Jolie's politics have matured in ways that other celebrities have yet to develop.

For example, in a 2007 *Newsweek* article, "Angelina Wants to Save the World," Jolie is quoted as explaining: "When I first started doing this, I thought I could save everybody . . . I was sure that there had to be a simple solution. Now I'm still in the field as much as possible, but spending more time in Washington. You can fight forever to open a tiny shop or vocational training center – and that's fantastic – but if the trade laws stay as they are, it's not really going to help" (Smith 2007). In other words, Jolie seems to be cognizant of the politics of being apolitical that, I have argued in this chapter, typify her work on the Thailand–Burma border. This irony may be indicative of the broader contradictions in celebrity and celebritized humanitarianism more generally. For example, within popular humanitarianism there is an inherent need to sell the story, the concert ticket or the chocolate bar (Ponte & Richey 2014; Igoe 2013). This need often requires a recognizable or consistent story about the relationship between the giver of aid and the perceived benefactor. If this story deviates, it runs the risk of not being recognizable to the consumer audience that the project depends on. Additionally, the possibility always exists that the alternative story – for example, of the colonial, structural or exploitative relationship between the North and South – insults the audience it seeks to recruit for its cause. The relationship between Jolie, the market and international politics is not without nuance. What this chapter has sought to demonstrate is that despite her personal politics – whatever those may be – the broader implications of her work have contributed to everyday geopolitical discourses among Burmese exiles that privilege the moral support of her celebritized concern over the political support of UNHCR as well as a broader, and relatively consistent geopolitical discourse of North–South relations.

Conclusions

Jolie's ability to "speak for" Burmese exiles and to popular audiences allows her to navigate the communicative circuits between the mundane and the elite spaces that collaboratively frame geopolitical discourses of North–South relations. It is "[B]y combining the celebrity's personal testimony of the suffering of others, with the celebrity's own 'star aura' (Chouliaraki 2011), the distance between the spectator and faraway others may be at least partially bridged" (Scott 2014, p. 4). Despite her ability to link the mundane and the elite through popular appeal, the political–material implications of her visits are less than clear.

Jolie's celebrated engagement with the refugee crisis along the Thai–Burmese border is indicative of the tendency among celebrity humanitarians to limit the extent of their radical horizon. In this way, Jolie's politics contribute to a broader geopolitical discourse of North–South relations that suggests that cosmopolitan chic and humanitarian sensibility are appropriate responses to international political, economic and social injustice. It is this problematic that it is at the core of the critique of Jolie's humanitarian intervention along the Thailand–Burma border. The everyday geopolitics of celebrity humanitarianism has obscured the continued physical as well as structural violence that has plagued the life of more than 140,000 exiled Burmese for more than three decades.

I do not dismiss the fact that Jolie's visits to the refugee camps have undoubtedly brought new attention from popular audiences in the North to the displacement crisis along the Thai–Burmese border, nor that her visits have engendered widespread moral support and a sense of social solidarity among Burmese exiles. Indeed, celebrities are important mediators between the elite and mundane and help lend credibility and popularity to social causes (Benwell et al. 2012). Despite positive indicators of her moral "success," popularity and public approval ratings, the material–political implications of Jolie's visits for Burmese exiles are less than clear. This is in part because the historical and structural causes of suffering are obscured by the focus on Jolie's personal experience of cosmopolitan and aestheticized compassion.

Finally, Jolie's role as a UNHCR Goodwill Ambassador is embedded in the same system that perpetuates the issues she is meant to help ameliorate. The incapacity of UNHCR to document new refugees along the border leaves thousands of Burmese exiles in a constant state of limbo where they are neither able to go back to Burma, nor to enter Thailand as citizens or relocate to a third country. Thus, Jolie's humanitarian visits to the Thai–Burmese border shed light on broader issues of development, inequality and cosmopolitanism by illustrating how her work reframes geopolitical discourses of North–South relations in ways that obscure history and politics.

Notes

1 Importantly, exiles from Burma include more than 130 ethnic and religious backgrounds. For the purposes of this chapter, I describe all exiles and residents in Thailand who were born in Burma as "Burmese" to indicate their country of origin rather than their ethnic and religious identity.
2 The country's official name was changed from Burma to Myanmar in 1989, not without controversy. While many countries in the region have accepted this name change, some countries continue to refer to the country as Burma.
3 cf. https://www.dvb.no/dvb-video/angelina-jolie-visits-refugee-camp-at-thai-burmese-border-myanmar/41749 [accessed on August 3, 2015].
4 T. Junod. 2010. Angelina Jolie Dies for Our Sins. *Esquire Magazine*. Available at http://www.esquire.com/women/women-we-love/angelina-jolie-interview-pics-0707 [accessed on May 19, 2014].
5 Look to the Stars. 2014. Angelina Jolie: Charity Work, Events and Causes. Look to the Stars: The World of Celebrity Giving [online]. Available at https://www.looktothestars.org/celebrity/angelinajolie [accessed on August 3, 2015].

6 Look to the Stars. 2014. Angelina Jolie: Charity Work, Events and Causes. Look to the Stars: The World of Celebrity Giving [online]. Available at https://www.looktothestars. org/celebrity/angelinajolie [accessed on May 19, 2014].
7 Look to the Stars. 2014. Angelina Jolie: Charity Work, Events and Causes. Look to the Stars: The World of Celebrity Giving [online]. Available at https://www.looktothestars. org/celebrity/angelinajolie [accessed on May 19, 2014].

References

Arnold, D. 2013. Burmese social movements in exile: labour, migration and democracy. In: M. Ford (ed.) *Social Activism in Southeast Asia*. London: Routledge, pp. 89–103.
Barron, L. 2009. An actress compelled to act: Angelina Jolie's Notes from My Travels as celebrity activist/travel narrative. *Postcolonial Studies*, 12, 211–28.
Benwell, M.C., Dodds, K. & Pinkerton, A. 2012. Celebrity geopolitics. *Political Geography*, 31, 405–7.
Biccum, A. 2011. Marketing development: celebrity politics and the "new" development advocacy. *Third World Quarterly*, 32, 1331–46.
Boltanski, L. 1999. *Distant Suffering: Morality, Media and Politics*. New York: Cambridge University Press.
Boykoff, M.T. & Goodman, M.K. 2009. Conspicuous redemption? Reflections on the promises and perils of the "celebritization" of climate change. *Geoforum*, 40, 395–406.
Brockington, D. 2014. *Celebrity Advocacy and International Development*. New York: Routledge.
Browning, B. 2013. *Infectious Rhythm: Metaphors of Contagion and the Spread of African Culture*. New York: Routledge.
Chouliaraki, L. 2006. The aestheticization of suffering on television. *Visual Communication*, 5, 261–85.
Chouliaraki, L. 2011. The theatricality of humanitarianism: a critique of celebrity advocacy. *Communication and Critical/Cultural Studies*, 9, 1–21.
Clarke, R. 2009. Travel and celebrity culture: an introduction. *Postcolonial Studies*, 12, 145–52.
Cooper, A.F. 2009. *Celebrity Diplomacy*. Boulder, CO: Paradigm Publishers.
Couldrey, M., Herson, M. & Brees, I. 2008. Burma's displaced people. *Forced Migration Review* [online] 30. Available at http://www.fmreview.org/burma [accessed on May 18, 2015].
Desjarlais, R. & Jason Throop, C. 2011. Phenomenological approaches in anthropology★. *Annual Review of Anthropology*, 40, 87–102.
Dittmer, J. & Gray, N. 2010. Popular geopolitics 2.0: towards new methodologies of the everyday. *Geography Compass*, 4, 1664–77.
Good, B. 1994. *Medicine, Rationality, and Experience: An Anthropological Perspective*. Cambridge: Cambridge University Press.
Goodman, M.K. 2011. Star/poverty space: the making of the "development celebrity." *Celebrity Studies*, 2, 69–85.
Goodman, M.K. 2013. iCare capitalism? The biopolitics of choice in a neoliberal economy of hope. *International Political Sociology*, 7, 103–5.
Hoffman, E.C. 1998. *All You Need is Love: The Peace Corps and the Spirit of the 1960s*. Cambridge, MA: Harvard University Press.
Horstmann, A. 2014. Stretching the border: confinement, mobility and the refugee public among Karen refugees in Thailand and Burma. *Journal of Borderlands Studies*, 29, 47–61.

Igoe, J. 2013. Consume, connect, conserve: consumer spectacle and the technical mediation of neoliberal conservation's aesthetic of redemption and repair. *Cultural Geography* 6, 16–28.

Jolie, A. 2003. *Notes from my Travels: Visits with Refugees in Africa, Cambodia, Pakistan and Ecuador.* New York: Simon & Schuster.

Jolie, A. 2004. Angelina Jolie's Thailand journal. *UNHCR – Thailand* [online]. Available at http://www.unhcr.org/cgi-bin/texis/vtx/home/opendocPDFViewer.html?docid=4a0 7ede06&query=angelina%20jolie%20thailand.

Kapoor, I. 2012. *Celebrity Humanitarianism: The Ideology of Global Charity.* Hoboken: Routledge.

Katz, C. 2001. On the grounds of globalization: a topography for feminist political engagement. *Signs*, 1213–34.

Kellner, D. 2010. Celebrity diplomacy, spectacle and Barak Obama. *Celebrity Studies*, 1, 121–3.

Krever, M. 2014. Angelina Jolie puts spotlight on Syrian refugees as UN Refugees chief warns Lebanon could collapse under burden. *CNN: Amanpour* [online]. Available at http://amanpour.blogs.cnn.com/2014/03/27/angelina-jolie-puts-spotlight-on-syrian-refugees-as-u-n-refugees-chief-warns-lebanon-could-collapse-under-burden/.

Littler, J. 2007. Celebrity CEOs and the cultural economy of tabloid intimacy. *Stardom and Celebrity: A Reader*, London: Sage Publications Ltd., pp. 230–43.

Littler, J. 2008. "I feel your pain": cosmopolitan charity and the public fashioning of the celebrity soul. *Social Semiotics*, 18, 237–51.

Lousley, C. 2013. "With Love from Band Aid": Sentimental exchange, affective economies, and popular globalism. *Emotion, Space and Society*, 10, 7–17.

Mattingly, C. 2010. *The Paradox of Hope: Journeys through a Clinical Borderland.* Berkeley, CA: University of California Press.

McKinsey, K. 2009. Angelina Jolie voices support for Myanmar refugees in Northern Thailand Camps. *UNHCR* [online]. Available at http://www.unhcr.org/print/498ab65c2.html.

Mostafanezhad, M. 2014. Volunteer tourism and the popular humanitarian gaze. *Geoforum*, 54, 111–18.

Naing, S.Y. 2014a. Burmese refugees criticize Thailand's push for quicker repatriation. *The Irrawaddy* [online]. Available at http://www.irrawaddy.org/burma/burmese-refugees-criticize-thailands-push-quicker-repatriation.html.

Naing, S.Y. 2014b. Repatriation thwarted by militarization in Eastern Burma: report. *The Irrawaddy* [online]. Available at http://www.irrawaddy.org/burma/repatriation-thwarted-militarization-eastern-burmareport.html.

Naing, S.Y. 2014c. Thai and Burmese officials to begin talks on repatriation. *The Irrawaddy* [online]. Available at http://www.irrawaddy.org/burma/thai-burmese-officials-begin-talks-repatriation.html.

Ponte, S. & Richey, L.A. 2011. (Product) RED: how celebrities push the boundaries of "causumerism." *Environment and Planning A*, 43, 2060–75.

Ponte, S. & Richey, L.A. 2014. Buying into development? Brand Aid forms of cause-related marketing. *Third World Quarterly*, 35, 65–87.

Repo, J. & Yrjölä, R. 2011. The gender politics of celebrity humanitarianism in Africa. *International Feminist Journal of Politics*, 13, 44–62.

Richey, L.A. & Ponte, S. 2008. Better (RED) than dead? Celebrities, consumption and international aid. *Third World Quarterly*, 29, 711–29.

Scott, M. 2014. The role of celebrities in mediating distant suffering. *International Journal of Cultural Studies*, available online May 8, 2014.

Smith, S. 2007. Angelina wants to save the world. *Newsweek*, 150, 46–53.

Street, J. 2004. Celebrity politicians: popular culture and political representation. *The British Journal of Politics & International Relations*, 6, 435–52.

Tan, V.T. & McClellan, M. 2014. US wraps up group resettlement for Myanmar refugees in Thailand. *UNHCR –Thailand* [online]. Available at http://reliefweb.int/report/thailand/us-wraps-group-resettlement-myanmar-refugees-thailand [accessed on May 18, 2015].

UNHCR. 2014. Angelina Jolie fact sheet. *UNHCR* [online]. Available at http://www.unhcr.org/pages/49db77906.html [accessed on February 15, 2014].

van Krieken, R. 2012. *Celebrity Society*, London: Routledge.

Vasquez, E. 2010. Do celebs like Jolie inspire voluntourism? *CNN: International* [online]. Available at http://edition.cnn.com/2010/TRAVEL/08/10/celebrity.humanitarian.travel/index.html.

Wheeler, M. 2011. Celebrity politics and cultural citizenship: UN Goodwill Ambassadors and Messengers of Peace. In: L. Tsaliki, C.A. Frangonikopoulos & A. Huliaras (eds) *Transnational Celebrity Activism in Global Politics: Changing the World?* Chicago: Intellect Ltd, pp. 45–62.

Wilson, J.A. 2010. Star testing: the emerging politics of celebrity gossip. *The Velvet Light Trap*, 65 (1), 25–38.

Yrjölä, R. 2011. The global politics of celebrity humanitarianism. In *Transnational Celebrity Activism in Global Politics Changing the World*. Chicago: The University of Chicago Press, pp. 175–92.

2

MADONNA IN MALAWI

Celebritized interventions and local politics of development in the South

Louise Mubanda Rasmussen

Introduction

"It was so special for someone like her to come visit this place . . . When she came, we expected that our lives would get better . . . [but] instead of receiving the blessings, we are now worse off. It all turned out very different from what we expected." Jimmy, a farmer from Chinkota village, Malawi where Madonna's Academy for Girls would have been located (field notes, September 22, 2012).

Madonna has been an active donor supporting international development interventions in Malawi since 2006. Her involvement in the country has been controversial in ways that help us to understand the impact of celebritized interventions on the local politics of development. The opening quotation from Jimmy expresses one aspect of this work, the local expectations and responses to development promises. Another aspect of celebrity humanitarianism is apparent at the level of elite politics. Here, Madonna's work in Malawi sparked considerable debate. On April 10, 2013 the Malawi State House press office issued the following statement:

> Granted, Madonna has adopted two children from Malawi. According to the record, this gesture was humanitarian and of her accord. It, therefore, comes across as strange and depressing that for a humanitarian act, prompted only by her, Madonna wants Malawi to be forever chained to the obligation of gratitude . . . Granted, Madonna is a famed international musician. But that does not impose an injunction of obligation on any government under whose territory Madonna finds herself, including Malawi, to give her state treatment.[1]

In response, Madonna issued a press statement justifying her humanitarianism:

> I came to Malawi seven years ago with honorable intentions. I returned earlier this month to view the new schools we built. I did not ever ask or demand special treatment at the airport or elsewhere during my visit. I will not be distracted or discouraged by other people's political agendas. I made a promise to the children of Malawi and I am keeping that promise.[2]

Two days later it transpired that the then President Joyce Banda had known nothing about the above statement.[3] Nevertheless, this highly publicized clash between Madonna and Joyce Banda marked the high point of the controversies that have continuously dogged the work of the Raising Malawi Foundation, which was established by Madonna and Michael Berg to support orphan care and education in Malawi. These controversies reflect how Madonna's humanitarian efforts have become entangled with local debates over development, aid and corruption.

In this chapter I examine these controversies as a case study on how celebritized development may interact with local politics of development in the Global South. As mentioned in the introduction, there is a need to better understand how publics in the South are engaged by celebrity mediation of development, and how celebrities come to intervene in existing politics and social processes, especially in terms of reinforcing or challenging the power dynamics of development aid. Because Madonna's personal role as a mother and Kabbalah[4] follower has intertwined with her humanitarian work, and because she has consistently sought to emblematize Raising Malawi through personal statements, donations and highly publicized site visits, the foundation and its work has become highly personified in Malawi. Analyzing the various views and voices debating Madonna's humanitarian work in Malawi reveals how such a personified celebrity intervention may illuminate the contradictions between how development is represented in the North and how it is experienced in the South, as well as how it may trigger local debates around development, elitism and corruption.

This chapter examines how Madonna's humanitarian work has been received in Malawi, and how these perceptions are connected to local politics of development. Based on six months of ethnographic research in Malawi, the chapter uses a mixture of informal conversations, participant observation, Malawian newspaper articles, online commentary, as well as interviews with Malawian NGO and government officials working to support "orphans and vulnerable children" (the scope of Madonna's interventions). I situate these perceptions in the context of Malawi's recent political history. In the mid-1990s the country went through a democratic transition, which was followed by liberalization of the media, and a massive growth of NGOs. The experience of both democratization and NGO growth has been highly ambiguous, as these developments have basically failed to deliver on their promises of greater political equality and better living conditions (Englund 2006; Swidler & Watkins 2009; Dionne et al. 2013).

I begin the chapter with a background section on the politics of development in Malawi, as well as an introduction to the Raising Malawi Foundation. Then follows a theoretical section focused on the question of celebrity authenticity and the depoliticizing effects of celebrity humanitarianism. The methodology section provides details of the ethnographic research I completed in Malawi. In the analysis I examine how Madonna's humanitarian work is debated in the country. I focus on drawing out the diversity of perceptions that characterize these debates, with the aim of exploring the contestations celebritized development may engender as well as the limits to whose voices are heard. I conclude the chapter by discussing how a controversial celebrity like Madonna functions in the intertwined elite politics of the Malawian regime and the development industry.

Context: the politics of development in Malawi

In the mid-1990s Malawi transitioned from a one-party state, which had been under the authoritarian rule of "Life President" Kamuzu Banda for almost 30 years, into a multi-party democracy. This political transition created a more open political climate, marked by a significant liberalization of the media and a massive growth of NGOs (Booth et al. 2006; Morfit 2011). However, corruption, authoritarian practices, political violence and attempts to co-opt and silence the most critical elements of civil society continue to characterize Malawian politics (Englund 2002; Khembo 2005; Power 2010). This means that international NGOs operating in Malawi must engage in careful political navigation (Englund 2006).

There are some local NGOs and civil society actors, such as the Catholic Church, who at times take very critical and vocal stands against the regime in power.[5] They do this at the risk of being met with police violence, arrest and public intimidation.[6] The local and international NGOs working with orphans and vulnerable children that I studied all pursued a more depoliticized form of service delivery and advocacy. One informant explained that it is more effective to engage in advocacy "from within" the government than to engage in a visible, activist critiquing. Based on the NGO's past experience, he claimed that if you openly criticize the government, you risk alienating yourself from key policy forums, and that the government will rather work against you then listen to your demands (interview, January 22, 2013). In my interviews with these NGO workers, they often made remarks such as: "we are just there to complement the government effort. They are the main duty-bearers" (interview, November 11, 2012). This language echoes the dominant international aid frameworks of "alignment with national priorities" and "donor harmonization" (OECD 2005). However, it also reflects how the Malawi government, under the pretext of these aid frameworks, can exert control over NGOs that are "out of line" (cf. Englund 2006, pp. 82–3).

Malawi's economy is highly reliant on donor funding. Up to 30 percent of the government budget comes from bilateral and multilateral development aid.[7]

International aid is, therefore, an essential factor in Malawian politics; an indispensable ressource in the pursuit of power and authority (Englund 2002, p. 19). In 2010–12, during the last years of former President Bingu wa Mutharika's rule, his increasingly authoritan practices made many of Malawi's most significant donors suspend or cut their budget support. When Mutharika died suddenly in April 2012, he was succeeded by Vice President Joyce Banda. Banda had in the meantime formed a new political party and become a vocal critic of Mutharika. She was eager to mend the relationship with the country's most important donors.[8] To do so, she had to accept a path of "economic recovery" mandated by the International Monetary Fund, which included the devaluation and floating of the Malawi Kwacha. The economic recovery package led to high inflation, a shortage of basic goods and a rapid rise in cost of living.[9] In the wake of these reforms Banda became increasingly unpopular. She was criticized for repeating the same tendencies as her predecessors: spending lavishly on foreign travel, political interference, nepotism and intimidating the opposition,[10] while people "are still dying of hunger, hospitals do not have drugs, people are jobless."[11] All the while she was backed by donors who praised her willingness to "recover the economy." These developments reveal how the intertwined elite politics of the Malawian regime and the development industry is an important theme in the local politics of development.

Another essential theme is the question of narrow donor agendas (Dionne et al. 2013). Like elsewhere in Africa, much donor funding to Malawi has shifted towards HIV/AIDS. From 1999 to 2005 funding for AIDS increased from 2 percent of total development aid to nearly 30 percent. Consequently, a significant share of Malawi's NGO growth has been among NGOs that deal with the AIDS epidemic, which includes the subfield of "Orphan Care" (Morfit 2011, p. 69). These dynamics reflect how international funding designed purposely for local AIDS NGOs may create a veritable market for such organizations, so that many are created primarily *because of* the opportunities international funding represents (Igoe & Kelsall 2005; Ferguson 2006; Swidler & Watkins 2009), which provides the important lesson that there are abundant resources in AIDS work for those who know how to "play the game."

Introduction to Raising Malawi

In 2006 Madonna became a player in the provision of aid to Malawi, when she started the Raising Malawi Foundation together with Michael Berg, co-director of the Kabbalah Centre. As stated on the foundation's website, its goal is "to bring an end to the extreme poverty and hardship endured by Malawi's 1 million orphans and vulnerable children once and for all."[12] Over the years the foundation has been involved in a range of projects from funding local orphanages and community-based orphan care initiatives to running a Kabbalah-inspired psychosocial support program for orphans and street children called Spirituality for Kids (SFK).

Recently, the fate of the Raising Malawi Academy for Girls has been at the center of both international and local controversies. US$15 million was devoted to the construction of this elite boarding school, which had been designed by a top architecture firm from New York.[13] The construction of the school began in 2009, and in April 2010 Madonna officiated over the "first brick laying" ceremony. But in November 2010, construction on the school site stopped. Raising Malawi's executive director, Philippe van den Bossche, had been fired a month earlier "amid criticism of his management style and cost overruns for the school."[14] He was replaced by Trevor Neilson, founder of the Global Philantrophy Group – a company that advises celebrities on their philantrophic endeavors. The implications of this change were – for reasons that have never been entirely clear – that the plan to build the Academy for Girls was dropped entirely. Additionally, over the course of 2011 the local offices in Malawi attached to the academy and the SFK programme were gradually closed down.

Madonna issued a statement in January 2011 which explained, "I realize that the plans we had in place for the Raising Malawi Academy for Girls simply would not serve enough children. My original vision is now on a much bigger scale. I want to reach thousands not hundreds of girls. I want to do more and I want to do it better."[15] This new strategy included building community schools across the country rather than one grand elite school.

During the closing down of the local office of the Academy for Girls, stories started circulating in the international press indicating that the office had had problems with "outlandish expenditures."[16] In a *New York Times* article, Trevor Nielson singled out Raising Malawi's former executive director, van den Bossche, and the prospective manager of the Academy, Dr. Anjimile Ntila Oponyo, as the culprits.[17] However, some US media reports indicated that stories like these were part of a smear campaign orchestrated by Nielson in an attempt to pressure Oponyo to accept termination without getting the severance pay her contract called for.[18] Incidentally, Oponyo is the sister of Joyce Banda, who as mentioned was Malawi's vice-president at this time. Following this apparent smear campaign, Oponyo and seven other staff members sued Raising Malawi for unfair dismissal and the non-payment of benefits.[19]

In January 2012 Madonna issued a statement presenting Raising Malawi's new school plans in more detail. The plan was to build ten "community schools" in Kasungu district in collaboration with buildOn – an American NGO that combines programs for underprivileged high school students in the US with the construction of village schools in developing countries.[20] These plans were criticized by the then minister of education, who claimed that when Madonna abandoned the Academy for Girls she did not inform them: "Now she decides to announce that she plans to build ten schools without getting authority from us again . . . We now feel like this is all about propping up her global image and not in our interest."[21] The minister thus indicated that Madonna was overstepping her boundaries as an international humanitarian in terms of not getting "proper authority" from the government, and by implication that Madonna's main interest was promoting herself, not supporting education in Malawi.

In November 2012 Banda's sister Dr. Oponyo was appointed principal secretary of education.[22] About two months later Raising Malawi announced that the ten community schools had been completed.[23] Then, a further few weeks after this announcement, the minister of education made a point of "clarifying" that what Madonna had built were new school blocks for existing government schools, rather than new schools as such.[24] This statement ignited a local debate over whether Madonna was lying about her accomplishments.[25] When Madonna went to Malawi in April 2013 to visit the new schools and some of the other projects she supports, the local and international press were keen to uncover new controversies, especially any relating to animosity between Madonna and the president. The visit culminated in the much-publicized clash between Madonna and Joyce Banda mentioned in the introduction.

Theoretical approaches to celebrity humanitarianism and local politics of development

How can we understand the strange public clash between the pop star and the President of Malawi? Conducting ethnographic fieldwork in Malawi has made it clear that there are a multitude of perceptions of Madonna's humanitarian work, which are defined by post-colonial cultural politics, as well as local debates over corruption, elitism and development. In order to explore these perceptions I take on two key themes in the literature on celebrity humanitarianism: the claim that such humanitarianism has depoliticizing effects, and the crafting of celebrity authenticity as a key concern. Subjecting these theoretical points to a different empirical context provides new insights, which I hope can contribute to developing this field further.

Critics like Littler (2008), Kapoor (2012) and Müller (2013) claim that celebrity mediation of development and humanitarianism has depoliticizing effects because it only further obscures or even rationalizes global structural inequalities. From a post-colonial perspective we can, moreover, point to the continuities between the "imperial heroes" and missionaries of colonial times and today's celebrity actors in how they lend moral righteousness to development as a benevolent project (Clarke 2009; Sèbe 2009). In Ferguson's (1994) Foucault-inspired analysis of how development works as an anti-politics machine, he shows how development discourses depoliticize poverty and inequality by turning such issues into technical problems that require the kind of technical solutions that only development experts can provide. Celebrities may in turn depoliticize global inequalities by casting development as both non-political and non-bureaucratic; representing interventions as simple, "cool," and building on emotional togetherness rather than politics or endless technical debates (Cameron & Haanstra 2008; Richey & Ponte 2011).

However, following Li (2007), I believe that we must see the depoliticization of development as a project, rather than a secure accomplishment. Combining governmentality analysis with a Gramscian approach, Li explores forms of contentious politics in Indonesia that defy the calculated attempts of development experts to direct conduct. I assume that, similar to expert discourses, the charismatic mediation of development may be "punctured by a challenge it cannot contain" (Li 2007, p. 11). By exploring how the debate on Madonna is linked to local politics of development, my aim is not to take depoliticization for granted as an effect, but to explore what kind of contestations celebritized development may make possible.

From the perspective of publics in the North the authenticity of celebrity actors is a central concern. Brockington shows how, in British NGOs, celebrity liaisons work to create "opportunities for celebrities to build long-lasting relationships with their organizations," which serve as the "basis for the most reliable performances of authenticity" (Brockington 2014, p. 96). Celebrity authenticity in this sense is about the public's (and the elite's) belief in the celebrity's genuine commitment to the cause and to the organization. Taking a discursive approach, Chouliaraki focuses on the *authentication strategies* celebrities employ. She analyzes celebrity as "a communicative practice that brings the offstage performance of celebrity (or the "persona") as an altruist together with his or her onstage performances of the voices of suffering as a message for action" (Chouliaraki 2013, p. 82). This means that the "truthfulness" of the celebrity's claims is something that is produced in "the course of his or her performances of aspirational dispositions of solidarity" (Chouliaraki 2013, p. 82). These aspirational discourses are primarily directed at Western publics as givers of aid, following the separation in humanitarian communication between spectators who watch at a distance and the "vulnerable others" they are encouraged to help (Boltanski 1999; Chouliaraki 2013, p. 27). No one has yet explored how such "vulnerable others," as well as publics in the South more generally, respond to strategies of celebrity authentication.

In this discursive arrangement Malawians are primarily positioned as "receivers" of aid, though some middle-class and elite Malawians may identity with a cosmopolitan, aspirational discourse of "helping the needy." When examining celebrity authenticity primarily from the receivers' perspective, I pay attention to how the "truthfulness" of Madonna's actions and intentions is evaluated, and consider how these debates are connected to local experiences of development practice. Inspired by post-colonial perspectives, I am concerned with identifying whether Madonna's humanitarian work produces resistance among Malawians towards the ways in which foreign actors speak on their behalf. In sum, by exploring how the question of Madonna's authenticity as a humanitarian actor is debated among different groups of Malawians, I aim to shed light on the opportunities for and limits to how a controversial celebrity project may enable a contentious politics of development critique in the local setting.

Methodology

I conducted fieldwork in Malawi for a total of six months in 2012–13 to explore local experiences of celebritized development. I focused initially on examining how Madonna, through her organization, Raising Malawi, is experienced as a donor in the local orphanages and community-based organizations supported by the foundation – in development jargon "local partner organizations." I conducted participant observation in two partner organizations for a total of two months in each. One of the organizations was a national NGO situated in the capital Lilongwe, the other a smaller, community-based NGO situated in a rural part of Central Malawi. Participant observation was focused on following the organizations' everyday practices, and it included conducting interviews with staff, volunteers and beneficiaries.

In order to position these experiences more broadly, I conducted interviews with a range of NGO and governmental officials working with support to orphans and vulnerable children. I also made four visits to Chinkota, the village adjacent to the site where the Raising Malawi Academy for Girls was supposed to have been built. I had informal conversations with the Chief and other residents of the village, and conducted five household interviews.

Finally, I conducted a supplementary media survey. I collected articles from the main print papers on topics such as donors, aid, government–NGO relations, orphan care and Madonna/Raising Malawi. The clash between Madonna and Joyce Banda happened at a time when I was not in Malawi. I therefore followed this debate online; I focused primarily on comments to articles from the main online newspaper the *Nyasa Times*, but also on a few Facebook groups and blogs. It is estimated that only 5.4 percent of the Malawian population has access to the Internet (Internet World Stats 2014). I assume, therefore, that online commenting is a practice confined to the relatively small middle class and elite in the country, as well as the diaspora. Apart from this overall categorization, I know little about the people who wrote these comments in a basically anonymous forum. Because of such methodological challenges, this data only serves as a supplement to the findings from my own fieldwork.

Debating Madonna – the humanitarian

In this analysis of how Madonna's humanitarian intentions and actions were debated in Malawi, I first explore the professional perspectives of NGO workers, before considering an additional variety of middle-class/elite viewpoints expressed in the online comments. Finally, I analyze some perceptions among the rural poor, based upon my interactions with beneficiaries and volunteers in one partner organization (the rural, community-based NGO) and the residents of Chinkota.

Madonna's change of plans

Initially, controversies related to Madonna's humanitarian work in Malawi mainly revolved around her adoptions. At the time I began my fieldwork in September 2012, it was clear that the change of plans regarding the construction of the Academy for Girls had become the defining feature of her humanitarian endeavor.

When I told one of my research assistants that I had an interest in Madonna's projects, he explained that:

> People had big expectations when Madonna was coming in. There were rumors that the school [the Academy for Girls] would enroll students from all over the country. So everyone was going to benefit, not just people living nearby the school. Now the school hasn't materialized. She was going to do another project and that didn't materialize either.
>
> *(field notes, October 7, 2012)*

I said that I believed she was now building community schools with another American NGO. My assistant replied that there were rumors that her other project didn't materialize either: "I don't remember exactly what it was, maybe those schools you said. It was in the newspapers. It was like the money she had promised – that organization didn't get it" (field notes, October 7, 2012).

Basing his statement on rumors, my assistant paints a picture of a widespread popular perception that Madonna is someone who makes grand promises that never materialize. He also points towards the great expectations a project of this size had raised among the population, and the dissonance they had experienced between Madonna's wealth, her fundraising efforts and the actual outcome of her projects.

FIGURE 2.1 A meeting of the village chief and community members in Chinkota. Photograph by Louise Mubanda Rasmussen.

Many of my informants were Malawian nationals who worked in NGO and government agencies with projects supporting orphans and vulnerable children. Their interpretation of Madonna's humanitarian work was shaped by professional development logic.

From a professional perspective, Madonna's conduct as a donor had been perceived as somewhat arrogant, as she had apparently failed to consult with the appropriate government actors as is expected of NGOs in Malawi. A program coordinator in an international NGO emphasized that she had not properly explained her change of plans regarding the Academy for Girls to the Malawian government, or to the public:

> . . . when you are up to something, a plot of that nature . . . it was like a process . . . there were meetings with Ministry of Education, recommendations, the approval, all that. Now somebody just said no, I have changed. It doesn't happen that way . . . people are trying to find out, is it about money? And people say that no-no-no, she had money to do that . . . but why did she change the deal? . . . She didn't give sufficient reasons for what she did.
>
> *(interview, October 17, 2012)*

While initially Madonna and Raising Malawi had drafted their plans for the academy together with the ministry, when Madonna "changed her mind" without giving a valid reason, he felt that this demonstrated a lack of respect towards local actors and for the promises she had made to the government and the wider population. Another program officer in the same NGO speculated that the local actors who had been involved in the process had given Madonna special treatment:

> . . . probably we were very . . . can I say emotional? . . . We were very, very eager to work with Madonna and then we missed some other very important protocol . . . probably we did not want to disappoint her . . . because if you have a new donor . . . when you are setting up a project, you listen to the donor and see how you want to assist that donor and then probably we were eager and did not look at those areas.
>
> *(interview, October 17, 2012)*

The use of "we" in this statement should be read as a general reference to the local actors involved in the process, because this informant had not been involved directly in negotiating the plans for the academy. The statement expresses his speculations about what had gone wrong, which, however, are interesting because they point towards an experience of the power dynamics between donors and local actors. Because local counterparts, in his experience, often attempt to please the donor in the initial contact it seems likely that when the donor was Madonna, local counterparts were so eager to please her that important protocol was overlooked. This speculation can be linked to popular perceptions of how Madonna received special treatment when she was allowed to adopt her second child from Malawi, because of her "commitment to helping disadvantaged children."[26]

Among these professional development workers there were, however, also some who defended Madonna's humanitarian work as well intentioned and useful. A program officer in another international NGO stressed:

> People have known Madonna because of the girl's school that collapsed, but I know her because of her foundation. The foundation has supported organizations here . . . and there was something called Spirituality for Kids. She has done a very good job . . . But the people who are not aware of her other projects are the ones who say she has not come to Malawi in earnest. That she has raised a lot of money abroad, but this money has not benefitted Malawi . . . So for me I don't have any problems with her. She has done a very good job for the children in Malawi.
>
> *(interview, November 15, 2012)*

Thus, his view is that the controversies surrounding the Academy for Girls have overshadowed all the other good work Madonna has done. He indicates that most Malawians know nothing about these other projects and that is why they become suspicious over the dissonance between the amount of money she has fundraised and the outcomes of her humanitarian work.

Online debates: promoting herself or acting as a well-meaning humanitarian?

In the online comments there was a similar overall division between a negative interpretation of Madonna's conduct as disrespectful and deceitful, and a positive interpretation of Madonna's ability to direct much-needed resources to Malawi's children. The tone in these comments was often more direct. From the negative side, here is one example from the tabloid Facebook site "Malawi Breaking News and Gossip":

> Madona [sic] should be the one to thank Malawi because she is using Malawi to enrich herself, the dollars that she raises in the name of Malawi do not equate to the amount she has spent on the blocks. The bulk of the money she claims to have been misappropriated was actually spent by herself and her entourage, let her give us the amounts she spent during her visits . . . Before Madona [sic] started her charity in Malawi, she was not making it on the Forbes millionaires list but now she is up there because she is getting good-will by using Malawi's plight.[27]

Taken together with the viewpoints analyzed in the previous section, it is clear that from the perspective of some aid receivers Madonna's authenticity is evaluated as a question of whether her achievements match her promises. From this perspective Madonna's "change of plans," the mismatch between the millions of dollars she has raised and the (perceived) limited tangible outcome (ten school blocks) all feed into the perception that she is merely using the poverty of Malawi to promote her own brand – or even to enrich herself. Such perceptions reflect how a personified celebrity initiative makes possible a kind of account-ability to the wider Malawian public, which other international NGOs are not subjected to, at least not to quite the same extent. The Malawian public rarely has access to the kinds of promises to Western publics upon which NGO pro-jects are built, but with a highly controversial celebrity initiative the relationship between such promises and on-the-ground accomplishments is propelled into local debate.

Among the critical online comments, the theme of Madonna's disrespect for local protocol and expectations of "special treatment" was also brought up. According to one comment:

> To all people of Goodwill, philanthropists, celebrities etc., as much as we appreciate the much needed assistance that you provide us, there are cer-tain protocols/policies that you should follow when you go to any coun-try . . . Do not come with the old colonialist mentality and think that Africans will bow down and wash your feet the minute you touch down on our soil. We are way past that . . . The fact that you can come and adopt African children and provide all the monetary or educational assistance does not give you the license to bulldoze yourselves into our sovereign countries and expect royal treatment.[28]

I read this comment as an explicit post-colonial critique, which highlights the con-tinuities in power relations between colonial rule and present-day philanthropy and celebrity humanitarianism. To this commentator, the power of money and fame that these actors command only reinforces the colonial mentality of them believing that they know what is best for poor others, without bothering to listen to their opinions. Thus, for some aid receivers, the authenticity of celebrity humanitarians is questionable because of their tendency to claim to speak on "their behalf," when they are in fact only seen to promote themselves and their own agenda.

However, among the online comments, the negative ones were actually out-numbered by those who defended Madonna's humanitarian actions as authentic. Many of these commentators juxtaposed Madonna's accomplishments with the self-serving behavior of the Malawian elite or the failure of the government to deliver basic services.

> A lot of rich Malawians give nothing back to the people. At least Madonna . . . is able to adopt "black" Malawian children who were at an orphanage and give them hope for the future. She is at least able to build some "school" blocks where some kids will learn. Let's give credit where it is due.[29]

> What Madonna promised is what government should be doing. Why does government collect taxes? There is no shying away from responsibilities.

> Maybe if you curbed useless foreign trips, hefty minister perks and cheap politics using taxpayers' money – then you could build schools.[30]

The first commentator seems to identify with a cosmopolitan notion of "giving to the needy" that she finds the Malawian elite rarely lives up to. The second commentator focuses on the failure of the government to live up to its responsibilities to deliver basic services, which are presented as connected to a corrupt, self-serving, populist politics. For such commentators, the work of international NGOs, philanthropists and celebrity humanitarians would probably generally be interpreted positively because of their perceived ability to bypass the political elite, and deliver goods and services to "the needy."

In April 2013, when the clash between Madonna and Joyce Banda was at its height, entirely different types of comments took up much space on the *Nyasa Times* site. These commentators defended Madonna in what came to be depicted as a personalized battle between her and Banda/Oponyo. Joyce Banda was extremely unpopular at this time; she was seen to be pushing ordinary Malawians into economic hardship, while repeating the same behavior as her predecessors. When she appointed her sister to a prominent position in the Ministry of Education this was seen as just one more indication that she was going down exactly the same path. The majority of these commentators interpreted Banda's (alleged) criticism of Madonna as a result of her attempting to defend her sister's interests:

> Oponyo Mtila is taking her personal grudges with Madonna and making them into a national issue. If she was fired by Madonna, then that is her problem. She should not be abusing her position at Ministry of Education like that. What a shame she is. And Joyce, stop protecting your little sister. How did she get this education job anyway? Nepotism basi.[31], [32]

The viewpoints I have analyzed in these two sections primarily represent voices of the middle class and the elite. These diverse perceptions of Madonna reflect how the intentions and actions of celebrity humanitarians may be evaluated as authentic in Malawi when seen against the backdrop of the self-serving behavior of the elite and an unaccountable and corrupt government unable to deliver basic services. However, the authenticity of celebrity actors may also be questioned when their promises are not matched by accomplishments and local protocols are not followed, which serves to confirm suspicions that celebrity humanitarians are only using Malawi's poverty to promote themselves, and that their behavior illustrates a continuation of colonial power relations, where foreign actors use their power to impose their own agendas.

Perspectives of the rural poor

In this section I analyze the viewpoints and experiences of some groups of rural poor. First I consider how some of the intended beneficiaries of Madonna's

FIGURE 2.2   A girl walks down a path in Chinkota, the village where Madonna's
Academy for Girls would have been located. Photograph by Louise
Mubanda Rasmussen.

humanitarian work perceived her, and then I analyze the experience of residents
of Chinkota, the village adjacent to the site where the Academy for Girls was supposed to have been built.

Beneficiary and volunteer perspectives

As mentioned, I conducted participant observation in a local partner organization,
situated in a rural part of central Malawi. The beneficiaries and volunteers in this
NGO appeared quite indifferent to the kinds of disputes covered in the previous
sections. The disconnection between their everyday quest for survival, and the discussions of Madonna's authenticity, does reflect, however, some of the persistent
inequalities of development practice.

During her trip to Malawi in April 2013, Madonna had paid a highly publicized visit to this organization. In interviews with the organization's volunteers
and beneficiaries, my assistant and I asked them if they had been present during
this visit and what it had been like. Some of the grandmothers supported by the
NGO had no idea who Madonna was, and one volunteer simply replied that "she
was azungu [white], and she was very happy because she was dancing with the
orphans" (interview, August 1, 2013). Such comments suggest that their experience and perception of Madonna is confined to that of the usual experience of a

donor performing a "site visit." These are familiar and highly ceremonial occasions when visitors from the city come to see the progress of the project, while the local organization makes sure to show off its success stories and round up huge crowds of local people to play the part of "happy beneficiaries"(cf. Richey 2008, pp. 129–35).

The beneficiaries' engagement with the NGO was structured by an everyday quest for survival. The NGO is primarily involved in organizing support groups for orphans and vulnerable children and their caregivers at around 40 "Community-Based Child Care Centers." My experience is that many beneficiaries participate in support groups in the hope their displays of active participation will benefit them when it is time for distribution of material benefits, such as food packets, shoes, clothes, notebooks, pens, etc. But since Raising Malawi – the organization's main donor – was gradually withdrawing their funding during this time, such distributions were becoming rarer and so too was the beneficiaries' attendance.

For the volunteers, their precarious work situation seemed their most immediate concern. One said that Madonna's visit "was good . . . only that it looked like the office never really emphasized our problems – maybe the issue of transport could have been solved by now" (interview, August 1, 2013). The "issue of transport" refers to the fact that some volunteers are charged with the responsibility of monitoring the activities of numerous child care centers, but receive no funds or means of transport to do so. Another volunteer talked about the great work they do as volunteers, "but do not get paid for it," even if "we all have our own problems at home." She emphatically appealed to us that as volunteers they should be "considered for training" (interview, July 18, 2013). These local volunteers are – apart from some of organization's paid staff – those who primarily run the support groups. As in other NGO-funded projects, these volunteers are mostly rural residents with limited educations, who volunteer in the hope of some compensation for their work and to gain experience and access training, which may eventually lead to more permanent employment in the NGO sector (see Swidler & Watkins 2009; Burchardt 2012; Maes & Kalofonos 2013). The fact that the "achievements" international NGOs promote as "theirs" are in large part made possible by using poor, underpaid labor was not a topic in the above debates, nor something that NGO workers are used to critically reflecting upon (Rasmussen 2013). For example, with regard to Madonna's new schools, no commentators dwelled on the fact that the blocks were primarily built by the villagers themselves.[33]

In sum, for these beneficiaries and volunteers, their connection to Madonna was mediated through their unequal relations to the NGO's management. They had limited insight into, and ways of influencing, how Madonna's humanitarian efforts affected them. Whether she was authentic or not did not matter as much as their attempts to position themselves towards getting something out of the erratic, unpredictable flows of donor funding.

Chinkota villagers: "what we want is to go back to talking with Madonna herself"

Chinkota is situated 15–20 kilometers outside the capital Lilongwe. The majority of the village's 200 households gave up farmland for the construction of the Academy for Girls. For most of these households, growing maize and tobacco on this land had constituted their primary source of livelihood. They had received some compensation for the land, but it was not enough to buy farmland elsewhere. My contact to Chinkota was established through a taxi driver who comes from the village. I went with him on my first visit, and the subsequent times with his brother "Jimmy"[34] who is also a taxi driver.

According to residents I talked to, Madonna had personally visited Chinkota to present her school-building plans to them. As indicated by the opening quote from Jimmy, this personal visit produced high expectations of what opportunities the school project might bring, generally spurring hope of improved living conditions.

Villagers presented me with different versions of what kind of compensation they had been promised and by whom. But it seems, at least, that there was initially some negotiation of compensation with representatives from Raising Malawi. Later the Department of Lands took over the process, and the compensation turned out to be much lower than the villagers had anticipated and thought they had agreed upon. A number of informants framed this experience as having lost their personal connection to Madonna. For example, Jimmy said:

> Madonna agreed with the people here on the amount of the compensation. They were expecting money to come from Madonna's side. But government people now came in . . . what they received was much less.
>
> *(field notes, September 22, 2012)*

Some residents explained that when they went to the District Commissioner's office to collect their compensation and they complained that it was not the right amount, they were shouted at: "Don't ask questions," they were told (field notes, October 7, 2012). When construction of the school started, some villagers tried to stop the bulldozers, as a way of protesting about their insufficient compensation. But the protests stopped when the police were called in and the villagers were threatened with arrest (field notes, November 17, 2012). According to the Village Chief, Raising Malawi has unofficially handed the land back to them, but since the ground has already been graded and the topsoil removed, only a small piece of the land was suitable for growing their crops.

For the households I interviewed the compensation from Madonna was not enough for them to buy a new piece of land, only to rent land for one season. When the money from selling the produce from that season ran out, villagers said that they remained without any other sources of income (household interviews, November 17, 2012).

FIGURE 2.3 Fields that were cleared for building Madonna's school in Chinkota. Photograph by Louise Mubanda Rasmussen.

During my visits, it was clear that the Chief and other residents were hoping that my presence might bring some attention to their plight. They had no hopes of the government authorities addressing their grievances, since it was evident to them that the government had "cheated" them of their rightful compensation. Villagers were used to the government "cheating people," Jimmy emphasized (field notes, September 22, 2012). Other residents speculated that "it appears there was coordination of some sorts between the local Raising Malawi staff, the lands department and the District Commissioner," indicating that half of the total amount allocated for their compensation had somehow disappeared into the hands of these people (field notes, October 7, 2012). Perhaps ironically, the one person in whom the villagers continued to have faith was Madonna. At the end of my first visit, the Chief said I should come back and take some pictures because perhaps Madonna would see them on the Internet. "What we want is to go back to talking with Madonna herself," he had said earlier (field notes, September 22, 2012). Thus, the Chief was expressing hope that Madonna could be held accountable for her failed promises, if they could only get in direct contact with her. While they had experienced Madonna's visit as instituting a personal connection to a benefactor who was concerned about their welfare, when matters were left in the hands of "government people" and local Raising Malawi staff, they experienced being at the mercy of corrupt and unaccountable forces, which poor people like them have no ways of opposing.

Conclusion: celebrities and elite politics in the South

This chapter has shown that when celebrity-led initiatives become highly personi-fied in the recipient country, a kind of "recipient public" is engaged. In contrast to Western publics' concern with emotional identification (Littler 2008; Chouliaraki 2013), recipient publics evaluate celebrity authenticity on different terms, compar-ing promises with accomplishments. In this way, a personified celebrity initiative may elucidate the contradictions between how development is represented in the North and how it is experienced in the South. Moreover, when the "failures" of Madonna's projects became an issue in the populist politics of a struggling regime, these contradictions ignited a broader political discussion of development, corrup-tion and elitism.

To some extent, then, this controversial celebrity intervention has opened up a contentious debate around the local politics of development. However, the degree to which the kind of "tabloid accountability" that characterizes every project in Malawi that Madonna gets involved with helps to raise broader questions about the power relations of development aid can be discussed. My interactions with professional development workers in Malawi suggest that the contentions around Madonna's humanitarianism constitute a challenge that professional development discourse can easily contain. Madonna might actually function like "the personal focus distracting attention" from central issues of power in development practice (cf. Tester 2010, p. 77). For the local discussions of corruption and elitism, the way in which the polemic increasingly came to be framed as a personalized clash between Madonna, Joyce Banda and Anjimile Oponyo serves perhaps only to confirm Malawians' widespread distrust of the endless intrigues of the political elite (Englund 2002, p. 15).

Even if we see contentious potential in the way some commentators critiqued the power relations of development aid and the self-serving behavior of the elite, the disconnect between the professional viewpoints and the media debate on the one hand, and the experience of the Chinkota residents and the beneficiaries and volunteers in the local partner organization on the other hand, reflect that there are fundamental inequalities in Malawi, and within the development industry, which are not questioned or even considered in these kinds of discussions. For example, apart from an occasionally brief reference to how the Chinkota residents had given up their farmland, their predicaments were essentially ignored in these middle-class viewpoints, thereby leaving out the voices of those who have probably been the most negatively affected by Madonna's "change of plans."

For the Chinkota residents, on the other hand, Madonna's personal visit to their village spurred hope in much the same way Angelina Jolie's visit did for Burmese exiles in the Thailand–Burma border zone (Mostafanezhad, this volume). In their marginal position, a personal connection to a celebrity promised connections to global structures of money and power, which they otherwise have virtually no access to. However, having now lost this connection, and having been cruelly disappointed, they are left with practically no avenues for having their complaints heard or addressed. Their opportunities for meaningful political participation seem extremely limited – could we imagine the Chinkota residents using this high-profile "land-grabbing" case to start off a collective struggle against Malawi's entrenched inequalities? Celebrity humanitarians can probably do just as little as international NGOs to fundamentally challenge such social and political inequalities. Neither can we, most probably, expect that celebrity humanitarians will be at the forefront of recognizing how development organizations in their own practices may reinforce such inequalities.

Notes

1 E. Ross. 2013. Madonna earns the wrath of Joyce Banda – full statement [online]. *The Guardian*, April 11, http://www.theguardian.com/world/2013/apr/11/malawi-madonna.
2 Madonna remains deeply committed to the children of Malawi despite government's accusations [online]. *Raising Malawi blog,* April 10, 2013, http://www.raisingmalawi.org/blog/entry/madonna-remains-deeply-committed-to-the-children-of-malawi-despite-governme/.
3 A. Harding. 2013. Malawi's president "furious" after Madonna criticized [online]. *BBC News,* April 12, http://www.bbc.com/news/world-africa-22123841.
4 Kabballah is a popularized version of Jewish mysticism that Madonna has been practicing since the late 1990s. Madonna's involvement with the Kabbalah Center in Los Angeles has been instrumental in raising the center's profile, especially among Hollywood stars.
5 For example, M. Musa. 2011. Bishop Zuza denounces dictatorship. *The Nation*, August 16.
6 For example, D. Chirwa. 2011. Mutharika attacks Bishop Zuzu. *Nyasa Times,* August 25; CONGOMA Press Release, 17th January Planned Demonstrations. *The Nation,* January 14, 2013.
7 M. Banda. 2012. Donors call for sacrifice. *The Nation,* September 21.
8 E. Phiri. 2012. Britain saved Malawi – JB. *The Daily Times*, December 19.
9 H. Mchazime. 2012; Cost of living hitting unattainable heights. *The Daily Times,* September 20; T. Khanje. 2012. IMF asks donors to swiftly aid Malawi. *The Daily Times*, October 15.
10 For example, A hollow nation. *The Daily Times*, September 21, 2012; T. Chapulapula. 2012. Queries over "JB" maize. *The Daily Times,* November 2, 2012.
11 Joyce and her donors. *The Daily Times*, November 2, 2012.
12 Raising Malawi. 2014a. About raising Malawi [online], http://www.raisingmalawi.org/pages/about.
13 V. Grigoriadis. 2011. Our Lady of Malawi [online]. *New York Magazine*, May 1, pp. 1–6, http://nymag.com/news/features/madonna-malawi-2011-5/
14 A. Nagourney. 2011. Madonna's Charity Fails in Bid to Finance School [online]. *The New York Times*, March 24, http://www.nytimes.com/2011/03/25/us/25madonna.html?_r=0.
15 Statement from Madonna [online]. *Raising Malawi blog,* January 11, 2012, http://www.raisingmalawi.org/blog/entry/statement-from-madonna/.
16 For example, D. Smith. 2011. Madonna's Malawi charity 'squandered millions' [online]. *The Guardian,* March 25, http://www.theguardian.com/world/2011/mar/25/madonna-malawi-charity-squandered-millions.

17 Nagourney. 2011. Madonna's Charity Fails in Bid to Finance School.
18 Grigoriadis. 2011. Our Lady of Malawi; W. Barrett. 2011. Madonna's Kabbalah disaster in Malawi [online]. *Newsweek*, April 3, http://www.newsweek.com/madonnas-kabbalah-disaster-malawi-66447.
19 Court dismisses Madonna plea to prevent Raising Malawi from being sued [online]. *Nyasa Times*, August 17, 2011, http://www.nyasatimes.com/2011/08/17/courtdismisses-madonna-plea-to-prevent-raising-malawi-from-being-sued.
20 Madonna honors commitment to help children of Malawi [online] *Raising Malawi blog*, January 30, 2012, http://www.raisingmalawi.org/blog/entry/madonna-honors-commitment-to-help-children-of-malawi/.
21 M. Hutchings. 2012. Malawi 'fed up' with Madonna, slams school plans [online]. *Reuters*, March 13, http://www.reuters.com/article/2012/03/13/entertainment-us-malawi-madonna-idUSBRE82C19N20120313.
22 Malawi President's sister Anjimile appointed PS Education Ministry [online]. *Nyasa Times*, November 7, 2012, http://www.nyasatimes.com/2012/11/07/malawi-presidents-sister-anjimile-appointed-ps-education-ministry/.
23 Madonna announces completion of 10 schools in Malawi in partnership with buildOn [online]. *Raising Malawi blog*, December 27, 2012, http://www.raisingmalawi.org/blog/entry/madonna-announces-completion-of-10-schools-in-malawi-in-partnership-with-bu/.
24 Malawi govt trashes Madonna schoolbuilding claim [online]. *Nyasa Times*, January 17, 2013, http://www.nyasatimes.com/2013/01/17/malawi-govt-trashes-madonna-school-building-claim/.
25 For example, S. Khunga. 2013. The truth about Madonna's schools. *The Daily Times*, January 23.
26 Madonna wins adoption battle [online]. *CBS News*, June 12, 2009, http://www.cbsnews.com/news/madonna-wins-adoption-battle/.
27 Pop icon Madona has accused Malawi government [online]. *Malawi Breaking News and Gossip*, April 5, 2013, https://www.facebook.com/MalawiBreakingNewsAndSports/posts/405567159542586?fref=nf&pnref=story.
28 Malawi State House responds to Madonna's outbursts: Full text [online]. *Nyasa Times*, April 10, 2013. Comment no. 19, http://www.nyasatimes.com/2013/04/10/malawi-state-house-responds-to-madonnas-outbursts-full-text/.
29 Madonna ends Malawi controversial tour: Accused of lying to the world on 'schools' [online]. *Nyasa Times*, April 7, 2013. Comment no. 21, http://www.nyasatimes.com/2013/04/07/madonna-ends-malawi-controversial-tour-accused-of-lying-to-the-world-on-schools/.
30 Madonna with David Banda, Mercy in Malawi classroom [online]. *Nyasa Times*, April 2, 2013. Comment no. 41, http://www.nyasatimes.com/2013/04/02/madonna-with-david-banda-mercy-in-malawi-classroom/.
31 '*Nepotism basi*' can be translated as 'pure/simple nepotism.'
32 Malawi State House responds to Madonna's outbursts: Full text. Comment no. 26.
33 buildOn and Raising Malawi provided the construction materials, transportation, skilled labor, project management, and construction plans. The community provided "a gender-balanced leadership team," volunteer labour, land, and local building materials. See Statement from buildOn on Schools Constructed in Partnership with Raising Malawi [online]. *Raising Malawi blog*, January 17, 2013, http://www.raisingmalawi.org/blog/entry/statement-from-buildon-on-schools-constructed-in-partnership-with-raising-m/.
34 A pseudonym.

References

Boltanski, L. 1999. *Distant Suffering: Morality, Media and Politics*. Cambridge: Cambridge University Press.

Booth, D., Cammack, D., Harrigan, J., Kanyongolo, E., Mataure, M., & Ngwira, N. 2006. *Drivers of Change in Malawi*. Overseas Development Institute, Working Paper.

Brockington, D. 2014. *Celebrity Advocacy and International Development*. London and New York: Routledge.

Burchardt, M. 2012. Faith-based humanitarianism: organizational change and everyday meanings in South Africa. *Sociology of Religion*, 74 (1), 30–55.

Cameron, J. & Haanstra, A. 2008. Development made sexy: how it happened and what it means. *Third World Quarterly*, 29 (8), 1475–89.

Chouliaraki, L. 2013. *The Ironic Spectator: Solidarity in the Age of Post-Humanitarianism*. Cambridge: Polity.

Clarke, R. (ed.). 2009. *Celebrity Colonialism: Fame, Power and Representation in Colonial and Postcolonial Cultures*. Cambridge: Cambridge Scholars Publishing.

Dionne, K.Y., Gerland, P. & Watkins, S. 2013. AIDS exceptionalism: another constituency heard from. *AIDS and Behavior*, 17 (3), 825–31.

Englund, H. 2002. *A Democracy of Chameleons: Politics and Culture in the New Malawi*. Uppsala: Nordic Africa Institute.

Englund, H. 2006. *Prisoners of Freedom: Human Rights and the African Poor*. Cambridge: Cambridge University Press.

Ferguson, J. 1994. *The Anti-Politics Machine: "Development", Depoliticization and Bureaucratic Power in Lesotho*. Minneapolis: University of Minnesota Press.

Ferguson, J. 2006. *Global Shadows: Africa in the Neoliberal World Order*. Durham, NC: Duke University Press.

Igoe, J. & Kelsall, T. 2005. *Between a Rock and a Hard Place: African NGOs, Donors and the State*. Durham, NC: Carolina Academic Press.

Internet World Stats. 2014. Internet users in Africa [online]. Available at http://www.inter networldstats.com/stats1.htm.

Kapoor, I. 2012. *Celebrity Humanitarianism: The Ideology of Global Charity*. London: Routledge.

Khembo, N.S. 2005. The multiparty promise betrayed: the failure of neo-liberalism in Malawi. *Africa Development*, 29 (2), 80–105.

Li, T.M. 2007. *The Will to Improve: Governmentality, Development, and the Practice of Politics*. Durham, NC: Duke University Press.

Littler, J. 2008. "I feel your pain": cosmopolitan charity and the public fashioning of the celebrity soul. *Social Semiotics*, 18 (2), 237–251.

Maes, K. & Kalofonos, I. 2013. Becoming and remaining community health workers: perspectives from Ethiopia and Mozambique. *Social Science & Medicine*, 87, 52–9.

Morfit, N.S. 2011. "AIDS is money": How donor preferences reconfigure local realities. *World Development*, 39 (1), 64–76.

Müller, Tanja R. 2013. The long shadow of Band Aid humanitarianism: revisiting the dynamics between famine and celebrity. *Third World Quarterly*, 34 (3), 470–84.

OECD. 2005. *The Paris Declaration on aid effectiveness and the Accra Agenda for Action*. Paris/ Accra: OECD.

Power, J. 2010. *Political Culture and Nationalism in Malawi: Building Kwacha*. Rochester, NY: University of Rochester Press.

Rasmussen, L.M. 2013. The fiction of sustainability: addressing the social consequences of AIDS through "civil society organisations" in Malawi. Presented at the 5th European Conference on African Studies, Lisbon.

Richey, L.A. 2008. *Population Politics and Development: From the Policies to the Clinics.* New York: Palgrave MacMillan.

Richey, L.A. & Ponte, S. 2011. *Brand Aid: Shopping Well to Save the World.* Minneapolis: University of Minnesota Press.

Sèbe, B. 2009. Colonial Celebrities in Popular Culture: Heroes of the British and French Empires, 1850–1914. In: R. Clarke (ed.) *Celebrity Colonialism: Fame, Power and Representation in Colonial and Postcolonial Cultures.* Cambridge: Cambridge Scholars Publishing, pp. 37–54.

Swidler, A. & Watkins, S.C. 2009. "Teach a man to fish": the sustainability doctrine and its social consequences. *World Development,* 37 (7), 1182–96.

Tester, K. 2010. *Humanitarianism and Modern Culture.* University Park, PA: The Pennsylvania State University Press.

3

MUHAMMAD YUNUS

A Bangladeshi aid celebrity

Anke Schwittay

I met Muhammad Yunus at a public lecture at the University of California, Berkeley in April 2002. It was a rather intimate affair in front of a small audience – it would be another four years before Yunus would win the Nobel Peace Prize – which allowed me to listen to his talk from the front row and shake his hand afterwards. Twelve years later what I remember most about him is his charisma: he was soft-spoken and humble, full of conviction and heart, and came across as powerfully committed. Others have been similarly struck by his genuine interest and affable nature. According to Alex Counts, head of the US Grameen Foundation, for example:

> Yunus owns a rounded, even pudgy face highlighted by expressive – some say magical – eyes and an eager smile. Visitors get the sense that he is a jolly man. Quick with a witty remark in any of the several languages he speaks, Yunus has the rare ability to make nervous strangers feel like long-lost friends in a matter of minutes.
>
> *(Counts 1996, p. 8)*

As these descriptions show, Yunus incites affect and compels care, through his persona, his work and his stories. In this chapter, I examine Yunus as an aid celebrity from the Global South (Richey & Ponte 2011). Yunus is the founder of the Grameen Bank in Bangladesh, which pioneered giving small loans to poor women so that they could start their own micro-businesses. What has become known as microlending[1] is the foundation of Yunus' aid celebrity status, together with his championing of the world's poor as microentrepreneurs. I argue that Yunus' success is partly based on his ability to present an affective persona and to effectively manage the sentiments of his global audience, from power brokers in international development organizations and national governments to everyday people. In other words, Yunus seems to have taken the dictum that "one must be affective in order to be effective" to heart (Mazzarella 2009, p. 299).

In this chapter, following a brief theory and methodology section, I situate Yunus' work with Grameen within his personal history that is firmly located in Bangladesh. In the next section, I present Yunus as a self-declared champion of the poor, whom he variously characterizes as bonsai people and natural entrepreneurs. Most importantly, through his work with Grameen he has become a voice for poor women in Bangladesh and beyond, narrating their difficult lives and salvation by microcredit. This led to the 2006 award of the Peace Nobel Price to Yunus and Grameen, which made him publicly known. In the last section, I explore the limits of his aid celebrity status, manifest in his fall from grace in Bangladesh and the increasing criticism of micro-debt.

Aid celebrity: theory and methodology

In this chapter I bring the literature on aid and development celebrities into con-versation with the literature on humanitarian affect. Yunus' status as an aid celeb-rity comes from the way in which his "identity has been made inseparable from [his] aid work" (Richey & Ponte 2011, p. 179). Yunus is the Grameen Bank and vice versa. In other words, the Grameen Bank provides him with a stage on which he can present his public persona, which he legitimizes through various authenti-cation strategies (Chouliaraki 2013). Indeed, for Chouliaraki, celebrity becomes a "communicative practice that brings the offstage performance of celebrity (or the 'persona') as an altruist together with his or her onstage performances of the voices of suffering as a message for action" (p. 82). As I show, Yunus has been masterful at authenticating and legitimizing himself and his work by channeling the voices of poor Bangladeshi women supposedly saved by microcredit. This is reinforced by his own insider status as a homegrown Bangladeshi development practitioner, whose life work has grown out of his life story. Yunus delivers these narratives to his multiple audiences, from the World Bank (WB) and national presidents to eve-ryday people supportive of microcredit, in powerful and persuasive ways.

One of his strongest, and at the same time most contentious, claims is that micro-credit is a simple solution to large-scale poverty alleviation (Counts 1996; Schwittay 2014). This has not only allowed him to build a microcredit movement, but also shows how aid celebrities are able to bring together diverse constituents for a cause through their embodiment of manufactured consensuses and their substitution of sim-ple moral truths for rational debate (Richey & Ponte 2011). The limits of this engage-ment were shown with Yunus' ill-fated attempt to enter formal politics in Bangladesh, which ultimately resulted in his ouster from Grameen. Trying to transform himself into a "politicized celebrity" who used "his fame as a form of political capital to . . . propagate partisan ideologies" (Wheeler 2013, pp. 60–1), which was thwarted by the Bangladeshi government, shows the boundaries of aid celebrities' power.

Yunus' appeal cannot be understood without reference to what is frequently referred to as humanitarian affect. Didier Fassin has argued for the existence of a "humanitarian emotion: the affect by virtue of which human beings feel personally concerned by the situation of others" (2012, p. 269). These sentiments are historically and temporally situated, forming structures of feeling (Williams 1976) that constitute subjects who "are more likely today to have sympathy for, and even to do something to alleviate, the suffering of people and animals distant from ourselves . . . than were men and women three centuries ago" (Laqueur 2009, p. 32). Such feelings have been created by individuals like Yunus and their organizations that "compel care" (Feldman 2010, p. 200). In addition, Yunus has contributed much to narrating the figure of the deserving, responsible female microentrepreneur as a worthy recipient of humanitarian sentiments.

While microcredit partakes in humanitarian affect, it also inflects it in particular ways. On the one hand, it is subject to the more general tension between the intimate connections on which this affect is built and the generic nature of monetary exchanges that make affect manifest, where money can only create minimal and abstract bonds (Boltanski 1999). On the other, because microcredit is based on a financial exchange, it can create connections to go beyond charitable impulses (Bornstein 2012). Lastly, microcredit and Yunus trade not in humanitarianism's "sad and sentimental stories" (Rorty 1993, p. 114), but in narratives of empowerment and entrepreneurial success. Through narrating his own encounters with the women who are the subjects of these stories, Yunus' own performance of care and compassion for the poor also mobilizes affective action in his followers (Chouliaraki 2011).

In line with Yunus' power as a storyteller, this chapter is animated by stories that have been told by and about Yunus, drawing on his autobiography *Banker to the Poor* (Yunus 1999) and several hagiographies (Bornstein 1997, 2005; Counts 1996) as well as more critical accounts of the Grameen Bank in Bangladesh (Rahman 1999; Karim 2011). Although widely celebrated as a successful poverty alleviation intervention, microcredit has in recent years been criticized for its questionable impact (Bateman 2010). In spite of the introduction of evaluation methods such as randomized control trials, the actual difference microcredit makes in recipients' lives is still contested (Banerjee & Duflo 2011). In addition, while microcredit proponents claim to empower women, on-the-ground studies have shown that women's use of loans is embedded in complex relations of kinship, labor and consumption, which complicate and sometimes negate the benefits women can reap from their loans (Kabeer 2001). A third critique centers on microcredit's links with neoliberalism, which have become more pronounced with the recent commercialization that has exposed poor people to financial risk and over-indebtedness (Roy 2012). Despite these debates around microcredit and its actual successes or limitations, Yunus became an aid celebrity because he personified microcredit's ability of enabling the poor to work themselves out of poverty.

Narrating a life in the Global South

While Yunus did not invent microcredit, which has existed in various localized forms for over 200 years, he took a small Bangladeshi experiment and transformed it into an international institution. By establishing the Grameen Bank in Bangladesh, where he lived and worked most of his life, in the late 1970s Yunus developed a model for how small loans could be given, especially to poor women, who until then had been excluded from formal banking services because of their lack of physical collateral and the strictures of Bangladeshi patriarchal society. Based on his belief in the abilities of his fellow Bangladeshis to enterprise themselves out of poverty, Yunus grew microcredit into a widely embraced global poverty alleviation intervention and in the process transformed himself from a local development practitioner into an internationally recognized aid celebrity from the Global South.

Early influences

Yunus' life and work, as represented in his autobiography (Yunus 1999), cannot be understood separately from the history and politics of his native Bangladesh. Yunus was born in 1940 in Chittagong, a commercial city of about three million people in what was then the southeast of the Indian state of East Bengal. He was the third of 14 children, of whom five died in infancy, and lived with his family in a small two-story house. His father, a devout Muslim, ran a successful jewelry business from the ground floor. He also insisted that his children study hard, which came easy to Yunus.

It was his forceful mother who exerted the strongest influence on him and early on instilled in him a sense of caring for the poor. Yunus remembers that:

> . . . full of compassion and kindness, Mother always put money away for any poor relatives who visited us from distant villages. It was she, by her concern for the poor and the disadvantaged, who helped me discover my interest in economics and social reform.
>
> *(Yunus 1999, p. 5)*

Another early influence was the headmaster of his Collegiate School; according to Yunus, "I had always been a natural leader, but Quazi Ahib's moral influence taught me to think high and channel my passions" (ibid. 12). As a good student, Yunus received a number of scholarships that would eventually earn him a Fulbright Scholarship to study at the University of Colorado Boulder and Vanderbilt University in Tennessee, where he earned a PhD in Economics in the late 1960s. This was not his first international travel, as he had already visited Canada, Japan and the Philippines as a Boy Scout. He credits Scouting with teaching him to be compassionate and spiritual, and to cherish his fellow human beings. Through these memories, Yunus has created a narrative of significant early influences that helped him become a compassionate and socially conscious person. According to him, they laid the foundations for his later work with the poor, which is thereby grounded in and authenticated by his Bangladeshi upbringing.

Yunus' nationalistic sentiments were awakened when, as a seven-year-old boy, he witnessed India's independence, with his family being strongly committed to Partition. As a result of the separation of India and Pakistan in 1947, Chittagong became located in East Pakistan. Twenty-five years later in the US, Yunus formed the Bangladesh Citizens' Committee to lobby political leaders there to support East Pakistan's movement for independence, which was being bloodily suppressed by the Pakistani army at the time. In 1972 Yunus returned home to a newly independent Bangladesh, and to the devastations of war and Cyclone Bhola. Committed to help rebuild his nation, he joined the new government's planning commission but became quickly disillusioned with its bureaucracy.

He left government service to become Head of the Economics Department at Chittagong University, which was located on the outskirts of the city and surrounded by the village of Jobra. As its poorer inhabitants slowly succumbed to the effects of the 1974 famine, Yunus was confronted with hunger and starvation on his daily journey to work (Yunus 1999). In attempts to alleviate this situation, he received small grants from the Ford Foundation to set up the Rural Development Project, where students could get hands-on learning through assisting villagers with agricultural technology development. By all accounts, students liked Yunus; as one of them remembers, "he had wide shoulders and he carried a big canvas bag over his shoulder. He had a car with no muffler. He also had a foreign wife" (cited in Bornstein 1997, p. 33). In the traditional and highly stratified Bangladeshi society, Yunus seemed an exotic and extraordinary individual to those around him, an image he fostered by his appearance and his activities.

Natural entrepreneurs?

Had Yunus not decided that his first love was teaching, he could have become a very successful businessman. After he graduated from his economics studies at Dhaka University at 21 years of age, he built and ran a successful printing and packaging business that monopolized the market in East Pakistan (Counts 1996). Even though he did not pursue this career, he has always been an ardent believer in the transformative power of entrepreneurship. During one of his speeches, Yunus called on his audience to "imagine a world where every human being is a potential entrepreneur . . . We will build institutions in such a way that each person is supported and empowered to create his or her own job" (quoted in Counts 1996, pp. 340–1). This vision of innate entrepreneurship also includes poor people, and especially poor women, whom Yunus regards as natural entrepreneurs. What they are lacking in their attempts to fulfill their entrepreneurial potential is access to financial capital, which makes microcredit an appropriate solution to this problem.

Yunus' notion of the poor as bonsai people best captures this belief.

> To me poor people are like bonsai trees. When you plant the best seed of the tallest tree in a flower-pot, you get a replica of the tallest tree, only inches tall. There is nothing wrong with the seed you planted, only the soil-base that is too inadequate . . . All it needs to get the poor people out of poverty is for us to create an enabling environment for them. Once the poor can unleash their energy and creativity, poverty will disappear very quickly.
>
> *(Yunus 2007, p. 247)*

A bonsai tree is a revealing and productive metaphor, albeit one that would probably mean little to poor Bangladeshis themselves. It grounds poverty in a context of carefully nurtured flora, in a state in-between nature and society that causes smallness. While Yunus draws attention to the way the growth of miniature trees is restricted by the pot environment in which they are placed, he does not mention the constant and long-term pruning of their crowns and roots to keep them small. The creation of a bonsai tree is an active process of ongoing curtailment, hinting at the daily vulnerabilities poor people experience in their struggles for survival. These are seen as external, violent interventions that intentionally keep poor people purposely small in means. On the other hand, characterizing poor people in terms of smallness evokes childlike qualities, and a certain degree of paternalism.

Importantly, for Yunus there is nothing inherently little about the poor, who start life with the same genetic potential as everybody else. It is the restrictive and restricting environment into which they are born that causes their smallness. Consequently, if given the right opportunities in the form of microcredit, poor people can realize their innate entrepreneurial potential and take charge of their own lives. Such beliefs feed into neoliberal agendas of state welfare retreat and decreasing formal employment opportunities, especially in the public sector (Weber 2004). In this context, microcredit has been promoted by the Washington Consensus as a safety net and pacification strategy, quelling potential unrest in the wake of Structural Adjustment Programs that wreaked havoc on poor livelihoods. Other critics have argued that Yunus' vision is based on a romantic view of the poor, who prefer the security of permanent employment at living wages to having their own businesses (Karnani 2007). What is celebrated as entrepreneurism are survival strategies, which, when supplied by microcredit, can at best only lead to miniscule improvements and at worst trap the poor in spiraling debt cycles (Guérin et al. 2013).

But this story is getting ahead of itself. In the early 1970s Yunus was just beginning to spend his time in Jobra, talking to poor (male) villagers in tea stalls, making a point of learning their names and getting to know how they lived and worked. Already Professor Yunus, as he came to be called, made himself known as a man of the people – accessible, approachable, unintimidating. In conservative and highly stratified Chittagong, that only reinforced his differences from the local establishment. Those years, then, mark the beginning of Yunus' celebrated status as champion of the poor.

The rise of microcredit

When Yunus began to experiment with giving small loans to some of those poor villagers, and especially to poor women, he broke not only social but also banking conventions. This forced him to experiment with different ways of reaching and organizing his borrowers. The result was the Grameen, or Village, Bank, which became Yunus' full-time occupation and his life's work, allowing him to make himself known as the *Banker to the Poor* (Yunus 1999). Growing Grameen from its local beginnings into an international financial institution, and creating a powerful narrative of how it is saving poor women from destitution earned Yunus and Grameen the 2006 Nobel Peace Prize.

The village bank

It was in Jobra in 1976 that the famous meeting with Sufiya Begum, which eventually resulted in the Grameen Bank, took place. The story of this meeting has been retold by Yunus, and others, on countless occasions, and has come to mark the moment of birth for both Grameen, and the modern microfinance movement.[2] Sufiya Begum, a 21-year-old mother of three, was crouching on the dirt floor in front of her hut weaving bamboo stools, as Yunus passed by. Striking up a conversation, he learned that it would take just 22 cents for her to become independent of the middleman who sold her the bamboo and bought her chairs for a pittance. In his autobiography, Yunus described the personal effect of the meeting as follows:

> Sufiya Begum earned two cents a day. It was this knowledge that shocked me. In my university courses, I theorized about sums in the millions of dollars, but here before my eyes the problems of life and death were posed in terms of pennies . . . I was angry, angry at myself, angry at my economics professors who had not tried to address the problem and solve it . . . I had never heard of anyone suffering for the lack of 22 cents. It seemed impossible to me, preposterous.
>
> *(Yunus 1999, p. 48)*

Here Yunus recounts having received an emotional shock to his core identity, showing how it was an affective reaction that jolted him into action. However, Yunus resisted the "impulse of charity," where images of poverty elicit often financial responses via various emotional registers (Bornstein 2012). Instead of giving Sufiya Begum the 22 cents, Yunus began to think how he could resolve the problem on a more permanent basis. In the end, he asked one of his students to make a list of all the people in Jobra who were dependent on middlemen; it came to a total of 42 people who had borrowed less than $27. "Sickened by the reality of it all," he gave the student $27 from his own pocket to lend to the people, and to be paid back whenever they were able (Yunus 1999, p. 50). He also began to envision an institution that would make such loans on a larger and more continuous scale. Yunus reacted with both his head and his heart, and the way in which microcredit enables similar double investments – financial and emotional – continues to make it appealing to everyday people (Black 2009; Schwittay 2014).

Over the years, Sufiya Begum's story has taken on the characteristics of a classical origin myth: "for the thousands of men and women who staff the Grameen Bank, the story of their organization's birth has the resonance of myth. Colleagues who were around at the beginning relate Yunus' experiences in Jobra the same way an old friend might describe Bill Gates' first attempts at writing his famous computer operating system" (Bornstein 1997, p. 32). This reference to Gates is no coincidence, as both men believe in the power of a humane capitalism to help eradicate poverty (Schwittay 2011). Such origin stories also play a good role in fostering company morale. In addition, Grameen's beginning story firmly puts Yunus at the center of the Grameen Bank and continuously reinforces the feeling that he created something that would make history, or, in his own words, "put poverty into the history museum" (Yunus 1999). Sufiya Begum's story thus constitutes the ground zero for the making of Yunus as an aid celebrity.

This feeling of extraordinariness has contributed to Yunus' status as a historical figure, who sees himself and is seen by others as set apart from everyday people by his exceptional achievements in the field of development. These achievements distinguish Yunus from media celebrities for whom engagement with development is an increasingly essential but still secondary part of their jobs (Goodman & Barnes 2011), and constitute him as an aid celebrity, whose fame is intimately tied to his values and work. Correspondingly, Yunus has been likened to people like Gandhi, J.F.K. and Martin Luther King Jr. (Bornstein 1997). All of them suffered for the causes they believed in and there is an element of personal sacrifice in Yunus' narratives as well, be it the loss of his first wife and daughter, who left him to move back to the US, financial costs or health problems. Indeed, he cites sacrifice as one of his core values (Counts 1996). On the other hand, the correlate of historical significance is immortality, and one anecdote tells of his exchange with a filmmaker who said to Yunus when she met him: "So you are mortal." He is said to have replied, "Don't be too sure" (cited in Bornstein 2005, p. 48). While outwardly remaining humble and modest, over the years Yunus appears to have become enamored with his own success story. To reconcile the resulting tension, Yunus has continuously presented himself as a champion of poor Bangladeshi women.

Giving voice to poor women

By arguing that "the poor know that credit is their only opportunity to break out of poverty" (1999, p. 59), Yunus articulates the needs of a generic population of poor people and thereby constitutes himself as one of its foremost advocates. Poor Bangladeshi women occupy a privileged place in this advocacy, and Yunus cultivates an image of being close to them, through his modest, local-style clothes, his down-to-earth demeanor and speech, and his frequent and well-publicized visits with poor borrowers. Photos of Yunus often show him sitting on the ground, smiling at the women surrounding him. Likewise, books about Yunus abound in descriptions of his village encounters with poor women, who become crucial props that reinforce Yunus' image as giving them not only the means to a better life, but also a voice and an identity.

Here is Yunus' version of the feelings of a poor woman getting her first Grameen loan:

> How does she feel? Terrified. She cannot sleep at night. She struggles with the fear of failure, the fear of the unknown. The morning she is to receive the loan, she almost quits. 25 dollars is simply too much responsibility for her. How will she ever be able to repay it? No woman in her extended family has ever had so much money. Her friends come around to reassure her . . . When she finally receives the 25 dollars, she is trembling. The money burns her fingers. Tears roll down her face. She never imagined it in her hands. She carries the bills as she would a delicate bird or a rabbit, until someone advised her to put her money away in a safe place, lest it be stolen. This is the beginning for almost every Grameen borrower. All her life she has been told that she is no good, that she brings only misery to her family, and that they cannot afford to pay her dowry. Many times she hears her mother or her father tell her that she should have been killed at birth, aborted, or starved. To her family she has been nothing but another mouth to feed, another dowry to pay. But today, for the first time in her life, an institution has trusted her with a great sum of money. She promises that she will never let down the institution or herself. She will struggle to make sure that every penny is paid back.
>
> *(Yunus 1999, pp. 64–5)*

This quote is long, but insightful, and not only because Yunus assumes the authority to speak for an ideal type woman borrower. Here, he personifies the voice of the suffering other, creating a proximity that is enabled by his work with Grameen and at the same time authenticates and legitimizes it. Using a highly affectively charged language that is common to many development celebrities (Chouliaraki 2011), Yunus presents receiving the first Grameen loan as a monumental, life-changing event in a poor woman's life. He thereby elevates Grameen, and by extension himself, to the position of a savior who gives poor women meaning and recognition, and indeed makes them into persons in their own right.

This narrative can be challenged in various ways. Firstly, it neglects the fact that it is likely that women have handled loans before, albeit from informal sources and probably not in such large amounts. Poor people have sophisticated financial lives and often juggle a considerable number of debt obligations and savings arrangements to manage the smallness, inconsistency and fluctuation of their incomes (Collins et al. 2009). In Yunus' narrative, by contrast, a Grameen loan is the beginning of a journey to freedom that transforms poor women from suffering victims into productive and responsible microentrepreneurs. While this might be the case for some women, for the great majority this transformation remains unrealistic and unrealized. Microloans might help to smooth consumption and cope with the hardship of poverty, but they rarely help women escape from poverty completely (Banerjee & Duflo 2011).

Secondly, Yunus' seemingly straightforward ability to communicate with poor women and express their feelings gives short shrift to the fact that Bangladesh is a Muslim country where many women observe *purdah*, or seclusion at home. Coupled with patriarchal social structures and conventional banking practices, this meant that in the early years most Grameen loans went to men (Yunus 1999). In the face of high default rates, however, women came to be seen as potentially more responsible and compliant borrowers.[3] Their recruitment was hindered by established gender norms, and purdah in particular, which meant that when Grameen's male loan officers came to the villages, women disappeared into their huts. Yunus found several ways around this, from hiring a Buddhist woman who was able to circulate freely and enter women's houses, to breaking purdah rules by entering them himself (Bornstein 2005).[4] Today, over 90 percent of all Grameen borrowers are women.[5]

Thirdly, while Yunus has promoted Grameen as empowering millions of poor Bangladeshi women, this narrative neglects kinship obligations of labor and consumption and gendered dynamics of shame and honor that circumscribe microloan recipients (Karim 2011; Rahman 1999). Often, women become conduits through which male loan officers exchange debt and repayment with male kin, while women are formally responsible for the loan and bear many of the negative consequences if payments cannot be made (Karim 2008). They can be subjected to peer pressure, surveillance and intimidations from the other members of their lending groups, who have to cross-guarantee each others' loans in the absence of physical collateral. In extreme cases, non-payment can lead to the loss of one's home. In spite of such documented negative effects, microcredit has until recently remained a celebrated development intervention.

Celebrating microcredit

Part of microcredit's success is that it appeals to the political left and right, the former lauding its bottom-up, participatory approach and the latter its entrepreneurial, self-reliance focus. Similarly, praise for Yunus has come from across the globe and the political spectrum:

> As a pitchman and a dreamer, he seems humble even when making grandiose claims, and, with his warm-heartedness, makes whatever he has to offer seem delightfully agreeable. At his talks, he regularly draws standing ovations from socially conscious progressives, business-oriented free-marketers, and numerous personalities in between.
>
> *(Engler 2009, p. 81)*

Public recognition was thus inevitable. The United Nations declared 2005 the Year of Microcredit. A year later Yunus achieved his greatest personal and professional triumph when he and the Grameen Bank were jointly awarded the Nobel

Peace Prize. This was not without its detractors. At the 2005 Boulder Institute, an important microcredit training program, various people opined that the reward should be going to Fazle Abed and BRAC, another NGO in Bangladesh that was established at around the same time as Grameen. Similar to Grameen, BRAC has grown into a large social welfare provider in Bangladesh, where NGOs form a "shadow state" (Karim 2008, p. 11). However, "BRAC, while much favored by the Washington consensus, did not enjoy the same global recognition. BRAC was not – as one of the Italian attendees at Boulder had put it so elegantly – as beloved and well-known as is parsley in Italy" (Roy 2010, p. 91). In other words, Abed is not as publicly visible and celebrated a figure as Yunus. Although clearly recognized in development circles for his important work, Abed is not an aid celebrity. Yunus, then, was rewarded as much for his self-presentation as for his work and the Nobel Prize cemented his status as an aid celebrity by making Yunus into a publicly recognized figure.

To receive the prize, which was jointly awarded to him and Grameen, Yunus traveled to Oslo with nine Bangladeshi women borrowers. During his acceptance speech, he declared that, "all borrowers of Grameen are celebrating this day as the greatest day of their lives." Once again, he gave voice to the feelings of several million poor Bangladeshi women, who in turn lent Yunus authenticity and legitimacy. Amidst the celebrations, however, storm clouds were already brewing. During the 2006 Microcredit Summit in Canada, where Yunus was treated to standing ovations, he proclaimed that "the era of showing profits is over . . . we will measure our success not on the rate of return on investment but by the number of people coming out of poverty" (quoted in Roy 2010, p. 90). But at its greatest hour of success, microcredit was beginning to be judged to be losing its way and actually harming poor women rather than helping them.

The limits of aid celebrity

Yunus is widely known and referred to as "Doctor Yunus," which highlights his academic credentials and social and cultural capital, but also marks him as an outsider in the banking and development world. Here, he has been trying to use his celebrity power to change some of the rules of the international development establishment.

Little wonder, then, that Yunus is also contentious, and nowhere more so than in his home in Bangladesh, where his political activity has caused his ouster from Grameen.

Changing the rules of international development?

In spite of being a homegrown Bangladeshi institution, Grameen would not have gotten off the ground without early institutional and financial support from the Ford Foundation and the United Nations' International Fund for Agricultural Development, which were joined by other funders over subsequent decades.

FIGURE 3.1   Doctor Yunus in Italy discussing social business, sustainable solutions for society's most important challenges in 2014. Photograph by Umberto Battaglia, from https://www.flickr.com/photos/cameradeideputati/14617800864/in/photostream/.

While accepting their soft loans, Yunus always resisted donors' involvement in Grameen's management, instead working to retain Grameen's independence and Bengali identity (Bornstein 2005). Indeed, Grameen is a rare example of a development practice originating in the Global South that has been taken up in the North as well (Roy 2010). As such, Grameen is a critical part of the Bangladesh consensus around microfinance that focuses on human development and social welfare.

In the 1980s Yunus tried to use Grameen's attractiveness to change some of the development industry's rules, just as he had changed banking rules in Bangladesh a decade earlier (Bornstein 2005). For example, when he received US$105 million to implement Grameen's Phase III from seven different international donor organizations, he insisted that they create a single office. Negotiations, which Grameen leadership conducted in a businesslike manner, took place in Bangladesh rather than the funders' countries as would have been customary. Grameen leadership insisted that funders' "oversight missions" became "joint reviews" and their recommendations were optional rather than mandatory. Donors were not used to such a lack of deference and gratitude.

What caused the greatest resentment, however, was Yunus' insistence that access to microcredit provides a simple solution to poverty eradication. As one US banker who has worked with Yunus recounted: "The reaction of the development community to Grameen went from disbelief to rage. They got so upset that Yunus would come in and say that it was so simple" (quoted in Bornstein 2005, p. 253). Microfinance's apparent simplicity is as much an operational as a strategic descriptor. Arguing that giving a woman a small loan will enable her to start a business and enterprise herself out of poverty is a far cry from how microcredit operates on the ground, but such arguments make it appealing to Northern publics, who remain supportive even in the face of increasing criticism. It shows how aid celebrities can often forge public consensus around their versions of development by substituting simple truths for complex issues (Richey & Ponte 2011). In the case of microcredit, Yunus' "obligatory success story" of poor women's entrepreneurial abilities promotes it as a common-sense approach to poverty alleviation (Schwittay 2014, p. 11).

In addition to the above-mentioned debates around the potential of microloans to (dis)empower women, the most persistent critiques have centered on the questionable economic impacts achieved by these loans, and the businesses they are supposed to fund. One economist and former microfinance practitioner argues that microcredit is based on a fundamentally flawed economic model, leading to a "de-industrialization, primitivization and informalization of the local economic base" in many of the countries that have embraced microcredit most enthusiastically (Bateman 2010, p. 117). The result is unsustainable bubbles that have been inflated by the expansion of a commercialized model of microfinance, which aims to build microfinance institutions that are attractive to mainstream, profit-seeking investors. Highly publicized borrower suicides in the wake of an Initial Public Offering of a microfinance bank in India, which greatly enriched its founders and investors while leaving poor borrowers in spiraling debt, has created some public awareness of the negative effects of microcredit and turned some proponents into critics (Biswas 2010). Yunus has been a vocal opponent of this commercialization, but without being able to stop or curtail it, it seems that he is no longer in control of his own creation. And because his celebrity status is tied to his work in microcredit, his persona has not escaped criticism.

Contentious politics

Yunus is the first to admit that support from the right people in positions of power in Bangladesh, be it in the government finance ministry, the Central Bank or national banks, has been crucial for the success of Grameen. In fact, Grameen Bank was founded in 1983 with the passing of a special law, the Grameen Bank Ordinance. To achieve this, Yunus has astutely managed to maneuver a politically charged terrain, all the while trying to keep Grameen itself away from formal politics. Staff members are forbidden to discuss politics with borrowers and Grameen has historically not wanted to be associated with any political party.

Yunus himself has had some forays into formal politics. In 1993, during a speech at the inauguration of a democratic forum, he offered a vision of a political party that would operate in a bottom-up manner and appeal to those who were alienated from traditional Bangladeshi politics. "With this speech, he had made himself a major political player. With a network of 12,000 employees and 1.6 million families who claimed membership in Grameen Bank, many knew that he had a potentially formidable political machine – a machine he had the capacity to mobilize" (Counts 1996, p. 135). In fact, loan officers always encourage borrowers, especially women borrowers, to exercise their right to vote, which many do in a bloc that makes the electoral power of Grameen borrowers highly visible during election time (Bornstein 2005).

After receiving the Nobel Peace Prize in November 2006, many people in Bangladesh were proud of Yunus for having put their country on the international map as the cradle of one of the most important global development interventions in decades:

> Professor Yunus' name was synonymous with symbolic prestige for Bangladeshis, the nation of floods and famines in the Western imagination. Many middle-class Bangladeshis, who had been disturbed by negative representations of Bangladesh in the Western press, believed that Professor Yunus would single-handedly turn the fate of Bangladesh around and make them feel proud as Bangladeshis.
>
> *(Karim 2011, p. 184)*

In early 2007 Yunus decided to use his star power to enter politics. When Bangladesh was being gripped by riots that led to a state of emergency, he announced his intention to start a political party called Citizen's Power. Different from most "celebrity diplomats" who take up political causes at a distance, Yunus aimed to become a political figure in his own country (Brockington 2014). In the context of the lack of capacity and credibility of the Bangladeshi government, he was trying to translate the social and cultural capital bestowed by the Nobel Prize into political capital, transforming himself into a "politicized celebrity" (Wheeler 2013).

Yunus' move was met with ambivalence; Karim recounts how a taxi driver in Dhaka told her "since you know him, could you please tell Professor Yunus not to get into politics. He has brought a lot of respect to our country. But our politicians are corrupt. If he gets into politics, he will lose the respect of the nation and the world" (cited in Karim 2011, p. 188). Around the same time, a group of Bangladeshi academics challenged Yunus, arguing that microfinance was a tool for the "protection and expansion of capitalism" by indebting people (Roy 2010, p. 93).

This was not the first time that microfinance had come under public attack in Bangladesh, although the politics of dissent are complicated by the fact that many university professors rely on NGO consulting jobs to bolster their meager academic incomes (Karim 2011).

Yunus abandoned his political ambitions only a few months later, but he had already alienated the country's leadership, especially because there were rumors that the military might support him (Harris 2013). From then on, any allegation against Yunus and Grameen were broadcast by the country's politicians. Perhaps appropriately for an aid celebrity, Yunus' downfall was spurred by a television program aired far away from Bangladesh, but with local and international repercussions for him and for the reputation of microcredit. In late 2010 a Norwegian television network showed a documentary called "Caught in Micro Debt" that reiterated many of the criticisms brought against microfinance, especially its high interest rates and questionable impact. This led to government-instigated legal cases against Yunus, and High Court appeals, which culminated in his forced resignation as Grameen's Managing Director in May 2011. Yunus himself called it a "black day in the nation's history . . . I can't summon words to express my sorrow" (quoted in Harris 2013, p. 230). Throughout these trials Yunus received much personal international support, mixed with concerns over government interference in Grameen Bank. He has, in turn, continuously insisted that "his only concern is to ensure the future of Grameen Bank's 8.3 million borrowers, almost all of whom are low-income rural women," once again drawing his own legitimacy from them (quoted in Wright 2011).

Yunus' fall from grace in Bangladesh shows that when aid celebrities try to become active outside their area of expertise, or to transform their status into political capital (Wheeler 2013), the limits of their power become manifest. Yunus' appeal did not lie in the formal political sphere, and that his party failed to attract significant public support also shows that many everyday Bangladeshis, like the taxi driver quoted above, saw his greatest effectiveness in the area of microcredit. In this case, the close association he had forged between Grameen and himself restricted his moves beyond development.

Conclusion

At a workshop bringing together the authors of this book, I was challenged to think whether microfinance would have developed without Yunus.[6] I still don't have a good answer to that question, but I do believe that Yunus' public persona and presentation have contributed much to making it into a popular cause, globally and locally (Schwittay 2014). I also believe that he has dedicated his life to convincing those in power of the validity of an idea that he himself has never publically questioned. Such conviction has material implications, especially when it becomes articulated with larger political–economic processes such as Structural Adjustment Programs, the celebration of neoliberal entrepreneurship and the rise of market-based approaches to development.

As a Bangladeshi aid celebrity, Yunus has a complicated relationship with his home country, at once close to it as the place where he grew up and built the institution that came to define him, and at the same time distant from it, as he received his PhD in the US and has spent much time abroad propagating his ideas of microcredit and social business to the world. Throughout all this Bangladesh, and especially its poor women, has remained the location that anchors his legitimizing and authenticating narratives. It is these narratives, and the images that accompany them, that continue to make microcredit a popular development strategy and cause for Northern publics, in spite of increasing criticism of it in newspapers and academic writings.

This is based on Yunus' message of simplicity and success, but also on microcredit's double appeal to supporters' heads and hearts. Creating investments in a financial and emotional sense is what makes Yunus and microcredit so powerful, as both are able to combine hard-nosed entrepreneurialism and financial logics with heart-warming stories of personal success against all odds. As a highly visible and charismatic spokesperson for microcredit, Yunus mediates between microcredit supporters and the development elite. Furthermore, his affective work for the poor helps his supporters to experience similar feelings vicariously. On the other hand, by giving a voice to the poor, he bridges the distance between them and their microfinance supporters. This shows the possibilities for aid celebrities to create connections and personal investments. However, these possibilities are limited by their attachment to personal charisma and to simplified stories of transformation.

Acknowledgements

Many thanks to Lisa Ann Richey for inviting me to the original workshop at Roskilde University, where the idea for this book was born. Her insightful comments, as well as those of other members of the Celebrity and North–South Relations Research Network made this a better article, although all errors are mine. I also thank Kate Boocock for her research assistance.

Notes

1 Throughout this chapter, I use the term "microcredit" on purpose, since Yunus is still best known for giving small loans to poor women. This is not to deny that microcredit has over the years changed into microfinance, where loans are complemented by savings, insurance, pension and remittance products, or that Grameen itself has diversified its offerings.
2 This narrative ignores the simultaneous experiments with microcredit in Indonesia by what was to become Opportunity International and in Brazil by USAID/ACCION.
3 This shift was also helped by the international Women in Development discourse of the time, which offered legitimacy and funding opportunities to the fledging Grameen (Karim 2008).
4 Given the necessity for loan officers to walk long hours to villages and spend much time in the company of strangers, the recruitment of female loan officers has been difficult, much to Yunus' chagrin (Bornstein 2005).

5 Globally women make up over 80 percent of all microloan recipients (Visvanathan et al. 2011).
6 I thank Dan Brockington for this provocative question.

References

Banerjee, A. & Duflo, E. 2011. *Poor Economics: A Radical Rethinking of the Way to Fight Global Poverty*. New York: Public Affairs.

Bateman, M. 2010. *Why Doesn't Microfinance Work? The Destructive Rise of Global Neoliberalism*. London: Zed Books.

Biswas, S. 2010. India's microfinance suicide pandemic. BBC News, December 16.

Black, S. 2009. Microloans and micronarratives: sentiment for a small world. *Public Culture*, 21 (2), 269–292.

Boltanski, L. 1999. *Distant Suffering: Morality, Media and Politics*. Cambridge: Cambridge University Press.

Bornstein, D. 1997. *The Price of a Dream: The Story of Grameen Bank and the Idea that is Helping the Poor to Change their Lives*. Chicago, IL: University of Chicago Press.

Bornstein, D. 2005. *The Price of a Dream: The Story of Grameen Bank and the Idea that is Helping the Poor to Change their Lives*, 2nd edn. Oxford: Oxford University Press.

Bornstein, E. 2012. *Disquieting Gifts: Humanitarianism in New Delhi*. Palo Alto, CA: Stanford University Press.

Brockington, D. 2014. *Celebrity Advocacy and International Development*. London: Routledge.

Chouliaraki, L. 2011. The theatricality of humanitarianism: a critique of celebrity advocacy. *Communication and Critical/Cultural Studies*, 9 (1), 1–21.

Chouliaraki, L., 2013. *The Ironic Spectator: Solidarity in the Age of Post-Humanitarianism*. Cambridge: Polity.

Collins, D., Morduch, J., Rutherford, S. & Ruthven, O. 2009. *Portfolios of the Poor: How the World's Poor Live on $2 a Day*. Princeton: Princeton University Press.

Counts, A. 1996. *Give Us Credit: How Muhammad Yunus' Micro-Lending Revolution of Empowering Women from Bangladesh to Chicago*. New York: Times Books.

Engler, M. 2009. From microcredit to a world without profit? *Dissent*, 56 (4), 81–7.

Fassin, D. 2012. *Humanitarian Reason: A Moral History of the Present*. Berkeley: University of California Press.

Feldman, I. 2010. The Humanitarian Circuit: Relief Work, Development Assistance and CARE in Gaza, 1955–1967. In E. Bornstein & P. Redfield (eds) *Forces of Compassion: Humanitarianism between Ethics and Politics*. Santa Fe, NM: SAR Press, pp. 203–26.

Goodman, M. & Barnes, C. 2011. Star/poverty space: the making of "development celebrity." *Celebrity Studies*, 2 (1), 69–85.

Guérin, I., Morvant-Roux, S. & Villarreal, M. (eds). 2013. *Microfinance, Debt and Over-indebtedness: Juggling with Money*. London: Routledge.

Harris, B. 2013. *The International Bank of Bob: Connecting our World one $25 Kiva Loan at a Time*. New York: Walker and Company.

Kabeer, N. 2001. Conflicts over credit: re-evaluating the empowerment potential of loans to women in rural Bangladesh. *World Development*, 29 (1), 63–84.

Karim, L. 2008. Demystifying micro-credit: the Grameen Bank, NGOs, and neoliberalism in Bangladesh. *Cultural Dynamics*, 20 (5), 5–30.

Karim, L. 2011. *Microfinance and its Discontents: Women in Debt in Bangladesh*. Minneapolis: University of Minnesota Press.

Karnani, A. 2007. Employment, not microcredit, is the solution. *Journal of Corporate Citizenship*, 32, 45–62.

Laqueur, T. 2009. Mourning, pity and the work of narrative in the making of "Humanity." In R. Wilson & R. Brown (eds) *Humanitarianism and Suffering: The Mobilization of Empathy*. Cambridge: Cambridge University Press, pp. 31–57.

Mazzarella, W. 2009. Affect: what is it good for? In S. Dube (ed.) *Enchantments of Modernity: Empire, Nation, Globalization*. London: Routledge, pp. 291–309.

Rahman, A. 1999. *Women and Microcredit in Rural Bangladesh: Anthropological Study of the Rhetoric and Realities of Grameen Bank Lending*. Boulder, CO: Westview Press.

Richey, L.A. & Ponte, S. 2011. *Brand Aid: Shopping Well to Save the World*. Minneapolis: University of Minnesota Press.

Rorty, R. 1993. Human rights, rationality and sentimentality. In S. Shute & S. Hurley (eds) *On Human Rights: The Oxford Amnesty Lectures*. New York: Basic Books, pp. 111–34.

Roy, A. 2010. *Poverty Capital: Microfinance and the Making of Development*. New York and London: Routledge.

Roy, A. 2012. Subjects of risk: technologies of gender in the making of millennial modernity. *Public Culture*, 24 (1), 131–55.

Schwittay, A. 2011. The marketization of poverty. *Current Anthropology*, 52 (S3), 71–82.

Schwittay, A. 2014. *New Media and International Development: Representation and Affect in Microfinance*. London: Routledge.

Visvanathan, N., Duggan, L., Wiegersma, N. & Nisonoff, L. 2011. *The Women, Gender and Development Reader*, 2nd edn. London: Zed Books.

Weber, H. 2004. The "New Economy" and social risks: banking on the poor? *Review of International Political Economy*, 11 (2), 356–386.

Wheeler, M. 2013. *Celebrity Politics: Image and Identity in Contemporary Political Communication*. Cambridge: Polity.

Williams, R. 1976. *Keywords: A Vocabulary of Culture and Society*. Oxford: Oxford University Press.

Wright, T. 2011. Yunus says borrowers are core of Grameen Bank. *Wall Street Journal*, March 24.

Yunus, M. 1999. *Banker to the Poor: Micro-Lending and the Battle against World Poverty*. New York: Public Affairs.

Yunus, M. 2007. *Creating a World Without Poverty: Social Business and the Future of Capitalism*. New York: Public Affairs.

4

SOPHIE'S SPECIAL SECRET

Public feeling, consumption and celebrity activism in post-apartheid South Africa

Danai Mupotsa

Picture the scene if you can, and if you struggle you are in luck as at least two media crews were present to carefully record the image of love and perfection to be broadcast on national television. Sophie Ndaba, tagged "socialite," celebrity actress and entrepreneur, comes on screen wearing an elaborate red gown to welcome us to her special "thanksgiving" celebration which will support her charity work with orphans in South Africa.[1] The details – which orphans, where they are, how they benefit, how many are involved – are rather vague and do not appear to matter for appealing to the viewer. The scene merely establishes that Sophie has a cause, and it is important to her. We know that this is a time for her to give back, because Sophie tells her story often in the national media, and she tells it well. She grew up in the foster care and orphanage system and aspired to one day be a social worker or a nurse and help others like herself. Only now she's done one better, she's a star. Three hundred and fifty of South Africa's celebrity elite are sitting patiently in neat rows separated by an aisle, to receive the "sudden surprise" that on this very special occasion Sophie will marry her beau, Reverend Keith Harrington (Pillay 2012). In a sweetheart neckline, satin mermaid dress, our "Queen" enters in person and we are all privy to this very public/private moment of intimacy as they exchange their wedding vows. Sophie later explains to the crew from *Top Billing*[2] that this was an important way for her to marry, as she grew up poor and she wanted to share her wealth with others.

Introduction

Sophie Ndaba came to the attention of the public as a much-loved single woman in the popular South African soap opera *Generations*. The television show has been the subject of much scholarly attention as one that signals the aspirations of an emergent, black and consumer, middle class in the post-apartheid era (see, for example, Motsaathebe 2009; Dentliner 1999; and Tager 2010). The television show enjoyed twenty years of unrivalled success, before coming to a dramatic and public end when the producer fired all of the actors following a labor dispute (see Pillay 2014 and Dennill 2014). The popularity of the show was closely tied to the way that it plotted the fantasies and disappointments of its viewers. The characters and interlocking narratives of romance and everyday life mirrored ordinary people's experiences of their own present realities. It is thus no wonder that the personal lives of the actors on the show came to be so important to its viewers. In addition to this, the storyline of the soap opera follows the history of South Africa, tracing social and political changes in a studiously timely fashion.

The post-apartheid narrative of a transformed or transforming citizenship in a broader neoliberal global environment sets the context for Ndaba to establish her status as a celebrity humanitarian. Sophie "travels" as an idea of both the possibilities for social and economic uplift and as a figure that translates to more global sentimental matrices of race, sex, gender and class. More specifically, Sophie works as a celebrity humanitarian in the South African context through histories that parallel the history of social change from apartheid to post-apartheid, but which also move beyond the simple equation that post-apartheid = freedom for black women. Black women's activism through these historical periods also included the production of images tied to consumption, beauty and fashion; as well as charity, social uplift and entrepreneurship. Ndaba's status as a mix of these elements is therefore hardly "new" to the "new South Africa."

Yet there are interesting ways in which we can understand Sophie's iconographic status at the present as tied to global sentiments of philanthropy and altruism that become part of celebrity brands (see Littler 2008). The storyline of the celebrity humanitarian as one who "gives back" runs simultaneously with a storyline of individual self-making. To be a good, moral subject who can change the world, this overcoming of a difficult past is often invoked. Celebrity is about a representation of the Self through both specific and strategic discursive practices that always already involve consumption and commodities, but affect us in a public sphere that demands the personal story. This chapter draws on a case study of the South African celebrity, Sophie Ndaba, to explore how African women celebrities interrogate the space of global celebrity humanitarianism by their own work with branding of proximity and distance. Understanding how Sophie Ndaba performs as a black, female celebrity in post-apartheid South Africa contributes to thinking about contextualized celebrity humanitarianism.

Context: a better life for all?

Race and gender are very important markers for what democracy means in South Africa. By the end of the colonial period, when the apartheid regime of "separate development" was instated into law in the new Republic of South Africa in 1948, citizenship was already substantially shaped around exclusive rights based on these criteria. Black women were multiply excluded as citizens (see Poinsette 1985). The race logic underpinning this state had a hierarchy of races: white, colored, Indian and African were the categories placed on its subjects. To be categorized "African" was an eviction notice, for once the boundaries of the new state were marked, an African man required a special pass to enter the city for work. African women were also confined geographically and restricted in multiple ways that shaped their possibilities as producers, consumers and citizens.

African citizenship was bound to newly constructed Bantustans, which were "separate states" (see Mager 1999; Moore 1994). The separation implied rigid hierarchies in social and economic relations. For black women, it was even worse (see Martin & Rogerson 1984). Bantustans as "native reserves" were imagined not only as the "true homes" of Africans, but were, for black women, the *only* homes. Black women were tied to the "home" by gendered logics (see McClintock 1991). While black women were not required to carry passes, neither were they welcome to reside in and work in the city (see Brown 1987). Black women's protests against the apartheid state were initially largely motivated by the state's moves to force black women to carry passes as well as the limited possibilities for work and economic or social power implied by the various apartheid laws.

Black women's protests against apartheid, leading up to the present nationalist phase where democracy was articulated, were framed around the multiple oppressions they faced (see Kemp et al. 1995). Race, class and gender came to be important when democracy was articulated in the new constitution of South Africa at the end of apartheid in 1994 (see Bond 2004). The inclusion of black women in the city, the suburb, or the corporate world serves then as a marker for the possibilities and failures of this new era. Black women's exclusion, inclusion and protest sets the stage for performances of contemporary celebrity humanitarianism in South Africa.

Sophie Ndaba's character "Queen Moroka" made her first appearance in the soap opera *Generations* in 1994 as a background character who was initially only contracted to appear in just four episodes. Ndaba went on to become the longest-serving actor on the show and her character became central to the story. Through her celebrity Ndaba has propelled herself into a narrative similar to that of the fictional plot, becoming an entrepreneur and public speaker on charity-related matters. In this heady mixture of fact and fiction, it is difficult to discern a distinction between the two figures; and Ndaba/Queen Moroka appears to be an attentively polished brand. Ndaba's 2012 wedding was followed shortly afterward by the very public failure of her marriage in 2013, and tabloid newspapers and magazines debated the intricate details of deceit and abuse.

Yet I remain drawn to the "romantic" scene that introduces this chapter because of the way it gathers together a range of logics tied to the work of celebrity, public memory, intimacy and citizenship in South Africa. Big, fat and fancy weddings are splashed across our television screens and newspapers in ways that frame them as illustrative of a broader politics of inclusion. The public/political branding of celebrity-cum-image of success-cum-activist, often with some rendering of a liberal feminist figure frequenting the landscape, achieves a high point when one of these latter stars as the bride on her own big wedding day.

Images of black women as celebrities and models of inclusion like this are revealing of the ways black women circulate, not simply as ideal consumers, but as consumable objects themselves (see Odhiambo 2008). Sophie markets or positions herself as a celebrity-cum-humanitarian, as her celebrity status is meant to reflect the success of the project of democracy as well as her ability to possibly "give back." The achievement of "overcoming" narrated in Sophie's personal story is vividly one about consumption. Signaling her "new" status with a big wedding, Ndaba is able to communicate her arrival at the status of citizenship by, simultaneously, her consumption as well as by her ability to share with others the possibility of this status (see Ingraham 1999; Otnes & Pleck 2003; Boden 2003; Otnes & Lowry 2003; Howard 2006; Mead 2007). She goes beyond herself by making her wedding an actual charity event to make the connection between her success and her ability to "give back" directly visible.

The soap opera *Generations* has garnered such keen interest because of the way it reflects the aspirations at the heart of post-apartheid relations. The show is centred on the entrepreneurial success of the Moroka family which mirrors the projected aspirations of the policy of Black Economic Empowerment (BEE). BEE policies were implemented with the intention to increase the proportion of the black middle class in the democratic period. Iheduru reads this policy as transforming from a compromise with white capital at the beginning of the democratic period to "democratise empowerment," to something viewed as more threatening at present (Iheduru 2004). The ruling African National Congress (ANC)'s strategy must be understood through its National Democratic Revolution (NDR), and Iheduru points to the incongruence between the macroeconomic policies of the ANC and the project of the NDR, as they have produced increased inequalities between a small black elite and the large poor and working classes. Southall (2004a), while aware of the tensions here, does not necessarily view these projects as incongruent: "the problem for the ANC is that the very success of the NDR will lead to the development of a black capitalist class and the major growth of the intermediate black middle strata," though the provision of education, wealth and upward mobility are consequential (see Nattrass & Seekings 2001). Southall's reading of the development of the black middle class here recognizes entrepreneurship not only as an unthreatening process of change in the new South Africa, but as embedded in longer histories of black capital (see Southall 2004b).

A "better life for all" is a notion imbued with aspiration for a citizenry that includes consumption as a marker of social change. The figure of the "black diamond," coined to refer to members of the new black middle class, signals the tensions of this aspiration. Both celebrated and reviled, this term was introduced by the Unilever Institute at the University of Cape Town who were principally interested in how to capture this new black middle class as a market (Unilever Institute 2008). Unilever reported the average income of the average "black diamond" to be 7,106 South African Rand per month in 2008[3] (Unilever Institute 2008).

As this figure is quite low, they add that it is important to consider that this is less about income and, for those interested in marketing, is more about spending power. Opting out of the language of class, these companies emphasize the notion of aspiration and, as such, consumption can be seen as part of an understanding of inclusion and a better life for all.[4]

Theoretical approaches to helping others: colonialism, consumption and celebrity

The definition of "celebrity" is contested, referring to a commodity itself that produces or performs its value through regimes of taste (see Clarke 2009). In this sense, the work or value of celebrity is also always already conditioned around the work of consumption. The celebrity is a figure produced through longer histories and technologies tied to colonialism, the spread of capitalism, and the processes broadly related to the "civilizing mission" of the various actors tied to the colonial enterprise, as "fame" itself was one of the key commodities of the cultural, economic and political economies of Europe's colonial regimes (Clarke 2009; see van Krieken in this collection). Processes of identification have also been important to the construction of celebrity, and how we consume a celebrity and, in turn, how we understand what celebrities teach us, or spread values about what or how to consume. For instance, Percy Hintzen argues that Product Red's campaign creates a demand for consumption, for those positioned in the global North to consume with good taste, or "naked freedom" the pleasures of the jungle (Hintzen 2008; also see Himmelman & Mupotsa 2008). That is, colonial rationality is sedimented within the logics of globalization, consumer culture and development aid.

This amalgam of development, global capital and the spread of consumer culture that scholars of celebrity colonialism trace has been referred to as "Brand Aid" by Richey and Ponte (2012). This form of branding commodities capitalizes on everyday life, they argue, for in everyday choices one can also achieve the work of "helping" others – abject Others in places far away, like Africa. In their analysis, celebrity acts, or works, as a conjunction between the commodities we consume and our desire for happiness, as it reconciles the contradictions of capitalism and inequality.

Primarily focused on "Northern" celebrities who do their humanitarian work in the "global South," scholars on celebrity colonialism have emphasized how Africa functions as an object in the political economy of symbolic goods. In this sense "Africa" is always already about the global North, "an Other," on which the West constructs its "civilisation, enlightenment and progress" (Abrahamsen 2012). In Abrahamsen's analysis, Brand Aid operates via "an Other"–"Africa" but does so somewhat differently from the civilizing mission of the past that was contained in a religious register, or obligation. Brand Aid is instead politically motivated by a concern about Africa that "has become part of the relentless self-invention of a particular kind of modern consumer" (ibid.). Celebrities produce their fame through the work of storytelling, or a "story factory" (Ponte & Richey 2014), which, through celebrity media, enable consumers of these texts, images and products to experience their consumption as part of a project of their own Self-making. Yet I wonder if the stories told about the Self in this version of celebrity humanitarianism can fit so neatly into the case of Sophie Ndaba in South Africa?

Sophie Ndaba's brand as a celebrity humanitarian is constructed through the impossible work of proximity and distance branding, which can be understood through Turner, Bonner and Marshall's analysis of celebrity:

> Celebrities are brand names as well as cultural icons or identities; they oper-
> ate as marketing tools as well as sites where the agency of the audience is
> clearly evident; and they represent the achievement of individualism – the
> triumph of the human and the familiar – as well as its commodification and
> commercialisation. Like all commodities, however, their trade needs to be
> organised and controlled and, as a result, the production and commercialisa-
> tion of celebrities has become an industry too.
>
> *(Turner et al. 2000)*

In the case of Ndaba, her position as a black woman and a consumer has the discursive effect of the celebrity "story factory" mirrored by her character in the fictional role she plays. Ndaba's performance substantively mirrors the public/private
aspirations of what individual lives could or should be in the contemporary South
African state.

Methodology: soap opera and self-making

This chapter provides an interpretive analysis of the public life of a popular South African soap opera star, read through an historical understanding of South Africa with particular attention to consumption and celebrity humanitarianism. *Generations* plays off the aspiration for a better life for all, and functions as a text that does not simply reflect broader social relations, but also offers powerful insights into the contradictions of contemporary South Africa. As Hofmeyr argues, it is "precisely in their fictionality" that texts such as the soap opera "offer powerful and condensed forms of social analysis" (Hofmeyr 2004). It is not only the aspiration around consumption, but that the texts also speak to ways the private life, or "family" is embedded in the democratic public private sphere (see Bystrom 2010).

The soap opera functions as an important narrative strategy. Soap operas as a genre have been examined as dramas built around a "female imaginary," through which women can identify:

> Soap opera invests exquisite pleasure in the central condition of a wom-
> an's life: waiting. Thus, the anticipation of an end becomes an end in itself.
> Hence it may be argued that soap opera narrative is circular rather than
> linear, thus opposing it to a traditional linear masculine narrative. Multiple

storylines make up single episodes and even in the case of a single storyline reaching a conclusion, an ultimate climax continually evades.

(Marx 2008)

In line with waiting, the storylines of many South African soap operas rely on narratives of aspiration, which have, since the 1990s, increasingly represented black subjects as professionals and semi-professionals, constituting an image of a transformed or transforming nation (see Cassim & Miguel 2001).

Public television and kinds of fictionalized and "reality-based" personal stories of everyday life have been around since the 1970s, when they were first introduced as working to produce a normative national consciousness. Following the introduction of democracy, one intention has been to construct a new national narrative predicated on transformation and new forms of national unity (Ives 2007). The "rainbow nation" of democratic South Africa produces a set of messages that sit atop tensions between the narrative of national unity and the neoliberal economic policies of the post-apartheid state, and thus the result becomes a commodification of unity. The storylines sold through public television come, therefore, to attempt to reconcile the narratives of unity, aspiration and consumption with the continued disparities in wealth and access.

Analysis: Sophie Ndaba as gendered celebrity commodity

Nuttall's analysis of black middle-class consumption, through "Self-styling," suggests that through consumption and styling the Self, a broader story of South African storytelling takes place (Nuttall 2004). The presentation of an individual, styled Self, in this reading is disseminated as a personal/public/private narrative. Reading Nuttall, Odhiambo pays particular attention to the place where black women as consumers get positioned in these public/private stories. Odhiambo argues that the black female body, subject to an intense gaze, "embodies both the value of the commodities that 'it' advertises, as well as offering itself as an object of consumption" (Odhiambo 2008). This gaze is not limited to the work of selling commodities, as in the case of Ndaba who through her celebrity comes to be representable in a feminist iconography. For instance, Ndaba responds to an interview in a feature article of *Agenda* in 2005:

> I believe that I have a fabulous full-figured African body. It's great when people tell me I look gorgeous, but I don't take too much notice when I am told I would look better if I was thinner. It was my decision to lose weight after my pregnancy because I felt that there was no need for me to carry around that much extra weight, and now I am happy with my body. I have researched surgical enhancement, in particular for the breast and the tummy. However, it involves a risk which I am not willing to take. I am comfortable with my body, and that is expressed through the way I walk and the way I relate to people. Having good self-esteem allows me to comfortably express my sexuality and femininity with my loved ones.
>
> *(Malinga 2005)*

Ndaba's selling of products is linked to performances of an embodied Self. The work of her body and her Self is read in relation to broader discussions about women, and her support of other women, vis-à-vis her success or ability to address personal yet broad social questions. The presentation of her body-work as a "woman of substance," is mirrored in a recent advertising campaign for the mobile phone network Cell C. She is the brand ambassador for its current campaign, and as part of this role and the company's "Take a Girl Child to Work" campaign, will spend the year mentoring a young woman (Thakurdin 2004).

Supporting charitable causes has been argued to be a way for celebrities to raise their public profile, so that we then view them as not completely "crudely commercial," as through acts of charity celebrities are able to reveal their compassion (see Littler 2008). Yet, implied in the communication of a compassionate Self who extends herself to less fortunate Others, is a distance.

In the case of Ndaba and many other comparable South African examples, the narrative is imbued with tales of self-improvement and empowerment facilitated by a social and economic environment that encourages the "entrepreneurial spirit" of women. There are long histories of black women's informal networks and organizations intended to build and share profit, alleviate poverty and enable forms of consumption. With a burgeoning industry of "corporate social responsibility," multinational companies operating in the country have capitalized on the idea of women as entrepreneurs.

For instance, Dolan and Scott examine the ways in which the global corporation Avon uses partnerships with women as a strategic development strategy with the intended goal of gender equality and poverty alleviation. These partnerships rely on the assumption that women are not only the primary consumers of certain household and personal goods, but also that the selling or marketing of these goods is an extension of immaterial women's labor (Dolan & Scott 2009). Ndaba's function as brand ambassador for a range of products replicates these assumptions, extended by her role in corporate responsibility programs that are explicit in their claims that consuming their products has the direct result of empowering other women as well.

Ndaba's very public wedding reflects how aspiration functions both through the display of consumption and desire for a better life, and through the cultural work of intimate exposure that shapes a public–private sphere. Forms of private exposure such as Ndaba's televised wedding are "performances of the self and the articulation of personal experiences, stories, and images as well as private or interior spaces" (Bystrom & Nuttall 2013, p. 308) that make the public sphere one framed by biographical stories that take shape, or take up space in architectures of South African public and social life. Ndaba's reality TV charity wedding, like *Generations* is a technology that both reflects and motivates aspirations of consumption and upward mobility (see Tager 2010), and reflects what the personal and private mean to the broader public. They tell new stories of "home" on television (see Coombes 2003), a technology that Ndlovu argues has progressively placed its interest in the family and interpersonal relationships, in ways that reimagine or reposition selfhoods, or bear the potential to "fix" them (Ndlovu 2013).

Ndaba's position as celebrity humanitarian does this "fixing" in public through stories about empowerment, consumption, development and entrepreneurship. By orientating her personal story in relation to her television character and other women "like her," giving back is a story about a better life for her and for all who are entangled within the soap opera's representational strategies.

The connection between empowerment and entrepreneurship as development, and the marketing of commodities is fraught. McClintock (1994) attends to the distinction between commodity racism and scientific racism. The commodities mass marketed in the projects of reinventing British national unity in her analysis

FIGURE 4.1   Admiral George Dewey washes his hands with Pears soap. Courtesy of US Library of Congress.

relied upon an evolutionary racism, a distancing or a difference, being imperial Others and the Victorian consumer.

The mass marketing of these commodities also relied on the cult of domesticity as McClintock reveals in her history of the "proper self," via the bar of soap:

> The story of soap reveals that fetishism, far from being a quintessentially African propensity, as nineteenth-century anthropology maintained, was central to industrial modernity, inhabiting and mediating the uncertain threshold zones between domesticity and industry, metropolis and empire.
>
> *(McClintock 1994)*

The marketing of soap and the invention of the "soap opera" that sold it, and the ideas of domesticity we inherit through history, are important as they do not only establish the market. McClintock urges us to see African consumption of commodities as directly intrinsic to the imagining of domesticity, gender and race differences, and territory in the colony and metropole (see Ally 2013). Furthermore, ideas about women's inclusion and empowerment get caught up in these histories.

Women's empowerment as an exercise in increasing women's agency and access to resources has generally been easily incorporated into development discourses under the assumptions of both consumption and domesticity as a natural realm of Self work for women. Ndaba, who extends her story of success into one about Self-making, entrepreneurship and giving back, gets locked into the narratives McClintock (1994) aims to historically problematize; but which are also central to how black women's success in philanthropy and business are strongly communicated in the South African public sphere.

Gqola suggests a different way of seeing the work of transition, a different method of reading the temporalities of cultural memory, expression and production whereby:

> Slavery, colonialism and apartheid are seen as moments along a continuum, and not as separate, completely distinct, and mutually exclusive periods. However, a continuum suggests linearity, which is undermined by the working of memory and ideology. In order to capture both the lineages across time suggested by the image of a continuum, as well as to complicate the ways in which these periods are embedded in each other and beyond.
>
> *(Gqola 2010, pp. 6–7)*

This method includes the possibility of "newness" in the stories being constructed, but also suggests work on memory, narrative, archive and history. In the case of figures like Ndaba, this means examining how her personal story speaks in forms of personal narrative that are particular to her social and political location as a black female celebrity, and how she does something different with the work of distance.

Consumption and/as giving back in the present

South African national broadcasters use the rhetoric of nation building, yet manage to incorporate conspicuous consumption as signaling the aspirations and achievement of personal and national prosperity. Thus, the implication of this media, corporate and nationalist interplay is that "the ideal national subject is no longer a politically active agent, but rather an upwardly mobile consumer" (Kruger 2010, p. 78). Programming serials that include soap operas have not only built upon the narrative of aspiration, but also often get labeled as education, and explicitly frame their incentives to be part of a project to produce the possibilities of self-realization. For example, the overtly "educational" series *Gaz'lam*, which predicates its narratives around self-actualizing characters whose sense of becoming productive citizens is then also subsumed into a binarized notion of "good" and "bad" consumption.

Yet consumption in the post-apartheid period is still convincingly a "new" possibility (Posel 2010), as the apartheid architecture systematically limited black consumption and movement. The significance of this is shown by the fact that consumer boycotts were central to political organization in the anti-apartheid movement (see Iqani 2012a,b). There is "a historically constitutive relationship between the workings of race and the regulation of consumption [as . . .] the making of a racial order was, in part, a way of regulating people's aspirations, interests and powers as consumers" (Posel 2010, p. 160). To understand the role that consumption plays in the imagining of the "new" South Africa necessarily requires that we attend to the central place it holds in the struggle for freedom. Ndaba's personal story of success in the present is, in this lens, not only about her inclusion. By simply articulating her arrival at consumption, she already politically performs the possibilities of this moment. It is particularly the case when we insist that consumption and the symbolic power tied to consumption connect the "racial politics of consumption [and] the 'civilizing mission' that traversed the continent, and were transformed along with shifting trajectories of economic development, class formation, and regimes of [. . .] distinction" (ibid.).

This is interesting and perhaps useful in disrupting the neatness of reading consumption and aspiration. Scholars of 19th-century South Africa have examined the ways that the civilizing mission intended to produce certain kinds of subjecthood, of good workers who consumed "well," or at least in a disciplined manner so that "good consumption," which would incidentally not be conspicuous, if in good taste, was part of the work of acquiring the status of being "civilized," or properly human. There are longer genealogies of discussions in the black press in South Africa, for example that frame black respectability and notions of the "proper" in consumer magazines from the 1950s like *Grace* and *The Township Housewife*. These reveal contestations about good and bad consumption, and good and bad taste (Ferreira 2011).

In *Grace* and *The Township Housewife* we can observe desire for proper consumption, tied to a Christian ethic of selfhood that corroborates these observations.

But they also contain a great deal of discussion in parallel about a selfhood that is entrepreneurial and is able to pursue fashions, and new consumer goods,[5] which corroborates the arguments posed by Burke who observes the entry of black subjects into wage labor as connected to the desire to consume new and domestic products, of the home and of the Self.[6]

Rather than having a view of black consumers as having a "new fetish" for consumption that we can assume to have a lateral relationship to whiteness, this historicized reading instead suggests that we read consumption of commodities of the Self and for the home as Self styling, as the appropriation of signs and symbols (see Magubane 2004). These are fertile grounds for reaching an understanding of how and why freedom in the democratic period is not necessarily incongruent with consumption.

More recent media texts and consumer magazines, even as they signal democracy as something that involves the entry of black women into new sites of work and consumption, attend to the longer historical manifestations of the relationship between the project of modernity and the struggle for freedom. They also trouble the potential dichotomy between giving back and consuming. These texts reflect the gendered aspects of the history of consumption in South Africa. Ndaba's work as a wedding planner, entrepreneur and general promoter of goods rests on the very possibility that consuming well is apolitical. Yet the historically present contestations about consumption in media texts about simple, possibly apolitical, things such as fashion reveal that there is more at stake:

> Beauty is an area where the consumer subject is exploited and the ideal that is reflected is Western white femininity and not an empowered emancipated black woman. In the February 1965 issue of *Grace*, a reader complains that "like most young girls of today [she] would also like to have [her] hair nice and straight" (Feb 1965, p. 26). More troubling, both magazines carry frequent advertisements for skin-lightening products that "no modern girl can be without." Another advertisement for skin-lightening creams in Grace distressingly states that: " ... you need a clear, light skin if you want to rise in life ..."
>
> *(Ferreira 2011, p. 64)*

Proper consumption and femininity is political. Furthermore, and without much explanation, the grounds for what is politically contested moves with ease from beauty and fashion to women's empowerment activities that promote "self-help" such as Ndaba's citing the Zenzele Women's Club. Zenzele, which translates as "help yourself," were collectives that organized educational activities in health, childcare, domesticity and consumption. They specifically intended to attend to responding to the racist state through a discourse of social and racial uplift (Ferreira 2011, p. 65). The political grounds for being fabulous, as Sophie Ndaba's celebrity stands historically "fits" with giving back to orphans, to other women, and even to herself.

Self and/as Other

In her analysis of the 2007 Product Red issue of *Vanity Fair,* Magubane draws a connection between coevalness and celebrity activism (Magubane 2008). Coevalness
refers to the contradiction inherent at the heart of anthropology as it places "those
who are talked about at a time other than that of the one who talks" (ibid., citing
Fabian 1996; see also Daley 2013). Magubane compares Bono the Irish musician
and Oprah Winfrey the American film star and producer, both connected to the
work of celebrity activism, who each narrate personal stories of their own experience in relation to their commitments to helping others, and asks:

> When Oprah and Bono invoke their own connections to a history of colo-
> nial subjugation as an explanation for what motivates their philanthropy, can
> it be read as an attempt to "share in the Other's past" and, in that way, stake
> a claim for their coevalness?
>
> *(Magubane 2007)*

Celebrity, consumption and luxury are framed in a personal story that is not simply a
tale of uplift, but has inherent to it a mode of explanation for sharing with those who
share a "past" time, or place with them. It is not simply that there is a sense of the Self
in relation to the Other that is at work in these representational practices, or a "psy-
chic interiorization," or a projection "whereby the darkest impulses of the European
Self are repudiated by attributing them to the Other" (ibid.). It is that there is always
a self-aware articulation of Self in relation to this Other when the celebrity story is
told. These figures tell personal stories that practice a tale of both the Self and the
Other, or at least intend to represent them both, recognizing the coevals in the time
and space of the Self. Someone like Sophie Ndaba presents us with a complex relation between Self and Other as a consumer. She speaks of herself in an assemblage
of I–you–us; coeval because it is a simultaneously individual and collective story.

Following the opening of the Oprah Winfrey Leadership Academy, Oprah
drew on her personal relation to the girls who would attend the school in an imagined familial relation, for instance claiming them as "surrogate daughters" who
would be the recipients of her motherly love. Ndaba's work with orphans is similar, drawing a relation between herself and motherless children. It is slightly distinct
as she signals herself as a "sister–daughter" in this imagined family. Citing oneself
as a sister or daughter or mother in relation to others in need, these women project
rather personal relations into broader social and historical relations of unfreedom in
South Africa as well as more globally.

If the closeness/distance, or coevalness, that these two figures attempt to draw
between themselves and the recipients of their philanthropy is framed as one of
"family," then Magubane's invocation of Squires' notions of black counterpublic
discourses might be useful (Squires 2002). This notion demands that we historically attend to legacies of "good public image" produced to counter racist imagery
of black subjects. Public image is complexly political and central to demands of

political and economic freedom both within the confines of a state like South Africa and beyond it in a world that systematically refuses to register race, class and gender as explicitly constitutive of the good, the proper and the included.

Thurman's account of Oprah's philanthropy in South Africa reads the emphasis on "Self-making" through her own personal narrative, which Ndaba similarly employs to suggest that it can be explained as part of the general neoliberal trend that holds individuals accountable for making good choices in relieving their own personal suffering. Thurman argues that Oprah "(mis)appropriate[s] individual stories and collective histories in order to construct a generic female biography; and that this is a dangerous project, insofar as it disregards the socio-political, economic and cultural differences that separate South African women from Oprah's primary target market" (Thurman 2008). I argue that Sophie Ndaba performs a similarly "dangerous project" within the divided society of contemporary South Africa.

Thurman reads this story factory of Self-making through the notion of a romantic utopia (Illouz 1997), yet there is a presentism to his analysis that is not his alone, and which reflects general assumptions about commodities and consumption, celebrity and Self without a deeper historical lens. The commodification of romance and the romanticization of commodities implied by the idea of the "romantic utopia" attend to the relationship between romance and commodity from the 19th century, and how popular mediated texts increasingly tie consumption to domesticity and the quest for romantic love.

Conclusions

The ways that celebrities like Ndaba operate have particular affects and effects concomitant with the historical moment in South Africa. Her personal story, along with a plethora of other personal stories, are indicative of the "home" and "nation" stories in the public sphere that reflect the project, or projections of the period of transition (Coombes 2003, p. 1). These personal stories that celebrity humanitarians like Sophie Ndaba use are premised on complex proximities between celebrities and ordinary people, or indeed those who possess the ability to consume and those who do not. So what conclusions might we draw about the work of proximity and distance in this specific form of celebrity activism?

Romantic love does, of course, in this fairytale achieve a "high" point on the wedding day, which is how I would read Ndaba's big staging of her arrival at the celebrity wedding-cum charity event. The soap opera, consumer magazines and other texts often rely on repeating nationalist stories of the present, progress and freedom. But they also need to be read via the romantic utopia because they interrupt the progress narrative of the nation and its "freedom." Weddings can be viewed as a representation of this freedom. Many scholars note the very low marriage rates in South Africa as signalling the depth of the divide between rich and poor (Hunter 2010). Yet it is not just the rich who marry in South Africa, as people negotiate through their various means, ways through which they can stage their entry into marriage; the ritual is one of the important ways that people stage or make a claim at belonging (see Mupotsa 2014). The 2012 wedding of actress and celebrity wedding planner Sophie Ndaba, staged as a "surprise" way for her to share her wealth with others who grew up poor like she did, speaks directly to the tensions related to the ways public intimacy, consumption and freedom are un-neatly breathed into discourses of broader belonging.

The soap opera narrative is not neatly linear, or progressive, and draws its viewers into complicated identifications that are aspirational and at times disappointing. One achieves the height of romance on the wedding day, but, as was in the case of Ndaba's actual marriage, is soon disappointed when it comes to a rather dramatic end. This structure of narrative is potentially non- and counternarrative, and is demonstrably one about waiting and the circularity of time. Ndaba's counterpublic story of "making Self while giving back," of familial/familiar Self and Others, demands attention both to present articulations of freedom within the scope of democracy, as well as other articulations that refuse to allow us to see them as simply Self-ish stories.

Notes

1 See http://www.sophiendaba.co.za/ [accessed on May 31, 2014].
2 *Top Billing* is a popular lifestyle magazine television show aired on the public broadcaster, SABC 3. The show features the lives of the rich and famous and Ndaba frequently appears as a guest celebrity wedding planner. The episode featuring Ndaba's nuptials has been removed from the website's archives, following the public fallout between Ndaba and her former partner. See http://www.topbilling.com/ [accessed on May 31, 2014].
3 Approximately US$635 per month.
4 See Krige (2012) who insists that the stereotyping of the black middle class as conspicuous consumers is the result of a sidelining of longer histories of social stratification among urban Africans.
5 See Ferreira (2011).
6 See Burke (1996).

References

Abrahamsen, Rita. 2012. Africa in a global political economy of symbolic goods. *Review of African Political Economy*, 13 (131), 140–2.

Ally, Shireen. 2013. Ooh eh eh . . . Just one small cap is enough! Servants, detergents, and their prosthetic significance. *African Studies*, 72 (3), 321–52.

Boden, Sharon. 2003. *Consumerism, Romance and the Wedding Experience*. New York: Palgrave.

Bond, Patrick. 2004. From racial to class apartheid: South Africa's frustrating decade of freedom. *Monthly Review*, March. 45–59.

Bonner, Philip. 2012. *The Black Elite on the Rand in the Interwar Years*. Seminar Presentation, NRF Chair in Local Histories, Present Realities February 22. University of the Witwatersrand.

Brown, Barbara B. 1987. Facing the "Black Peril': the politics of population control in South Africa. *Journal of Southern African Studies*, 13 (2), 256–73.

Burke, Timothy. 1996. *Lifebuoy Men, Lux Women: Commodification, Consumption and Cleanliness in Modern Zimbabwe*. Durham, NC: Duke University Press.

Bystrom, Kerry. 2010. The public private sphere: family narrative and democracy in Argentina and South Africa. *Social Dynamics*, 36 (1), 139–52.

Bystrom, Kerry & Nuttall, Sarah. 2013. Introduction. *Cultural Studies*, 27 (3), 307–32.

Cassim, Shahida & Miguel Monteiro, Miguel. 2001. Black role portrayals in South African television advertising. *Ecquid Novi: African Journalism Studies*, 22 (1), 106–23.

Clarke, Robert. 2009. The Idea of Celebrity Colonialism: An Introduction. In Robert Clarke (ed.) *Celebrity Colonialism: Fame, Power and Representation in Colonial and Postcolonial Cultures*. Newcastle-upon-Tyne: Cambridge Scholars Publishing, pp. 1–12.

Coombes, Anne E. 2003. *History after Apartheid: Visual Culture and Public Memory*. Durham, NC: Duke University Press.

Daley, Patricia. 2013. Rescuing African bodies: celebrities, consumerism and neoliberal humanitarianism. *Review of African Political Economy*, 40 (137), 375–93.

Dennill, Bruce. 2014. Life after Generations. *The Citizen*, October 1, http://www.citizen.co.za/250943/life-after-generations/ [accessed on November 14, 2014].

Dentliner, Lindsay. 1999. The representation of "South Africanness" in the locally produced television production, *Generations*. Thesis submitted in partial fulfillment of the requirements of the degree of Master of Arts. Grahamstown: Rhodes University.

Dolan, Catherine & Scott, Linda. 2009. Lipstick evangelism: Avon trading circles and gender empowerment in South Africa. *Gender & Development*, 17 (2), 203–18.

Fabian, Johannes. 1996. *Time and the Other: How Anthropology Makes Its Object*. New York: Columbia University Press.

Ferreira, Nicolette. 2011. *Grace* and the *Townships Housewife*: excavating Black South African women's magazines from the 1960s. *Agenda*, 25 (4), 59–68.

Gqola, Pumla Dineo. 2010. *What is Slavery to Me? Postcolonial/Slave Memory in Post-apartheid South Africa*. Johannesburg: Wits University Press.

Himmelman, Natasha & Mupotsa, Danai. 2008. (Product) Red: (re)Branding Africa? *Journal of Pan African Studies*, 2 (6), 1–13.

Hintzen, Percy C. 2008. Desire and the enrapture of capitalist consumption: Product Red, Africa and the crisis of sustainability. *Journal of Pan African Studies*, 2 (6), 77–91.

Hofmeyr, Isabel. 2004. Popular literature in Africa: post-resistance perspectives. *Social Dynamics*, 30 (2), 128–40.

Howard, Vicki. 2006. *Brides, Inc.: American Weddings and the Business of Tradition*. Philadelphia: University of Pennsylvania Press.

Hunter, Mark. 2010. *Love in the Time of AIDS: Inequality, Gender and Rights in South Africa*. Bloomington: Indiana University Press.

Iheduru, Okechukwu C. 2004. Black economic power and nation-building in post-apartheid South Africa. *The Journal of Modern African Studies*, 42 (1), 1–30.

Illouz, Eva. 1997. *Consuming the Romantic Utopia: Love and the Cultural Contradictions of Capitalism*. Berkeley: University of California Press.

Ingraham, Chrys. 1999. *White Weddings: Romancing Heterosexuality in Popular Culture*. New York & London: Routledge.

Iqani, Mehita. 2012a. *A Genealogy of the "Black Consumer" in post-Apartheid South African Media: Counterpoints to Discourses of Citizenship*. Conference Presentation at ENEC VI, the 6th Brazilian Meeting on Consumption Studies. 12–14 September. Escola Superior de Propaganda e Marketing, Rio de Janeiro, Brazil.

Iqani, Mehita. 2012b. Spazas, Hawkers and the status quo: black consumption at the margins of media discourse in post-apartheid South Africa. *Animus: Revista Interamericana de Comunicação Midiática*, 11 (22), 4–30.

Ives, Sarah. 2007. Mediating the neoliberal nation: television in post-apartheid South Africa. *ACME Editorial Collective*, 6 (1), 153–73.

Kemp, A., Madlala, N., Moodley, A., & Salo, E. 1995. The dawn of a new day: redefining South African feminism. In Amrita Basu (ed.) *Social Change in Global Perspective*. Boulder, CO: Westview Press, pp. 131–61.

Krige, Detlev. 2012. The changing dynamics of social class, mobility and housing in black Johannesburg. *Alternation*, 19 (1), 19–45.

Kruger, Loren. 2010. Critique by stealth: aspiration, consumption and class in post-apartheid television drama. *Critical Arts*, 24 (1), 75–98.

Littler, Jo. 2008. "I feel your pain": cosmopolitan charity and the public fashioning of the celebrity soul. *Social Semiotics*, 18 (2), 237–51.

McClintock, Anne. 1991. "No longer a future in heaven": women and nationalism in South Africa. *Transition*, 51, 104–23.

McClintock, Anne. 1994. Soft-soaping empire: commodity racism and imperial advertising. In George Robertson (ed.) *Travellers' Tales: Narratives of Home and Displacement*. New York & London: Psychology Press, pp. 128–52.

Mager, Anne K. 1999. *Gender and the Making of a South African Bantustan: A Social History of the Ciskei*. Portsmouth: Heinemann.

Magubane, Zine. 2007. Oprah in South Africa: the politics of coevalness and the creation of a black public sphere. *Safundi: The Journal of South African and American Studies*, 8 (4), 373–93.

Magubane, Zine. 2008. The (Product) Red man's burden: charity, celebrity, and the contradicitons of coevalness. *Journal of Pan African Studies*, 2 (6), 102.1–102.25.

Magubane, Zine. 2004. *Bringing the Empire Home: Race, Class, and Gender in Britain and Colonial South Africa*. Chicago, IL: University of Chicago Press.

Malinga, Nkululeko. 2005. Women of substance. *Agenda*, 19 (63), 58–9.

Martin, V.M. & Rogerson, C.M. 1984. Women and industrial change: the South African experience. *South African Geographical Journal*, 66 (1), 32–46.

Marx, Hannelie. 2008. South African soap opera as the other: the deconstruction of hegemonic gender identities in four South African soap operas. *Communication*, 34 (1), 80–94.

Mead, Rebecca. 2007. *One Perfect Day: The Selling of the American Wedding*. New York: Penguin.

Moore, Henrietta. 1994. Households and gender in a South African Bantustan: a comment. *African Studies*, 53 (1), 137–42.

Motsaathebe, Gilbert. 2009. Gendered roles, images and behavioural patterns in the soap opera. *Generations. Journal of African Media Studies*, 1 (3), 429–48.

Mupotsa, Danai S. 2014. White Weddings. Thesis submitted in fulfilment of the requirements of the degree of Doctor of Philosophy. Johannesburg: University of the Witwatersrand.

Nattrass, Nicoli & Seekings, Jeremy. 2001. "Two nations"? Race and economic inequality in South Africa today. *Daedalus*, 130 (1), 45–70.

Ndlovu, Thabisani. 2013. Fixing families through television? *Cultural Studies*, 27 (3), 379–403.

Nuttall, Sarah. 2004. The Y Generation in Rosebank, Johannesburg. *Public Culture*, 16 (3), 430–52.

Odhiambo, Tom. 2008. The black female body as a "consumer and consumable" in current *Drum* and *True Love* magazines in South Africa. *African Studies*, 67 (1), 71–80.

Otnes, Cele C. & Lowry, Tina M. 2003. *Contemporary Consumption Rituals: A Research Anthology*. New York: Psychology Press.

Otnes, Cele C. & Pleck, Elizabeth. 2003. *Cinderella Dreams: The Allure of the Lavish Wedding*. Berkeley and Los Angeles: University of California Press.

Pillay, Claudia. 2012. Sophie's Special Secret. *Drum Weddings*, Issue 1, Spring/Summer, 12–19.

Pillay, Verashni. 2014. Earth to Vavi: There are worse labour issues than *Generations*. *Mail and Guardian*, September 16, http://www.mg.co.za/article/2014-09-16-earth-to-vavi-there-are-worse-labour-issues-than-generations [accessed on November 14, 2014].

Poinsette, Cheryl L. 1985. Black women under apartheid: an introduction. *Harvard Women's Law Journal*, 93, 95–119.

Ponte, Stefano & Richey, Lisa Ann. 2014. Buying into development? Brand aid forms of cause-related marketing. *Third World Quarterly*, 3 (1), 65–87.

Posel, Deborah. 2010. Races to consume: revisiting South Africa's history of race, consumption and the struggle for freedom. *Ethnic and Racial Studies*, 33 (2), 157–75.

Richey, Lisa Ann & Ponte, Stefano Ponte. 2012. Brand Africa: multiple transitions in global capitalism. *Review of African Political Economy*, 39 (131), 135–50.

Southall, Roger. 2004a. The ANC & black capitalism in South Africa. *Review of African Political Economy*, 31 (100), 67–84.

Southall, Roger. 2004b. Political change and the black middle class in democratic South Africa. *Canadian Journal of African Studies*, 38 (3), 521–42.

Squires, Catherine R. 2002. Rethinking the black public sphere: an alternative vocabulary for multiple spheres. *Communication Theory*, 12 (4), 446–8.

Tager, Michele. 2010. The black and the beautiful: perceptions of (a) new generation(s). *Critical Arts*, 24 (1), 99–127.

Thakurdin, Karishma. 2004. Actress Sophie Ndaba plans to be a good mentor. *The Heat Show*, May 30, http://thejuice.co.za/top-stories/actress-sophie-ndaba-plans-to-be-a-great-mentor/ [accessed on August 4, 2014].

Thurman, Christopher. 2008. Oprah, the Leavisite: a caveat for feminism and women's studies in South Africa. *African Studies*, 67 (1), 101–20.

Turner, Graeme, Bonner, Frances & Marshall, David P. 2000. *Fame Games: The Production of Celebrity in Australia*. Cambridge: Cambridge University Press.

Unilever Institute. 2008. *The Black Diamond*, http://www.uctunileverinstitute.co.za/research/black-diamond/ [accessed on January 27, 2015].

5

CELEBRITY PHILANTHROPY IN CHINA

The political critique of Pu Cunxin's AIDS heroism

Johanna Hood

> Because you are a celebrity, the common people recognize you. You utter one
> word, do one thing, and you have the power to have an influence. This ability
> to have an effect [on people] comes with being a celebrity.
>
> *(Pu Cunxin de lücheng 2006)*

Over the past several decades there has been a rapid increase in celebrity advocacy
on issues of Western humanitarian concern, particularly concepts of democracy,
human rights and health. This has been facilitated by the establishment of major
international development bodies, which became conduits for channeling aid and
exerting power after World War II, such as the United Nations (UN), the World
Health Organization (WHO) and the World Bank. Celebrity advocacy in Euro-
American societies has also been assisted by the popularization of television, which
provided a new and accessible medium through which celebrities could become
known, and establish their fan bases. These events and conditions appear to have
provided unique opportunities for celebrity involvement in health and other social,
political, economic and environmental issues. They not only mark a turning point
in the rise of celebrity presence beyond the silver screens, podiums and platinum
charts (Epstein 2005; Richey & Ponte 2008; Turner 2004, 2007) but also serve to
highlight the inadequacies of the loose yet widely quoted definition of celebrity as
a person "who is known for [their] well-knownness" (Boorstin 1972, p. 57).

In contemporary society, the platforms and media technologies through which
celebrity figures impact on issues of public interest grow by the day. Celebrities
now extend their reach beyond spaces traditionally ascribed to their area of expertise and are busily involved doing their "part" for humankind by using their fame
for apparent wider community benefit. They mobilize and attract huge global
audiences to the particular causes they support. By raising publicity and capital they

are able to influence governmental and organizational policy and practices in the distribution of scarce research and aid resources. For example, Midge Ure and Bob Geldof's massive Live Aid and the later Live 8 concerts raised hundreds of millions of dollars for food aid and encouraged the G8 leaders to address issues of debt relief, trade, aid and HIV/AIDS (Watt & Sharman 2006). Some celebrities have become active in a range of leadership roles in international policymaking. Geldof holds political appointments, such as membership in the Commission for Africa and the Africa Progress Panel, which were established to ensure that international commitments to Africa are met (Africa Progress Panel 2008). Globally, celebrities have increasing political influence, and demonstrations of philanthropic spirit are almost a compulsory part of the celebrity's public image.

Large development organizations also promote celebrity activism on issues of contemporary disease and poverty as a desirable feature of development practice. The United Nations Children's Fund (UNICEF), one of the first organizations to

FIGURE 5.1   In China, HIV/AIDS was one of the first causes celebrities were allowed to endorse, and many are now involved in HIV awareness campaigns and benefits. Su Youpeng, his assistants and security, together with journalists and plainclothes and uniformed police race to an event endorsed by UNAIDS, IFRC and the China Red Cross. Su made a brief appearance to sing against HIV-based discrimination. Photograph by Johanna Hood at Bird Nest Stadium during the capital's busy week of activities and endorsements around World AIDS Day.

enlist celebrities to promote their mandate in the 1950s through campaigns involving film stars like Danny Kaye and Audrey Hepburn, explains the development of their celebrity-based ambassadorial system as follows:

> Fame has some clear benefits in certain roles with UNICEF. Celebrities attract attention, so they are in a position to focus the world's eyes on the needs of children, both in their own countries and by visiting field projects and emergency programmes abroad. They can make direct representations to those with the power to effect change. They can use their talents and fame to fundraise and advocate for children and support UNICEF's mission to ensure every child's right to health, education, equality and protection.
>
> *(UNICEF 2006)*

This institutionalized practice has promoted the phenomenon of celebrity activism and fan identification with the consumption of celebrity-endorsed activism. Prominent examples of recent individual celebrity advocacy/philanthropy include: TV host Oprah Winfrey's very own *O Philanthropy*; U2 rock star Bono's involvement in orchestrating the (RED)™ brand; and Angelina Jolie's ambassadorial relationship with the UN (Angelina Jolie's Story 2005; O Philanthropy 2007; What Red is 2006). The Look to the Stars: The World of Celebrity Giving website claims that as of 11 May 2015, there were "2,076 charities, 3,532 celebrities and counting" involved in causes and organizations to change the world (www.looktothestars.org).

In the context of global celebrity activism, this chapter focuses on celebrity mechanisms in China's public health realm. It first examines the emergence of celebrity activism around health issues in the international arena and within the controversial and problematic state management of HIV/AIDS in China. It then turns to the rise of "HIV/AIDS heroes" in the People's Republic of China (PRC) where the co-production and consumption of what Lisa Ann Richey and Stefano Ponte call "aid celebrities" now occurs (2008, pp. 711–29). I focus on one of China's AIDS heroes, the actor Pu Cunxin, drawing from over 300 articles written on Pu over the past five years, as well as from personal observation during fieldwork in China in 2003–08, to explore the emergence and significance of his fame within its local context.

An examination of Pu Cunxin's media identity reveals some unique features of the operation of Chinese aid celebrity. Pu's efficacy as a contemporary Chinese aid celebrity does not rely solely on his status as an actor or popular cultural figure – social positions which, until this past century, were often poorly regarded in China. In fact, an examination of his case suggests that the power or impact of an aid celebrity cannot be measured strictly with reference to the realm of pop culture and popular perception (Alberoni 1972; Fong 2005, p. 119). Pu Cunxin's uniqueness derives from his conformity with state visions of celebrity involvement in the promotion of public health, while simultaneously raising tacit social criticism of state inadequacy in the same arena. He also gains popularity by evoking centuries-old notions of the kinds of heroism and civility that can be expected from the cultivated classes. Pu's status as a Chinese-style aid celebrity thus problematizes Boorstin's well-referenced understanding of celebrity that: "We can make a celebrity, but we can never make a hero" (1972, p. 48).

Celebrity health activism and the cultivation of HIV knowledge in China

In the mid-1980s the potential of celebrities to impact on public understandings of illness became dramatically apparent in the USA. Having starred in films such as *The King and I*, *The Ten Commandments* and *The Magnificent Seven*, Yul Brynner's 1985 involvement in an anti-smoking public service announcement marked the first celebrity endorsement of public health campaigns against lung cancer (Yul Brynner 2007). In the same year, movie star Rock Hudson's declaration that he was dying of liver cancer also shocked fans around the world. Hudson had established himself as an icon of masculine strength in a distinguished acting career, appearing in such films as *Magnificent Obsession*, *Giant* and *A Farewell to Arms*. His later admission that he was dying of AIDS, and his suspected homosexuality, transformed the public's understanding of HIV/AIDS. The international fame of both men also made public discussions of their imminent deaths from lung cancer and AIDS intensely personal to audiences around the world.

Richard Schickel's work, *Intimate Strangers* (2000), suggests that celebrities such as Brynner and Hudson were able to serve as authoritative and persuasive voices in the then nascent health awareness campaigns due to the public's familiarity with the cinematic celebrity as an "intimate stranger." However, examining the processes through which the celebrity achieves this intimacy is critical to understanding the nuances that both bind and differentiate the phenomenon of celebrity in differing contexts. Accounting for the phenomenon of the aid celebrity requires not only a consideration of the international processes that support the construction of celebrities as activists, but also an examination of the local contexts in which the actions of a given celebrity are situated. The more recent case of the Chinese actor and aid celebrity, Pu Cunxin, underscores the necessity of examining celebrity in ways that enable us to account for differences, not just within what Graeme Turner (2004, p. 17) describes as the multiple domains of *a* culture, but also *across* the continuities and differences between cultures, and also between the sociocultural norms and the politico-economic and historical contexts which define each context.

Almost 15 years after the deaths of Brynner and Hudson, Pu Cunxin, a Chinese movie celebrity and Communist Party (CCP) member, was said to be picking peaches when he received a phone call from staff in China's Ministry of Health asking him to become involved in a HIV/AIDS awareness campaign. Pu admitted that at the time he was not terribly familiar with HIV/AIDS, but agreed to be involved in what later turned out to be the first HIV/AIDS public awareness poster (*gongyi guanggao*) using a Chinese celebrity (Beijing qingnian zhoukan 2007). From then on, Pu began his highly visible commitment to serving the Chinese people and the Chinese nation and his philanthropy now dominates Chinese media discussions of him.

Pu is a self-proclaimed aid celebrity and has established his own charities to support his chosen causes. He has promoted drug prohibition and voluntary blood donation and was invited to sit on the board of directors for the China Youth Development Fund as well as the China Welfare Fund for the Handicapped. He now "fully devotes himself to helping AIDS orphans" (Beijing qingnian zhoukan 2007). Pu also engages with and promotes emergent narratives on corporate social responsibility and philanthropic business culture in China. He is involved in a variety of product advertisements and ensures that donations from every product he endorses are passed to his charities of choice (Li Xiangquan 2003; Ping 2006; Chengdu shangbao 2006; Zhi 2007, p. 29; Beijing ninzao 2007).

There are a number of features specific to HIV/AIDS that make it a particularly productive site for Chinese celebrity engagement. Despite the fact that there are several more infectious and more prevalent diseases in China, such as hepatitis and tuberculosis, only HIV/AIDS has attracted carnival-like publicity and only HIV/AIDS has designated celebrity heroes mobilizing the population to its cause. In part, the considerable attention HIV/AIDS attracts derives from the international focus on this illness, a trend that is not limited solely to China (Butt 2002; Richey & Ponte 2008). Famous international dignitaries such as former UN Secretary General, Kofi Annan, and former US President, Bill Clinton, have both made official visits to China to promote programs on HIV prevention and anti-discrimination. In 2007, the Bill and Melinda Gates Foundation won permission to begin HIV/AIDS-based aid programs in China (Sohu 2004; Sohu 2003; Bill and Melinda Gates Foundation 2007).

International credibility is a major accessory to Chinese celebrity, and Pu Cunxin has emerged from this globally informed, but locally mediated space as a celebrity aid hero. Pu both benefits from and contributes to the industry and political system that sustains him. His actions demonstrate that celebrity is far more complex than a simple "onslaught of consumerism" (Fong 2005, p. 119) or a "broadcasting of fame" (Epstein 2005, p. 20).

Since the detection of China's first HIV case in the mid-1980s, the rate of infection, policy response and its implementation have been inconsistent and differ regionally. Initially, there was widespread resistance to acknowledging the prevalence of HIV in China. There were few reliable information sources available to the public and those that existed cultivated a host of transmission myths regarding HIV. This information vacuum and the media's sensationalized stories promoted a culture of fear and ignorance that is proving difficult to transform. Urban legends abound (e.g. Deng & Ke 2002; Ruo 2002), HIV-positive Chinese suffer tremendous discrimination and high rates of suicide (Peng 2005; Shao 2006). Moreover, those who fall into designated at-risk categories are reluctant to be tested for fear of the consequences if a positive test result is exposed (Chen 2006, p. 20). Pu Cunxin's HIV/AIDS activism and advocacy is situated in this difficult and uneven terrain.

During the past decade, international bodies have provided financial incentives to promote HIV/AIDS awareness projects across the PRC. Additionally, the Chinese government and various collaborators have tried to reduce moral panic about the disease by re-authoring a biomedically-oriented and less threatening narrative of the virus and its transmission paths. Official media outlets and educational and health institutions have produced short films, pamphlets, posters, comics, and newspaper and magazine articles aimed at increasing public knowledge of the disease, many of which feature Pu Cunxin. Workers in HIV circles have increasingly called for the Chinese media to adopt a more "responsible" role in reportage on HIV/AIDS (Sohu jiankang 2006a; Jing 2007). As a result, in their everyday experiences Chinese citizens now find themselves encouraged to "love and care" (*huxiang guan'ai*) for the HIV-positive.

Recent state action on HIV/AIDS in China was prompted in part by the socio-economic cost and international embarrassment of the Party-state's mismanagement of the outbreak of Severe Acute Respiratory Syndrome (SARS) in 2003–04. This event is widely acknowledged as being the catalyst for changing top-level politicians' attitudes toward HIV/AIDS (Yu 2007). The government is revising many of its legal and bureaucratic frameworks to ensure the welfare and rights of the HIV-positive and their families. State medical facilities are required to provide voluntary confidential HIV testing services. Life-extending anti-retroviral medication also is to be free of charge under the "four frees and one care policy" (*si mian yi guanhuai*) (Zhu & Zhou 2004). Inspired by nationalism, government research funds are invested in seeking a cure for HIV/AIDS through traditional Chinese medicine and doctors explore innovative treatment regimens across differing medical traditions to provide care to those who cannot afford it otherwise. These actions demonstrate China's "modernness" and are designed to contribute to improving its international image and domestic leadership legitimacy (Hood 2011).

Local interest groups (*minjian zuzhi*) have also emerged to focus on issues of concern relating to HIV/AIDS. Many of these groups have encountered considerable difficulty in gaining state approval to operate as official non-governmental organizations (NGOs, *feizhengfu zuzhi*) and instead function as business enterprises (*qiye*). The Party-state tolerates this practice, even though their activities are not typical of business enterprises. The local Chinese who staff these organizations are usually conversant in international development acronyms and network regularly with other international and national HIV/AIDS bodies. They also are successful in obtaining international funding for their various projects.

In addition, the newly liberalizing media and creative industries sectors contribute to public awareness on HIV/AIDS. Local and international documentaries have been produced which address aspects of HIV transmission in China. For example, *Huri* [Tiger Day] (2002), a documentary by the anthropologist Zhuang Kongshao, addresses the Yi minority's drug rehabilitation ritual and community resiliency. It received recognition at the 16th Belfast International Public Health Conference and Film Festival in 2005 as well as by the China–UK HIV/AIDS Prevention and Care Project. Later, Hong Kong director Ruby Yang and

New York producer Thomas Lennon won a 2007 Oscar for their China AIDS Media Project documentary, which addresses the impact of China's blood-selling scandal on the most vulnerable, *The Blood of Yingzhou District* (2006). These productions drew further international attention to China's growing HIV/AIDS problem and stimulated significant debates within the country (Bu k la 2007; Yan Lieshan 2007). Similarly, the Internet has become a significant site for information exchange in China through the emergence of HIV-positive and activist blogs and sites that address HIV risk and transmission (Sina.com 2008; Yu 2007; Zhu Liya boke 2008). Some of these sites encourage China's netizens to pose questions anonymously (Liu 2005).

Under an officially sponsored unified battle against the spread of HIV/AIDS in China, these various projects amalgamate international and local knowledge and development practices. Members of NGOs, "enterprise-NGOs," government-organized NGOs (GONGOs) and academics provide the workforce for this battle.[1]

FIGURE 5.2 Tents set up for select NGOs, GONGOs and people's organizations to share information about HIV in a secure area adjacent to a stage where celebrities, including those with party memberships, performed for World AIDS Day. Ordinary people could not gain access to the venue or free condoms, posters, kites shaped like red ribbons, and print material – some with caricatures of celebrities encouraging the reduction of stigma and increased voluntary testing – until the celebrities departed. Most organizations displaying at this event were supported by local and international funding, and staffed by local employees and volunteers. Photograph taken in Beijing by Johanna Hood on November 30, 2008.

Moreover, the Party-state, supported by many of those working on HIV including Pu Cunxin, is trying to draw big business into health-oriented philanthropy (Hao 2005; Jing 2006; Zhang & Zhang 2005). Taken as a whole, these trends suggest that the PRC's management of public health problems is increasingly approximating practices approved by WHO and the UN in other developing nations. But at this particular juncture of policy, law, medicine, social intervention, big business and development practice, a phenomenon has arisen in China that brings new dimensions to the discussion of celebrity health activism in China and internationally. This is the phenomenon of the "AIDS Hero" (*kang'ai yingxiong*).

The "AIDS hero" and the cultivation of Pu Cunxin

The Chinese-language term *kang'ai yingxiong* [AIDS Hero] is not found in any contemporary dictionary, but it litters the HIV media. It is used to describe those dedicated to HIV activism in China. These heroes, often in conjunction with state health authorities and/or on behalf of "the Chinese people," participate in a "war" against HIV/AIDS. Those atop the hero list compiled by one of China's popular weeklies, *Renwu zhoukan* [VIP Weekly], are both male and female and range from prominent local politicians like Wu Yi; to Taiwan-born HIV/AIDS researcher Dr. David Ho; to China's local health practitioners Drs. Gui Xi'en and Gao Yaojie,[2] whose heroic status is not unlike that of the much-revered Canadian doctor of the Sino-Japanese War, Norman Bethune. A key characteristic of China's AIDS heroes is that their engagement with disease control in China has allowed them to become known, widely recognized and celebrated in society and in contemporary media discourse.

Although traditional heroes became known through oral or literary traditions, contemporary heroes rely on media technologies. Public awareness of HIV issues has increased as images of the AIDS heroes are broadcast via the media on television shows and dramas about HIV, and through their regular appearances in the press, in hospitals and clinics and at public, private and state information events. China's adoption of the annual World AIDS Day (1 December) has added to this coverage. In the weeks before and after 1 December media coverage of China's AIDS heroes increases in intensity and culminates in a commemorative performance broadcast on China's Central Television Station. The program's format is similar to Spring Festival television broadcasting events and includes ceremonies, songs, dances and speeches. It is a significant mechanism for increasing public recognition of the AIDS heroes (Zhou 2006).

Of all China's AIDS heroes, Pu Cunxin stands most visibly above the others. Although not necessarily the most active, he is the most publicized AIDS hero for his dogged promotion of HIV education and social acceptance of China's HIV-positive. In an interview in 2006, Pu is noted as saying:

> One person is nothing of great significance. A person's strength lies in their well-being. To be very well-off is of great significance. Yet no matter how

we perform as actors, stars, or social celebrities, when working to promote AIDS awareness we can be of extraordinary use. Over the past few years we've really been able to show that we can make a difference.

(Sohu jiankang 2006b)

Born in 1953, Pu grew up in an acting household in Beijing. During the Cultural Revolution (1966–76), and like many celebrities of his generation, Pu gained his acting experience while in the state-run Heilongjiang production–construction corps where, among his other duties, he acted in plays. He returned to Beijing in 1977, became a CCP member in 1978, and then gained entrance to the prestigious Naval Academy Theatre Troupe. Pu's talents are diverse: he sings, acts, and recites poetry. He gained fame through appearances in immensely popular television series such as *Zuihou de guizu* [The Last Aristocrats], *Yingxiong wuhui* [Unrepentant Hero] and *Lailai wangwang* [Come and Go]; big screen movies such as *Xizao* [Shower]; and dramas like *Chaguan* [Teahouse].

Significantly, Pu Cunxin was the first Chinese celebrity to appear in an educational movie about HIV, *Jiaru you mingtian* [If There's Tomorrow], and the first to feature in a commercial TV series about the virus. The series, *Shileyuan* [Losing Paradise], unfolds around the tragedy of a stoic yet family-oriented businessman who mysteriously was infected by HIV. He has since featured in a second commercial TV series about HIV, *G xianshang de yongtandiao* [Aria in G].

Pu attends and gives speeches at HIV/AIDS events where his presence attracts fans and journalists. He was a major attraction at a candle-lighting memorial ceremony in Beijing's *Gongti* bar area that I attended in May 2007, and at an induction ceremony for HIV/AIDS volunteers at Beijing's People's University the following June. Attendees bustle around and try to capture a signature from or a picture of themselves with this popular actor and AIDS hero at the end of such events (Chongqing chenbao 2006). The success of Pu's star endorsement of HIV education campaigns prompted the Ministry of Health to invite other celebrities to join the fight against AIDS, such as female folk singer and now China's first lady, Peng Liyuan and female actor, Jiang Wenli (Sohu jiankang 2006a; Zhang Xiaohe 2006). State-guided philanthropic action is a growing feature of the dynamics of celebrity in China today.

The efficacy of Pu's engagement in enhancing understandings of HIV is difficult to determine, and the motives behind his very visible role are not without criticism (Lin 2004), but, according to staff members involved in Beijing's HIV organizations, "the degree of Pu's impact on popularizing HIV as an issue is unquestionable" (Interview, anonymous respondents, May 22 and October 10, 2007). In my encounters with people from all walks of life in China, there are few who do not know that superstar/AIDS ambassador Pu Cunxin is involved in China's fight against AIDS and against the discrimination faced by HIV-positive sufferers. Between 2002 and 2007, I gathered hundreds of articles on Pu's HIV/AIDS activities and a quick search on China's Google or Baidu Internet portals yields thousands of articles, websites and blogs about Pu's humanitarianism. In one article

Pu defends his efforts as follows: "I want to take the stage, and take it in a big way, and seek the limelight in a big way too. If I don't assume a more prominent or loftier stance as an AIDS prevention publicist, then I won't be effective" (Pu cited in Chu 2006).

A conversation I had with a 20-year-old female migrant from rural Sichuan who was working on a Beijing university campus reveals the extent of the connection between Pu and HIV/AIDS awareness issues. Although she was unable to tell me how HIV was transmitted, and maintained that Sichuan was HIV/AIDS-free – "AIDS? We don't have that in Sichuan" – she was, nonetheless, acutely aware that Pu was active in HIV/AIDS prevention efforts. As she helped me copy media about Pu and asked questions about these and my interest in HIV, she informed me "I already know that he attends lots of AIDS activities."

Pu is credited with having deep knowledge about HIV/AIDS and his fame positions him as an authoritative voice at a level not commonly associated with Euro-American movie celebrity health advocates. Pu educates state leaders about HIV/AIDS, endorses official campaigns, and serves as an advisor on HIV publications.

FIGURE 5.3 Fans, journalists and volunteers dispersing and flying red ribbon kites after Pu Cunxin sang and gave a short motivational talk "I have a dream. I hope that one day we, together with all HIV positive, will live in a world without discrimination" for a World AIDS Day performance and information event sponsored by UNAIDS, IFRC and the China Red Cross. Photograph taken by Johanna Hood outside the Beijing National Stadium on November 30, 2008.

A commentary by Pu prefaces the *Diaries of an AIDS Girl*, which details the experience of HIV-positive university student, Zhu Liya (pseudonym) (Zhu 2006). His expert opinion appears in China Youth Development Foundation educational materials as well as in a variety of UN publications (Huang 2007; Liu 2005; Sun 2003; Zhang Xu 2003). He appears on condom packages and alongside the head of the prestigious Chinese Academy of Science, Zeng Yi, in posters and educational publications about HIV for students.

Despite his frequent adoption of expert roles, Pu has no relevant educational credentials to offer advice on health, which typically are prerequisites for legitimate involvement in a public campaign or for holding formal positions of power in China. His acceptability to the Party-state most likely emerges from his status as a member of the CCP. Without this imprimatur, the Party-state may not have solicited his initial support.

As in many other fields, CCP membership facilitates the individual's ability to be promoted and rise to prominence and is often a prerequisite for positions of social and political power. For example, Pu could not have served as Dean of Beijing's top performance academy without being a Party member. In this regard, the case of Pu Cunxin demonstrates the interaction of China's celebrity systems with the publicity machinery and information systems of the Party-state. However, the creation of Pu as an AIDS hero also draws on longstanding Chinese conceptions of prominent individuals and the roles they play in society.

Heroism, civility and philanthropic acts in China

At first glance, China's AIDS heroes and the modern techniques of hero production appear to have emerged out of conditions specific to a rapidly changing society. The heroes' fight is an active one and is staged by state and society against a modern disease that requires new techniques of sociopolitical involvement and management. New forms of technology are bound up in this process – television, technical performances and the Internet are necessary to facilitate publicity and discussions about these new social figures. This situation has produced new forms of social recognition and subjectivity. China's AIDS heroes exhibit progressive humanitarian thinking and for the most part maintain correct political affiliations. Their media personas and celebrity status reflect modern forms of activism, identity management and community engagement, such as concerns over public health.

Pu Cunxin embodies and performs ideals of modern-day celebrity activism and citizenship. He is cultured and educated in performance and fine arts, but is also aware and concerned about issues that extend beyond the stage. Media interviews demonstrate that he participates in international events and awareness raising, and his efforts are rewarded at both local and international levels.[3] Pu's public statements further vouch for his physical and intellectual quality (*suzhi*) as well as his cultured, civilized (*wenming*) outlook (on *suzhi*, see Anagnost 2004; Kipnis 2006; Yan 2003). He engages with issues of HIV/AIDS and with China's emergent culture of business philanthropy.[4]

But an examination of Pu's persona also reveals how established conceptions of heroes or moral exemplars may be reinvented to meet contemporary purposes and concerns. On assuming control of China in 1949, the CCP adopted an interventionist role in the art of hero production through the promotion of model workers and exemplary citizens, even though many such models were elected locally and based on real-life events and achievements. Popular examples included localized Stakhanovite model heroes, such as Lei Feng and even those spun of socialist realist thread, such as Li Shuangshuang and her revolutionary canteen, written in 1959 by Li Zhun (2007). The Maoist Party-state used model heroes to support massive sociopolitical intervention programs and heroic individuals were praised for their physical resilience and dedication to hard labor and self-sacrifice (Feng & Shao 1994; Hsia 1963; Sheridan 1968; Stranahan 1983; Zaniello 1977). In the post-1978 reform era, these exemplary figures have evolved into model economic citizens (*jingji laomo*; *jingji bangyang*), reflecting current values – wealth accrual and/or economic acumen (Zhang Xueli 2005; Tan Siliang 2007; Yang Haiyu 2007). These changes suggest that the celebrity politics of the contemporary moral exemplar often resonate with established sociocultural and political traditions.

Regardless of the fact that Pu is a CCP member and that his entrance into HIV/AIDS publicity was orchestrated by the Ministry of Health (*Pu Cunxin de lücheng* 2006), his persona unites past oral, literary, Confucian and heroic traditions with the post-1949 heroes who served diverse political purposes. As an arts and culture superstar activist, Pu has no *exact* historical replica. But his public persona shares similarities with earlier figures who gained state and public recognition for their dedication in pursuit of a sanctioned cause. The recognition and honors bestowed on the AIDS heroes as well as on model workers and citizens (*laomo, bangyang*), exemplary youth (*jieqing*) and exemplary women (*nüjie*), among others, have historical precedence. As Mary Sheridan (1968, p. 47) notes in her study on heroism in the Maoist era: "[t]he emulation of heroes in China is not a communist invention. It was a mainstay of Confucian education in the form of stories about great emperors, generals, poets, magistrates and filial children. This technique of emulation was never abandoned, even when China entered more modern times."

Appreciating the historical moral economy within which Pu's actions circulate enables us to critically engage with his contemporary persona as a celebrity AIDS hero and to better understand his social significance. The AIDS hero is reminiscent of a rich history of famed individuals, and the roles Pu performs and the social functions he fulfills have deep historical roots. In addition to being akin to this century's "model citizens and workers," the AIDS hero is like the Confucian scholar (*junzi, shi* or *caizi*) and knight errant (*youxia*). James Liu (1967, p. 11) notes of the knight errant that they were "inspired by an altruistic spirit and a strong sense of justice and . . . acted on a universalistic principle." The knight errant "placed a moral code above the law" and both the Confucian scholar and knight errant "came into being as a matter of social necessity" (Liu 1967, pp. 10, 15). All figures, the AIDS hero included, have the following notable features: they uphold distinct moral codes; help the vulnerable; place the needs of nation, society or family over their own; remain aloof from worldly appetites; and desire recognition for their righteousness. Further, the heroes, past and present, are recognized for their upstanding actions and bravery, and all critique social and/or state practices – a point to which I return in the conclusion.

By drawing distinct parallels with Pu's public persona and the earlier models, heroes and knights errant, I suggest that Pu should be placed along an evolving trajectory that stretches back in Chinese history and social traditions. The legendary righteousness and bravery by which heroic figures are characterized have roots in Han Chinese literature and oral traditions stretching from the Warring States period (475–221 BCE) and the Han dynasty (206 BCE–220 CE), up until contemporary times (Hanan 1980; Liu 1967; Yeh 1989). These famed individuals are found in classics like the Han dynasty's *Records of the Historian* (Sima 1961) and the 1879 *Tales of Magistrate Bao* (Shi 1997) and are mirrored in contemporary AIDS heroes.

The identifiable continuity of Pu's persona with the past is readily found in his statements declaring that he is motivated by a sense of greater public service and social good. Although Pu most often operates in conjunction with the state, he is involved in helping the state reform its attitudes toward HIV and stresses he does so *for society*. For example, Pu claims:

> The work I do is to let society – including all levels of government and the public – know the high degree of importance of this issue [HIV]. I want to make each Chinese person know that AIDS really is not far from any of us . . . on the one hand we must make people aware of the ideology [surrounding AIDS], while on the other hand spread AIDS awareness in order to make people understand how to avoid transmitting it or getting infected with AIDS . . . Aside from [realizing] the imperative that AIDS patients get respect, eliminating social discrimination and caring for persons with AIDS is work that benefits all of the society.
>
> *(Pu cited in Peng 2005)*

Pu's persona is marked by selflessness and dedication to the HIV/AIDS cause. This is reflected in article titles like "Pu Cunxin, serving the public is my lifestyle" and "Pu Cunxin, AIDS publicist: the important role in my life." He is often quoted as prioritizing society's needs over his own, and is exceptionally generous with his time and financial resources (Jiankang shouce 2007; Sohu jiankang 2005; Zhang & Wang 2006). For example, he supports AIDS orphans in their schooling, finds employment for HIV-positive people who suffer discrimination, and purchases hundreds of handicrafts from HIV-positive families (Peng 2005; Yi 2004). In addition, Pu refuses to accept advertising contracts unless companies first donate to his charitable causes (Li Xiangquan 2003; Zhang & Wang 2006). Regarding his role in the television series about AIDS, *Shileyuan*, Pu stated that he "believes that all he has done really is truly worthy [of the effort] . . . that it is his dutiful responsibility to be publicly involved in the socio-medical aspects of HIV" (Wang & Wu 2002).

As the very first celebrity figure in China to adopt the AIDS cause as his responsibility (*zeren*), Pu often is described as humble, yet courageous (*yonggan*) and as cultured and refined (*siwenren; ruya*) (*Pu Cunxin de lücheng* 2006; Lin 2004). His courage is a distinguishing feature in a time when others have cowered in the face of HIV (see Anagnost 2006; Yu 2007). Pu declares he "does not fear AIDS," which further contributes to his heroic qualities (Chu 2006; Peng 2005; Wang & Wu 2002).

Recognition systems commonly measure success by one's ability to become known through one's actions and Pu has been undeniably successful in this respect. The constitution of his persona and the ways people engage with his reputation show that Pu is both widely known and desires recognition for himself and for his causes. He is sometimes criticized for his tendency to take the limelight (*zuoxiu*). However, at a major event in Beijing, fellow movie star publicist, Cai Guoqing (2007) encapsulates Pu's fame as follows: "He is China's first AIDS publicist. Over many years, he has devoted himself entirely to HIV publicity and education, as well as to charitable acts of helping and caring [for the HIV-positive]. His impact is found across almost the whole of China." An article on Pu's activities in 2004 further highlights some of these characteristics and the popular recognition of his activities and talents:

> Once, Pu Cunxin and Sun Daolin went to Nanjing to participate in a Tang *shi* and Song *ci* poetry recital. While they were on the train a few middle-aged and elderly ladies saw them and pointed to Pu Cunxin saying, "Look quickly, it's him, that AIDS guy." . . . Other people heard this and snickered in amusement. Pu Cunxin couldn't help but laugh himself, saying: "It is fine if people can't remember the roles I've acted or think what my name is, so long as they understand AIDS and how to prevent it. This is the impact I want to have. All those public billboard advertisements lining the streets can't be for naught!"
>
> *(Yi 2004, p. 36)*

Descriptions of Pu's appearance and manner also establish resonances between his modern public persona and the heroic models and erudite traditions of the past. At public events the handsome Pu is charismatic, yet soft spoken and always impeccably dressed. He presents himself as intelligent, kind, compassionate and aware, as well as youthful and physically fit (Zhang & Wang 2006). Pu is described as a gentleman who possesses an acute sense of justice, responsibility, moral duty and righteousness (Li Xiangquan 2003; Peng 2005; Beijing qingnian zhoukan 2007). Moreover, Pu emerges as selfless and detached from any of the pleasures typically associated with star celebrity on the arts scene (*wenyi mingxin*), and rarely discusses his family attachments (Huang 2003, p. 70; Liu 1967). Like his predecessors, Pu's persona is marked by stoicism and is often imbued with qualities that exceed the expected norms of human behavior (Huang 2003, p. 72). Pu successfully balances an incredibly rich acting career with his heroic identity and role.

Conclusion: heroes emerge in troubled times

The cultivation and delivery of Pu Cunxin's AIDS heroism in contemporary China calls attention to the cultural specificity of celebrity. On the one hand, an examination of Pu's case allows the obvious similarities between Chinese and Western celebrity humanitarian activism to be highlighted, such as the role of China's consumer culture in fuelling the celebrity industry and health becoming a space for activism. On the other hand, Pu's embodiment of *suzhi* (quality) and other desirable characteristics specific to his local moral world highlights the limited nature of Boorstin's theorizing of the celebrity as an amoral actor, a "new category of human emptiness" and someone who, unlike the accomplished hero, is merely known for their "well-knownness" (1972, p. 49, 57).

Locally, Pu may be seen as a modern celebrity hero with modern aspirations and a passion for modern causes. Through him, we learn how celebrity in China changes and how we need to continuously update our understanding of the ways in which mass media, internet technology and the state come together to bear on the present through very different mediums than those of the literary and oral history traditions of the past. Additionally, an understanding of past discourses on heroism and upstanding individuals, and how these have changed over time, allows us to better understand not just celebrity in China, but how to use Pu to engage the contemporary concerns of the Chinese state and society. As Martin Huang (2003, p. 64) points out, although no two social models are the same, their stories may be used to reflect the social conditions and problems of the societies and times in which their narratives unfold.

In this regard, Pu demonstrates how health is increasingly presented as an issue of importance to China's economic security and social stability. His numerous media appearances, and media reportage about him, need to be situated amidst a time when China's struggling health system is undergoing serious reform and when attitudes toward HIV are changing. His comments need to be understood through a framework in which HIV has been construed as a serious threat to the long-term stability and prosperity (*shuaibai*) of the Chinese people and nation (Zhuang Tao 2001). In a very short period of time, HIV/AIDS has developed from an issue that was shrouded in secrecy to a mainstream political agenda. The management of HIV/AIDS now demonstrates the necessity of Party-state intervention and the legitimacy of its rule. Pu's philanthropy as a model citizen is a consistent theme of his involvement in an era and an arena where philanthropy and harmony are to be cultivated, illustrating the Chinese state's growing concern to foster the generosity of its citizens.

Remembering that Pu's persona shares continuities with the Confucian scholar, the knight errant and other heroes of the past, we may better understand this present production of the AIDS hero in light of its social function and critique of injustice and inequality. As the Chinese adage tells, "heroes emerge in troubled times" (*luanshi chu yingxiong*) and Pu's evocation of the heroic figures of China's past informs his celebrity status as a "critical" AIDS hero. However, national borders do not concern this hero, and the "war" he fights goes beyond HIV/AIDS to touch on sensitive issues of corruption, the health of the nation and access to scarce economic, political and welfare resources. By helping the socially, politically, economically and now biologically vulnerable, like the majority of the HIV-positive in rural China who have yet to see compensation for selling their blood to the state, he struggles to rectify the consequences of insufficient state provision and an uneven distribution of wealth and power in China's modern era of economic reform.

This heroism endears Pu Cunxin to audiences and readers and directs us to the long-standing capacity of the hero to serve as a medium for social critique, as well as to the greater irony of his political cultivation in his current role. Pu's fans have come to know he embodies HIV advocacy. Doubts about the efficacy of his mission, such as comments by the UNAIDS Executive Director Peter Piot who declared, "I've just come back from China where most young people have barely a clue about how HIV is transmitted" (Piot 2007), miss the larger significance of Pu's role. We should not simply take rates of popular knowledge of HIV's transmission paths as the sole measure of his success. We also need to consider his subtle critique of an inadequate, albeit improving, Party-state as a significant achievement. The Party-state does have a definite bearing on the shape of Pu's public persona and the limits of his activities. They influence where he donates his time, money and efforts, and the scope of his comments on the areas of current HIV/AIDS policy that require improvement. Nonetheless, Pu serves as a subtle critic of governmental policies and failures to act, and as a result he sets a new precedent for celebrities in China to follow. Through his charity and personal generosity, the courageous, handsome, stoic, intelligent and morally minded AIDS hero appears to stand up for the little people when others and the state have failed.

Notes

1 GONGOS are NGOs with Chinese state characteristics and governance, for example, the Beijing-based China HIV/AIDS Information Network (CHAIN). CHAIN maintains a public library of HIV/AIDS resources, manages a daily press release in both Chinese and English that summarizes HIV/AIDS reportage or major non-controversial developments, and it employs several HIV-positive staff (Chain.net.cn 2007).
2 China's most well-known AIDS heroes are: (1) Wu Yi, the first Vice Premier to enter the epidemic area of Henan province's Wenlou village; (2) Ma Shenyi, HIV-positive superdad; (3) Du Zong, a Columbia and Harvard graduate who gave up a successful career to dedicate himself to the fight against AIDS (he is also a self-identified homosexual who often speaks out about discrimination, a consideration which local media often ignores); (4) Dr. Gui Xi'en of Wuhan University South Central Hospital, one of the first to identify HIV in Henan's AIDS villages; (5) Yu Jian, a reporter who exposed the blood selling scandal; (6) Dr. Gao Yaojie, who although retired works tirelessly to treat and educate people about HIV/AIDS; (7) Dr. Gao Yanning, a Fudan University Professor who has recorded thousands of narratives of HIV-positive farmers and works to increase social and academic involvement in the issue; (8) Pu Cunxin; (9) Dr. He Dayi, a Taiwanese researcher who discovered the HIV cocktail therapy; and (10) Ma Shiwen, a public health worker

who leaked confidential documents about the condition of HIV in Henan. Slideshows and brief biographies of eight of the AIDS heroes can be found online, see 2006 shijie Aizibingri 2006.

3 Pu's efforts are rewarded at the local level in part because his activist actions are non-confrontational (*Jiankang shouce*, 2007; Sohu jiankang 2005; Zhang and Wang 2006). This contrasts with the actions of Dr. Gao Yaojie, the people's AIDS hero (*minjian kang'ai yingx-iong*), who is presented as more of a caring yet confrontational activist in the media and as such receives considerably less state support for her activities and accolades (Hu 2007; Li Jianhong 2007).

4 Pu's remarks about the importance of donating to support the less fortunate also fall within safe state-endorsed boundaries (Sohu jiankang 2006a; Hao 2005; Xu 2007; Zhang Xueli 2005). Officially endorsed courses on the cultivation of a philanthropic culture are now available for business enterprises. These typically employ a deficit approach that assumes that the shape of contemporary philanthropy should follow that of donation and corporate social responsibility (Cui 2005; csr.org 2007; Tang 2006). These reports make no comment on how philanthropy was differently expressed in China in the past.

Images available online

Zhongguo renkou xuanchuan jiaoyu zhongxin et al. 2004. *Jinggao: Beijing aizibing jinru kuaisu zengzhangqi*, [Warning: AIDS in Beijing has entered a period of rapid growth], http://www.bj.xinhua.org/bjpd_tpk/2004-12/01/content_3317145.htm [accessed on March 3, 2015].

Zhonghua renmin gonghe guo weishengbu. 2003. *AIDS: Aixin hehu shengming xingdong diyu aizi*, [AIDS: Love and protect life, action against AIDS], http://photo.sohu.com/21/77/Img213817721.jpg [accessed on March 3, 2015].

Zhonghua renmin gongheguo weishengbu & Qingdao Lundun she Duleisi youxian gongsi. 2004. *Aizibing ziyuanzixun jiance lijiliren*, [VCT: helping yourself is helping others], http://pic30.nipic.com/20130615/8708506_155146028372_2.jpg [accessed on March 3, 2015].

References

Africa Progress Panel. 2008. Africa's development: promises and prospects, http://www.africaprogresspanel.org/pdf/2008%20Report.pdf [accessed on September 8, 2008].

Alberoni, F. 1972. The powerless elite: theory and sociological research on the phenomenon of stars. In D. McQuail (ed.) *Sociology of Mass Communications*. Harmondsworth: Penguin, pp. 23–51.

Anagnost, A. 2004. The corporeal politics of quality (suzhi). *Public Culture*, 16 (2), 189–208.

Anagnost, A. 2006. Strange circulations: the blood economy in rural China. *Economy and Society*, 35 (4), 409–29.

Angelina Jolie's story. 2005. United Nations information database, April 2, http://www.un.org/works/goingon/refugees/angelina_story.html [accessed on October 10, 2007].

Beijing ninzao. 2007. *Zhong-wai shige langsonghui: mingxing jiqing songmingpian* [Sino-foreign poetry recital: celebrities enthusiastically recite famous works from memory], Beijing dianshitai, transcription, April 10, http://www.btv.org/btvweb/yzlm/2007-04/10/content_168412.htm [accessed on November 4, 2007].

Beijing qingnian zhoukan. 2007. *Pu Cunxin: gongyi shi wo shenghuo fangshi* [Pu Cunxin: serving the public is my lifestyle], 6 September, http://bjqn.ynet.com/article.jsp?oid=23788009&pageno=1 [accessed on September 7, 2007].

Bill and Melinda Gates Foundation. 2007. *Major commitment to expand HIV prevention in China*, Global Health, November 14, http://www.gatesfoundation.org/GlobalHealth/Pri_Diseases/HIVAIDS/Announcements/Announce-071114.htm [accessed on September 18, 2008].

Boorstin, D. 1972 [1961]. *The Image: A Guide to Pseudo Events in America.* New York: Atheneum.

Bu k la. 2007. *Tianya zatan: Guanzhu aizibing gu'er Yingzhou de haizi huo Aosika zuijia jilu duanpian jiang* [Tianya chitchat: Concern for AIDS orphans. Blood of Yingzhou District wins Oscar for Short Documentary], *Tianya shequ*, February 26, http://www.tianya.cn/new/publicforum/Content.asp?idWriter=0&Key=0&strItem=free&idArticle=868694&flag=1 [accessed on October 29, 2007].

Butt, L. 2002. The suffering stranger: medical anthropology and international morality, *Medical Anthropology*, 21 (1), 1–24.

Cai Guoqing. 2007. *Opening ceremony speech for university student HIV prevention campaign.* People's University, Beijing, June 18.

Chain.net.cn. 2007. *Zhongguo hongse dai wang* [China's red ribbon net], http://www.chain.net.cn/ [accessed on October 29, 2007].

Chengdu shangbao. 2006. *Pu Cunxin gongyi jijin xian Aixin* [Pu Cunxin's Aixin Public Welfare Fund gives love to others], April 17, http://www.cphcf.com/list.php?id=1802&type= [accessed on October 20, 2007].

Chen Jiu. 2006. *Zhengyi zhong de Zhongguo xing nanti* [Debates around China's tough problems with sex] *Xin zhoukan,* November 15, 20–3.

Chongqing chenbao. 2006. *Mingxin weiyuan zao meiti weidu: renmin dahuitang guangchang cheng zhanchang* [Celebrity Party members cause media barricade: the Great Hall of the People's Square becomes a battleground], March 4, http://news.sohu.com/20060304/n242122022.shtml [accessed on October 29, 2007].

Chu Donghua & Zhang Yicheng. 2005. *Anning jiangli: "jingji laomo"* [Anning awards: "Model Economic Workers"], *Yunnan ribao*, http://www.yn.gov.cn/yunnan,china/73469366967992320/20050129/19200.html [accessed on September 16, 2008].

Chu Ge. 2006. *Pu Cunxin he Yan Qinghao xuanchuan fang'ai: yong hongsidai chuandi wennuan xinxi* [Pu Cunxin and Yan Qinghao publicize AIDS prevention: Using the Red Ribbon to pass on heartening news], *Sohu yule*, December 12, http://yule.sohu.com/20061204/n246783346.shtml [accessed on November 4, 2007].

csr.org. 2007. *Qiye shehui zeren tongmeng* [Corporate Social Responsibility Alliance], http://www.csr.org.cn [accessed on November 5, 2007].

Cui Shengxiang. 2005. *Qiye shehui zeren yuanhe queshi* [Why is there a corporate social responsibility deficiency?], *Renmin wang*, November 8, http://theory.people.com.cn/GB/49154/49156/3836786.html [accessed on October 25, 2007].

Deng Ke & Ke Li. 2002. *Tianjin Aizibing huanzhe chi zhen zha ren shijian diaocha* [Investigating the Tianjin incident: AIDS sufferer continues to use needles to prick people] *Nanfang zhoumo*, January 25, http://news.sina.com.cn/c/2002-01-24/455264.html [accessed on September 13, 2003].

Eastday.com. 2006. *shijie Aizibingri: Zhongguo kang'ai yingxiong*, http://big5.eastday.com:82/gate/big5/photo.eastday.com/slideshow/20061201_6/index3.html [accessed on September 8, 2008].

Epstein, J. 2005. The culture of celebrity, *Weekly Standard*, October 17, 19–25.

Feng Di & Shao Dongfang. 1994. Life writing in mainland China (1949–1993). *Biography*, 17 (1), 32–55.

Fong, F. 2005. Celebrity in China. In J. Cooper & K. Burry (eds) *Celebrity: International Association of Entertainment Lawyers*. London: Five Eight/Frukt, pp. 121–2.

Hanan, P. 1980. Judge Bao's hundred cases reconstructed. *Harvard Journal of Asiatic Studies*, 40 (2), 301–23.

Hao Yachao. 2005. *Weihe 99% Zhongguo qiye bu yuanyi zuo cishan* [Why 99% of Chinese enterprises are unwilling to do philanthropy], *Fazhi zaobao*, November 28, http://www.chinalegalnews.com.cn/legaltimes/20051128/1401.htm [accessed on November 4, 2007].

Hood, J. 2011. *HIV/AIDS, Health and the Media*. London: Routledge.

Hsia, T.A. 1963. Heroes and hero-worship in Chinese communist fiction. *China Quarterly*, 13, 113–38.

Hu Jia. 2007. *Gao Yaojie bei feifa goujin di shi'er tian: guanfang huangyan huiying guoji shehui zhixun* [Gao Yaojie's illegal detention reaches day twelve: Party-state lies in response to request for further detail by international community], *Minzu Zhongguo*, February 11, http://minzhuzhongguo.org/Article/ShowArticle.asp?ArticleID=809 [accessed on September 16, 2008].

Huang Fang. 2007. *Pu Cunxin: 5 nian lai zui manyi de ti'an yu shangliu de yihan* [Pu Cunxin: five years of highs and lows], *Xinhua wang*, March 10, http://news.sohu.com/(2007)0310/n248634755.shtml [accessed on November 11, 2007].

Huang, M. 2003. From Caizi to Yingxiong: imagining masculinities in two Qing novels, *Yesou puyan* and *Sanfen meng quan zhuan*, *Chinese Literature: Essays, Articles, Reviews*, 25, 59–98.

Jiankang shouce. 2007. *Pu Cinxin: yibeizi yufang aizibing xuanchuanyuan* [Pu Cunxin: I want to spend a lifetime promoting AIDS prevention], July 27, http://www.jk-sc.cn/sex_69/15384.shtml [accessed on July 28, 2007].

Jing Jun. 2007. HIV/AIDS discussion panel. *The Bookworm Public Lecture*, Building 4, Nan Sanlitun Road, Beijing, April 5.

Kipnis, A. 2006. Suzhi: a keywords approach. *China Quarterly*, 186, 296–313.

Li Jianhong. 2007. *Zhuhe Gao Yaojie yisheng chenggong fu Mei ling jiang* [Congratulations to Dr. Gao Yaojie on successfully getting to the USA to receive her award], *Minzhu Zhongguo*, March 14, http://minzhuzhongguo.org/Article/ShowArticle.asp?ArticleID=976 [accessed on October 18, 2007].

Li Xiangquan. 2003. *Dabao wei "Aizi gu'er" gai xinjia: Pu Cunxin juankuan xian aixin* [Dabao cosmetics builds home for "AIDS orphans": Pu Cunxin donates to Aixin endowment], *Beijing qingnian bao*, December 9, http://news.xinhuanet.com/edu/2003-12/09/content_1220590.htm [accessed on October 18, 2007].

Li Zhun. 2007 [1959]. *A brief biography of Li Shuangshuang*, trans. J. Hood & R. Mackie. *Renditions*, 68, 47–73.

Lin Haihui. 2004. *Zhongguo diyi yufang aizibing xuanchuanyuan* [China's first AIDS prevention publicist], *Jiefang ribao*, November 19, http://www.hwxz.com/ShowContent.aspx?ArticleID=9727 [accessed on October 18, 2007].

Liu, J.J.Y. 1967. *The Chinese Knight-Errant*. London: Routledge and Kegan Paul.

Liu Jianqiang. 2005. *Zhongyangdang xiaoli de aizibing guannian jiaofeng* [Contesting conceptions of AIDS at the Central Party School], *Nanfang zhoumo*, June 23, A6.

O Philanthropy. 2007. Oprah.com, http://www.oprah.com/ophilanthropy/ophilanthropy_landing.jhtml [accessed on October 27, 2007].

Peng Shengting. 2005. *Pu Cunxin: Aizibing xuanchuanyuan; wo rensheng de zhongyao juese* [Pu Cunxin, AIDS publicist: the important role in my life], *Beijing zhoubao*, November 24, http://news.xinhuanet.com/society/2005-11/24/content_3830238_1.htm# [accessed on November 24, 2005].

Ping Huan. 2006. *Pu Cunxin: "Pu Cunxin Aixin gongyi jijin": gongyi shi yizhong AAzhi xingwei* [Pu Cunxin: "Pu Cunxin's Aixin Public Welfare Fund": public welfare is a type of double Dutch], Sanyuefeng, 8, http://qkzz.net/Announce/announce.asp?BoardID= 16500&ID=403646 [accessed on October 16, 2007].

Piot, P. 2007. *Introductory speech, Joint Learning Initiative on Children and HIV/AIDS*, Harvard Medical School, September 24. Transcript posted on AIDS ASIA yahoo group, October 2.

Pu Cunxin de lücheng [The journey of Pu Cunxin]. 2006. Dongfang shikong yangshi guoji, CCTV, Video, December 1, http://www.cctv.com/video/dongfangshikong/2006/12/dongfangshikong_300_20061201_3.shtml [accessed on October 20, 2007].

Richey, L. & Ponte, S. 2008. Better (Red)TM than dead? Celebrities, consumption and international aid. *Third World Quarterly*, 29 (4), 711–29.

Ruo Yu. 2002. *Zhimian Aizibing: Aizi huanzhe chi zhen zha ren* [Facing AIDS: AIDS sufferer continues to prick people], *Nanfang zhoumo*, January 25, http://news.southcn.com/community/shzt/aids/zhimian/200201250356.htm [accessed on August 8, 2003].

Schickel, R. 2000 [1985]. *Intimate Strangers*. Chicago: Ivan Dee.

Shao Jing. 2006. Fluid labor and blood money: the economy of HIV/AIDS in rural central China. *Cultural Anthropology*, 21 (4), 535–69.

Sheridan, M. 1968. The emulation of heroes. *China Quarterly*, 33, 47–72.

Shi Yukun. 1997 [1879]. Tales of Magistrate Bao and his valiant lieutenants, in *Selections from Sanxia Wuyi*, trans. S. Blader. Hong Kong: Hong Kong University Press.

Sima Qian. 1961 [n.d.]. The biographies of the wandering knights and the biographies of male favorites. In *Records of the Grand Historian: Han Dynasty Vol. II*, trans. B. Watson. New York: Columbia University Press, pp. 409–23.

Sina.com. 2008. Wei *aizibing fangzhi nuli yisheng* [A life dedicated to combating AIDS], http://blog.sina.com.cn/u/1406703434 [accessed on August 8, 2008].

Sohu. 2003. *Kelindun jiejian Zhongguo aizibing bingdu ganranzhe Song Pengfei* [Clinton receives China's, AIDS virus infectee, Song Pengfei] *Sohu.com*, November 10, http://news.sina.com.cn/c/2003-11-10/14152105427.shtml [accessed on November 10, 2003].

Sohu. 2004. *Annan canguan Beijing aizibing zixun jiance dian* [Annan pays visit to Beijing AIDS Sentinel Site], October 13, http://health.sohu.com/20041013/n222462901.shtml [accessed on October 16, 2004].

Sohu jiankang. 2005. *Xuanchuanyuan Pu Cunxin he ertong youxi bisai chang'er ge* [Publicist Pu Cunxin and children playing games and singing kid's songs], June 2, http://health.sohu.com/20050602/n225790188.shtml [accessed on October 4, 2007].

Sohu jiankang. 2006a. *Aizi fangzhi xuanchuan women zuole shenme?* [What have we done to raise awareness of AIDS prevention?], May 18, http://health.sohu.com/s2006/aizibing fangzhi/ [accessed on September 16, 2008].

Sohu jiankang. 2006b. *Pu Cunxin: wei xuanchuan aizibing fangzhi wo bupa chu fengtou* [Pu Cunxin: I'm not afraid of the limelight when it is for publicizing how to prevent and cure AIDS], May 18, http://health.sohu.com/20060518/n243295701.shtml [accessed on July 2, 2007].

Stranahan, P. 1983. Labor heroines of Yan'an. *Modern China*, 9 (2), 228–52.

Sun Lu. 2003. *Pu Cunxin ti'an guanzhu "aizi" wenti: Gong Li, Pan Hong qi qianzi* [Pu Cunxin promotes concern for "AIDS" problem: Gong Li and Pan Hong also sign up], *Zhongguo xinwen wang*, March 9, http://ent.sina.com.cn/s/m/2003-03-09/1610136551.html [accessed on December 5, 2005].

Tan Siliang. 2007. *Tamen shi Hunan yejie zuiqiang shi xiong* [They are the ten most powerful of Hunan's entrepreneurs], *Sanxiang dushi bao*, May 24, http://www.hnce.com.cn/news/rdjj/hnxw/2007/5/24/7109910356934.htm [accessed on November 4, 2007].

Tang Jiansheng. 2006. *Hexie xiaofei huanjingzhong de qiyezeren* [Corporate social responsibility and the consumption environment of a harmonious society], *Renmin wang*, March 13, http://theory.people.com.cn/GB/49154/49156/4191633.html [accessed on November 4, 2007].

Turner, G. 2004. *Understanding Celebrity*. London: Sage.

Turner, G. 2007. Diana and the cult of celebrity we enjoy. *Britannica Blog* Where Ideas Matter, August 22, http://blogs.britannica.com/blog/main/author/gturner [accessed on October 15, 2007].

UNICEF 2006. Goodwill Ambassadors, article database, http://www.unicef.org/people/people_ambassadors.html [accessed on November 4, 2007].

Wang Chen & Wu Ran. 2002. *Changchun yaohe Shileyuan. Pu Cunxin: fangzhi aizi bupa chufengtou* [The cry of Changchun Shileyuan. Pu Cunxin: not afraid to take the stage for the prevention and cure of HIV], *Sina Yingyin yule*, May 15, http://ent.sina.com.cn/v/2002-05-15/83437.html [accessed on November 3, 2007].

Watt, P. & Sharman, T. 2006. Mission unaccomplished: one year on from Gleneagles is the G8 hitting its targets on debt, trade and aid?, *Actionaid.org*, www.actionaid.org.uk/doc_lib/g8_1-report.pdf [accessed on September 7, 2008].

What Red is. 2006. *The Persuaders, LLC*, http://www.joinred.com/red/ [accessed on August 8, 2008].

Xu Yongguang. 2007. *Zhongguo minjian cishan juanzeng duanque de yuanyin fenxi ji jjianyi* [Analysis and recommendation regarding China's deficiency of public charitable donations], *Zhongguo jijinhui tonxun*, 8, June 28, http://www.cydf.org.cn/gb/tongxun/database/showtongxun.asp?newsid=4141 [accessed on October 4, 2007].

Yan, H. 2003. Neoliberal governmentality and neohumanism: organizing suzhi/value flow through labor recruitment networks. *Cultural Anthropology*, 18 (4), 493–523.

Yan Lieshan. 2007. *Zenyang bangzhu geng duo "Yingzhou de haizi"* [How do we help more "Children of Yingzhou"?] *Sohu pinglun*, March 13, http://star.news.sohu.com/20070313/n248685497.shtml [accessed on November 4, 2007].

Yang Haiyu. 2007. *Yingxiao nüjie: Zhongguo tongxinye jinguobang* [Distinguished enterprise women: exemplary women of China's communications industry], *Tongxin shijie*, 9 (March 12), 30–7.

Yang, R. 2006. *The Blood of Yingzhou District*, Documentary film, 39 minutes. China HIV/AIDS Media Project: Thomas Lennon Films.

Yeh, W. 1989. Dai Li and the Liu Geqing Affair: heroism in the Chinese Secret Service during the war of resistance. *Journal of Asian Studies*, 48 (3), 545–62.

Yi Lijing. 2004. *Pu Cunxin wei AIDS zuoxiu* [Pu takes the limelight for AIDS], *Renwu zhoukan*, December 1, 36.

Yu, H. 2007. Talking, linking, clicking: the politics of AIDS and SARS in urban China. *positions*, 15 (1), 35–75.

Yul Brynner. 2007. *The Yul Brynner Head and Neck Cancer Foundation*, http://www.head-andneck.org/psa.htm [accessed on October 22, 2007].

Zaniello, T. 1977. The popular hero in contemporary China. *Journal of Popular Culture*, X (4), 902–7.

Zhang Na & Zhang Youyi. 2005. *Liu da yuanyin zhang'ai qiyi juanzeng reqing* [Six main reasons barring the welcoming of [charitable] contributions], *Zhongguo fazhi*, November 28, http://www.chinalegalnews.com.cn/legaltimes/20051128/1401.htm [accessed on October 10, 2007].

Zhang Xiaohe. 2006. *Mingxing tuiguang aizibing zhishi Pu Cunxin, Cai Guoqing shang anquantao fengmian* [Celebrities promoting understanding of AIDS. Pu Cunxin and Cai Guoqing on condom packaging], *Sohu yingyin yule*, December 6, http://ent.sina.com.cn/s/m/2006-12-06/12091358530.html [accessed on December 7, 2006].

Zhang Xueli. 2005. *Zongbianji Liu Youping: cishan gongyi zai Zhongguo mianlin si da zhang'ai* [Editor-in-chief Liu Youping: the four major obstacles to public philanthropy], *Gongyi shibao*, November 28, http://www.chinalegalnews.com.cn/legaltimes/20051128/1401.htm [accessed on October 15, 2007].

Zhang Xu. 2003. *Pu Cunxin de ti'an* [The case of Pu Cunxin], *Zhongguo funübao*, February 25, Issue 3895.

Zhang Ying & Wang Binbin. 2006. *Pu Cunxin: tiaojin "renyi" zhe guo zhou* [Pu Cunxin: dabbling in the "arts" pot of porridge], *Nanfang zhoumo*, February 16, D25–6.

Zhi Hui. 2007. *Aixin zhaoliang meigeren de shengming "Aixin Chedui" kaijin Hunan zhong miequ* [Compassion lights up everybody's life: "motorcade of kindness" enters Hunan's hardest hit disaster area], *Beijing yule xinbao*, September 6, 29.

Zhou Shanyi. 2006. *Shijie aizibing ri: Zhongguo kang'ai yingxiong* [2006 World AIDS Day: China's AIDS heroes], *Dongfang wang*, December 1, http://photo.eastday.com/slide-show/20061201_6/index.html [accessed on January 1, 2007].

Zhu Liya. 2006. *Aizi nüsheng riji: An HIV Girl's Diaries* [sic]. Beijing: Beijing chubanshe.

Zhu Liya boke [Blogger Julia]. 2008. *Sina.com*, http://blog.sina.com.cn/zhuliya [accessed on August 8, 2008].

Zhu Yu & Zhou Tingyu. 2004. *Shenme shi "Simian Yiguanhuai"* [What are the "Four Frees and One Care"?], *Xinhua wang*, December 1, http://news.xinhuanet.com/health/2004-12/01/content_2282000.htm [accessed on October 29, 2007].

Zhuang Kongshao. 2002. *Huri: Xiao Liangshan minjian jiedu shijian* [Tiger Day: popular practice of drug detox], Documentary film. Beijing: Institute for Anthropology, Renmin University of China.

Zhuang Tao. 2001. *Aizibing dui shehui yingxiang you duo da?* [AIDS: How large an impact on society can it have?], *Shidai chao*, 27, 27.

PART II

Celebritization, participatory democracy, and the donor North

6

BEN AFFLECK GOES TO WASHINGTON

Celebrity advocacy, access and influence

Alexandra Cosima Budabin

In 2014 Hollywood actor and director Ben Affleck went to the US capital, Washington DC, to speak to the US Senate Foreign Relations Committee. He was not called to speak about filmmaking but rather about the increasing violence in the Democratic Republic of Congo (DRC). Since the founding of his Eastern Congo Initiative (ECI) in 2010, Affleck has been called three times to speak as an expert witness. For his third appearance, Affleck sat alongside ambassadors, academics, and the US Special Envoy for the Great Lakes Region and Congo. He spoke about his organization's economic development efforts and pushed Congress and the Obama Administration to sustain its leadership in the DRC. As a celebrity humanitarian, Affleck displays his intent to be more than a beacon for cameras and speak about important matters. His appearance in DC is illustrative of the opportunity for celebrities and their organizations to gain access and build influence in a particularly post-democratic fashion. As a result, the implications of Affleck's efforts prompt vital questions about the role of celebrity, power and politics in international humanitarianism.

Among the larger field of celebrity humanitarians, a small but growing number have started development organizations, crafting exclusive platforms that focus attention on underreported areas and promote unique visions for interventions in the Global South. At the helm of their own NGOs, celebrity humanitarians are expanding their engagement by mediating across contexts in the North and South. Following Brockington's (2014) use of Crouch (2004), I adopt a post-democratic lens to situate and understand Affleck's ability to found his organization, gain access, and build influence. The term "post-democratic" characterizes politics in Western countries where public participation is dependent on "top-down publicity campaigns" that are directed by political elites, often acting in concert with corporate entities (Crouch 2004, pp. 19–20). I contend that the access and influence of celebrity-led organizations reflects a post-democratic context, where political and financial elites are able to propel select individuals like celebrity humanitarians. The establishment of ECI benefited from an exclusive network of celebrities such as Bono and philanthropists like Howard Buffett, while receiving funding from corporations like Google. The presence of this privileged dynamic deserves enquiry for positioning celebrities to mediate humanitarianism between the Global North and South.

This chapter considers Hollywood actor and director Ben Affleck as a celebrity humanitarian by examining the organization he created, the Eastern Congo Initiative (ECI). With the help of the strategic consultancy firm williamsworks, Affleck co-founded ECI to spur social and economic development in the DRC. Despite the relative youth of ECI, the organization has received extensive validation and access. ECI's capacity for influence is wide as it seeks to direct the relationship between the US and the DRC. In the North Affleck raises funds from elite circles, educates political elites, and lobbies the US Congress to shape foreign policy towards the DRC. In the South, Affleck instead focuses on identifying and supporting local partners through ECI grants without direct engagement in politics. ECI also conducts research with the humanitarian agency US Agency for International Development (USAID) to identify potential grantees for foreign donors. This chapter poses the following questions: How does the access and influence of a celebrity humanitarian such as Affleck reflect post-democratic politics in the US? With what consequences for economic and social development in East Congo?

To address this question, I make two primary arguments: (1) the case demonstrates the logic of post-democratic politics in the Global North by illustrating how celebrity actors are able to parlay their celebrity status to establish their own organizations and gain access to policymaking circles; (2) the political advocacy exercised by select individuals like celebrity humanitarians has serious consequences for economic and social development, particularly in the area of accountability. Celebrity humanitarians are positioned to influence interventions in the South by coalescing elite support in the North, both political and financial, for a celebrity figure rather than following more traditional paths of public consultation and evaluation. As a distortion of democratic ideals, the web of political and financial players behind the celebrity humanitarian creates an imbalance in the fair representation of interests, in particular crowding out the Southern recipients. Thus, celebrity-led interventions shape the Global North's understanding of humanitarianism in ways that preclude accountability for stakeholders in the Congolese context.

This chapter is organized as follows: first, I briefly introduce the case study background of the eastern Congo. I ground my analysis of celebrity humanitarianism in US elite politics in relevant literature around celebrity advocacy, the post-democratic context, and the US political environment. I examine Affleck's entry into development causes, the establishment of ECI, and the efforts of the strategic consulting firm williamsworks. I then explore ECI's dual objectives around US advocacy and grant-making in the DRC in order to understand how celebrity humanitarianism mediates elite politics across the Global North and South. Finally, I address how celebrity-led NGOs are emblematic of post-democratic politics and why this matters for humanitarianism.

Background on the case

The DRC is the second least developed country in the world according to the 2013 *Human Development Report.*[1] Following independence in 1960 the DRC's artificial borders, drawn across previously unmarked territories, failed to establish authority and order over various political, ethnic, and regional divisions. Neighboring countries, colonial powers, armed groups as well as multinational corporations fight for control over DRC's extensive natural resources (Eichstaedt 2011). Policies of liberalization, privatization, and structural adjustment have produced a central government with both enduring lack of state capacity to maintain order along with overcapacitated mechanisms for exploiting its local population. Since 1997 the cycle of violence in the Great Lakes region, stemming in part from refugees escaping Rwanda's genocide, enveloped six neighboring countries and, to a lesser extent, France and the US (Prunier 2010). Recent conflict has taken the lives of over five million.[2] Today, while a fragile peace exists over most of the DRC, the eastern section of the country continues to be plagued by unrest and bitter discord between the Congolese government and numerous armed groups. The UN's largest peacekeeping mission has been in the country since 2003 and helped organize democratic elections in 2006. But peace talks and extensive international intervention have failed to quell the violence, address the humanitarian crisis, and return the rule of law.

Within the world of US advocacy, conflict in the DRC has received less attention than other star-studded efforts around Darfur, South Africa, and Uganda. The conflict has been underresearched, underreported, and "when remembered, largely misunderstood" (Paddon 2010, p. 322). Sporadic, albeit intense attention to conflict minerals and to sexual violence against women has led only to a narrow definition of the challenges the country faces, often resulting in misguided policy solutions around the rebuilding of state authority (Autesserre 2012). This dovetails with US policy, which focuses on political stability. A focus on celebrity engagement is not to detract from the materiality of the problems in the eastern region of the DRC. Rather, misrepresentations about the DRC further raise the stakes of celebrity humanitarians who are potentially able to shape US policy and donor relations towards the country.

Literature review

This case study is situated in a body of work that examines and problematizes the ways in which celebrities have moved beyond their day jobs as entertainers and athletes to become advocates for humanitarianism, delving into the areas of foreign aid, charity, human rights, and development. Advocacy around humanitarian issues can encompass fundraising, speaking to the media, and addressing policymaking bodies. Previous scholarship has examined celebrity humanitarians and their advocacy as celebrity diplomats and celebrity ambassadors on behalf of international organizations like the UN (Cooper 2008; Wheeler 2013), humanitarian agencies, corporations (Richey & Ponte 2011), and NGOs (Brockington 2014). Celebrities are credited with drawing media attention (Huliaras & Tzifakis 2010; Hawkins 2011) and increasing fundraising.[3] For NGOs in particular, celebrity humanitarians have become an integral part of communication strategies, acting as the public face for organizations and their campaigns (Goodman & Barnes 2011). I extend this understanding of celebrity humanitarianism by focusing on celebrity advocacy efforts within the emergence of celebrity-led NGOs. I draw on Brockington's (2014) analysis of post-democratic politics as a useful lens through which to understand the environment that makes it possible for celebrity humanitarians to establish their own organizations and enter political circles. I also contextualize the US political environment for celebrity witnesses before Congressional hearings.

The rationale behind celebrity humanitarian engagement in advocacy is straightforward. First, a celebrity "seeks to influence the exercise of political power by way of their fame and status" (Street 2012, p. 347). Whether on behalf of pet causes or in response to the appeals of a needy group, the intent is to enter decision-making arenas to effect social and political change. Second, the means by which celebrities gain access is their presumed popular mass appeal and political capital. Deftly straddling two separate audiences, celebrities "have the power to frame issues in a manner that attracts visibility and new channels of communication at the mass as well as the elite levels" (Cooper 2008, p. 7). While a celebrity's actual ability to mediate between the public and elites remains somewhat of a mystery, celebrities do demonstrate the enviable ability to gain access to elite circles of national and global governance. At the international level, Cooper (2008) has traced the development of "outsider-insider" status of celebrities with mass appeal who enter rarefied spaces on the international stage like the United Nations, the White House, 10 Downing Street, and Davos. Celebrities like Bob Geldof, Bono, and Angelina Jolie enter into elite policy circles in the North to discuss third world debt, poverty, and refugees. Such encounters are covered heavily in mainstream and digital media. Overall, these practices suggest a dual relationship between political and celebrity power: celebrities wish to gain access in order to build influence while decision-makers associate themselves with celebrities to draw on their mass appeal.

Yet the role of celebrity humanitarians in the political process is controversial and prompts normative debates around legitimate democratic processes. For many observers, celebrity advocacy is a positive development for global issues. If celebrities are capable of using their popular appeal, then they offer the possibility of bringing the public to the realm of politics (Cooper 2008). This "bottom-up" view invigorates democracy by regarding the celebrity as a key interlocutor: educating the public on challenging issues while also channeling their preferences to the political realm. Wheeler regards celebrities as bringing about "new forms of engagement which indicate a dialectical transformation of high-politics with a more populist approach to cultural citizenship" (2013, p. 29). Trailed by media coverage and a wide fan base, the celebrity figure brings transparency into policy processes, leading to greater accountability of decision-makers.

For others, the presence of celebrities in political processes signals a concentration of elite power that is anathema to democracy. Brockington (2014, p. 37) argues that celebrity has gained in visibility and influence, especially among NGOs, as "part of the performance and display of elite-dominated post-democracies". Rather than represent the interests of the majority, celebrities can be seen as another category of select individuals that exercise greater influence than the mass public. Thus, the deeper entrenchment of celebrity humanitarians perpetuates a "post-democratic order" that obfuscates power and privilege, strengthens top-down political processes, and closes down disagreement and conflict without popular input (Kapoor 2013, p. 37). Accountability in this instance is attenuated; the celebrity is not beholden to his or her public in the same manner as the elected official. And when the stakeholder public is located elsewhere, as in humanitarianism, there are even weaker grounds for accountability of celebrity advocacy. Misguided proposals and ineffective interventions will not endanger a celebrity, whose position is assured by both financial and political elites.

Celebrity-led organizations are a recent and growing phenomenon that offer the possibility for greater autonomy to a celebrity humanitarian. There have always been celebrity humanitarians who have enjoyed more independence without ties to an established organization or campaign. Cooper's taxonomy of "celebrity diplomats" distinguishes celebrities who operate as "freelancers" in their engagement in international affairs with a sense of individual autonomy such as US talk show host Oprah Winfrey. In some cases this list includes celebrities who adopt such controversial positions that freelancing is their only option – as, for example, in the case of US actress Jane Fonda (Cooper 2008, pp. 7–8). But the decision to found an organization offers celebrities the possibility to set a firm foundation for activism, signal a long-term commitment to an issue, and build credibility in the policymaking world.

In the past decade, a handful of celebrity humanitarians have chosen to create organizations to highlight neglected areas and issues. This group includes singer and entertainer Madonna's establishment of Raising Malawi in 2006 to draw attention to education (see Rasmussen in this volume). In 2010, following the earthquake in Haiti, the actor Sean Penn created the J/P Haitian Relief Organization, which is focused on local relief efforts and sustainable development (see Rosamond in this volume). Similarly, actor Matt Damon advocates for water delivery and sanitation through his organization water.org. Celebrity-led organizations have the potential to invigorate the democratic process by using a celebrity figure's mass appeal to translate the complexity of international aid and development initiatives for both public and elite audiences.

But celebrity-led organizations reflect a post-democratic environment by enabling the celebrity humanitarian to benefit from elite networks to secure funding, guidance, and political access. This access and influence is bestowed on a person whose issue area is unrelated to their occupation as actor or entertainer. For example, after years of working on behalf of the Jubilee 2000 campaign, Bono established DATA (Debt, AIDS, Trade Africa). He did so with start-up funding from the Bill & Melinda Gates Foundation and the financier George Soros. Philanthropists appear eager to fund these celebrity enterprises while political elites offer early endorsements and invitations to enter decision-making processes. As a reinforcement of elite politics, any celebrity inclusion in national and global governance venues is regarded as a means to build popular legitimacy for politicians, not celebrities, but herein lies the rub; Brockington (2014, p. 8) reminds us that celebrities are "members of those elites" with the mixed task of speaking "for the people" while also being used by the political and financial elites to speak on their behalf to the people. If, as Brockington (2014, p. 8) underscores, "celebrity advocacy matters because it is a means of speaking to power," then whose power is being reflected: that of the people who raised the celebrity to his/her position or that of the elites that give the celebrity a platform for making mass appeals?

The case of Affleck demonstrates the particularities of the US political context, where celebrities have engaged with democratic processes. Congressional hearings are considered a prime space of influence for interest groups, ahead of letter-writing campaigns or electoral contributions (Demaine 2009, p. 88). For advocacy groups, congressional hearings have become popular vehicles for media and public attention although coverage and influence is often over-estimated (Thrall et al. 2008, p. 375). Within the US an increasing number of celebrities have participated in social and political advocacy by addressing a congressional hearing before committees of the Senate or House of Representatives. Over 500 celebrities have testified before Congress, with the frequency of appearances doubling after 1980 to about twenty a year (Thrall et al. 2008, p. 374). Most celebrity appearances have taken place before committees dealing with domestic issues: less than 5 percent of celebrity witnesses testified before committees dealing with foreign relations (Senate) or international relations and foreign affairs (House) (Demaine 2009, pp. 141–3). While Affleck is among a large group of celebrities to testify before Congress, his appearances on behalf of humanitarian issues in the DRC stands apart.

To a large extent, congressional appearances by a celebrity assure the transparent nature of democratic processes and the possibilities for popular input. Appearing as a witness involves the delivery of oral and written statements, a question and answer period, reports and exhibits as well as other correspondence and materials. The entire transcript is then made public. Congressional hearings are also sites for assessing accountability, offering insight into the thinking of congressional representatives and, through debate, the inactions and missteps of the US government are brought to light. But the ways in which a celebrity is invited to appear before Congress deserve scrutiny. The extensive and costly network of lobbyists and special interests behind celebrity humanitarians like Affleck challenges the integrity of democratic processes by positioning the advocacy and issues of select individuals favorably. The next sections closely explore the case of Ben Affleck and the ECI as a celebrity-led NGO that exemplifies the relationship between elite networks and public accountability.

Methodology

The case study is built upon a content analysis of the activities, finances, and communications of Ben Affleck and ECI. I examined the coverage of Affleck in mainstream media between 2007 and 2014. Affleck has explained his own motivations and agenda for ECI in editorial writings, short documentaries available on YouTube, and statements delivered to Congress. Charting ECI involved a review of its website, organization materials, tax returns, and annual reports. Congressional records furnished some of the information regarding ECI's lobbying activities. ECI was created by the strategic consulting firm williamsworks, which has published information about its client. However, publicly-available information about ECI's grant-making, elite supporters, and operational expenditures was limited. This was further complicated by the fact that ECI uses a third-party fiscal sponsor to make the most of its fiscal outlays. Deductions into the elite network behind ECI are drawn through williamsworks testimonials as well as Internet searches. Indeed, the lack of information about ECI serves my argument about the absence of accountability obtainable for a celebrity-led NGO and its mediation of North–South relations. From the body of material available, I drew a purposive sample to demonstrate how the establishment and activities of Affleck and ECI signal a post-democratic context.

Affleck takes up the cause of eastern Congo

By 2006 Hollywood actor and director Ben Affleck had become linked to over a dozen domestic and international charities and NGOs.[4] In 2008 Affleck began suggesting that fundraising alone, in particular around Africa, was insufficient and potentially counterproductive. While attending a charity event, Affleck remarked that fundraising in the West discounted the efforts of would-be recipients in Africa to formulate their own solutions: "I think sometimes that gets out the message disproportionately that this is a place just full of misery and awfulness and suffering and it does a disservice in a way to 800 million people on a continent."[5] At around the same time, Affleck chose to focus his energies on the DRC, which was motivated, in part, by the excess attention given to the situation in Darfur; he reasoned, "I thought a lot of people are advocating on Darfur. I'd just be a very small log on a big fire. I started getting interested in Congo and I thought, this is a place where I can have a really big impact."[6] Here, Affleck exhibits his confidence in his celebrity status and the potential to make a difference pursuing his own agenda.

Affleck embarked on a series of steps to build expertise, reading widely and paying frequent visits to the DRC. During his nine trips to eastern Congo, he visited refugee and IDP camps, hospitals, and gold mines. He describes meeting with "warlords and peacemakers, survivors and aid workers."[7] It appears that many of Affleck's site visits were coordinated by the United Nations. This self-education took place in the public eye; ABC News accompanied Affleck on his third fact-finding mission, and he penned an essay for the network's website with reflections on the constraints and possibilities of his engagement. Anticipating criticisms of his commitment, Affleck wrote:

FIGURE 6.1   Ben Affleck (second from right), actor from the United States, with members of the United Nations Mission in Democratic Republic of Congo (MONUC) Press and Information Office (PIO), and the Disarmament, Demobilization, Rehabilitation and Reintegration (DDRR) office, during a sensitization campaign targeting the Democratic Liberation Forces of Rwanda (FDLR) based in the east of the country. UN Photo/Marie Frechon.

It makes sense to be skeptical about celebrity activism. There is always the suspicion that involvement with a cause may be doing more good for the spokesman than he or she is doing for the cause. I welcome any questions about me and my involvement, but I hope you can separate whatever reservations you may have from what is unimpeachably important about this segment: the plight of eastern Congo.[8]

In this statement, Affleck displays recognition of the troubled category of celebrity humanitarianism by attempting to deflect attention away from his celebrity background. This includes redirecting any suggestions that Affleck's efforts are self-serving. To build his credibility as a development specialist, Affleck shows off his local knowledge and connections, naming local groups and international organizations involved in the region. He regularly cites statistical data from the UN and the International Rescue Committee in his presentations. In his writings Affleck also demonstrates belief that his celebrity status has the potential to make an impact on the DRC. As we will see, while Affleck engaged in a public exercise of educating himself as a seeming "freelancer," there were powerful actors working behind the scenes to direct his activities and amass elite endorsement.

Williamsworks and Affleck co-found an organization

Affleck's decision to form an organization, and the manner in which ECI came into being, reflect the post-democratic context of elite concentration of power. Despite the existence of other NGOs and campaigns addressing social and economic development in the DRC – such as Friends of Congo and Raise Hope for Congo – Affleck sought his own organization that would benefit from his celebrity status.[9] This act ignores Congolese efforts and past experiences in order to forge a unique approach. ECI was crafted not from inside the eastern Congo, but in the offices of a strategic advisory firm based in Seattle, Washington State. Established in 2004, the firm williamsworks boasts impressive political connections and financial ties. The CEO and founder, Whitney Williams, worked for then US First Lady Hillary Clinton. Her mother served in the Montana State Senate and her father was a congressman for nine terms. Fees per year run in the hundreds of thousands of dollars.

Williamsworks appears to both work for and draw upon its client base, a collection of select individuals. Their website proudly proclaims: "williamsworks was founded on the belief that we can improve countless lives by partnering with extraordinary people."[10] Williamsworks advises foundations led by prominent philanthropists and politicians, including the Bill & Melinda Gates Foundation (Bill Gates was the founder of Microsoft) and the Bill, Hillary, and Chelsea Clinton Foundation (Bill Clinton is the former US president; Hillary Clinton is a former Senator and Secretary of State and candidate for the 2016 Democratic presidential nomination). They also consult for nonprofit organizations and corporations like Google.org, Nike Foundation, and TOMS Shoes. Within the marketplace for strategic consulting, williamsworks has built a sturdy reputation in its decade of operation. The firm consults for other celebrity-led organizations like ONE, led by the musician Bono, and Water.org, co-founded by Affleck's childhood friend and actor Matt Damon. Indeed, it was Bono who introduced Affleck to williamsworks.[11] This network of US political and philanthropic elites along with corporate entities forms the foundation for Affleck's advocacy and ECI's activities.

Williamsworks' mission and strategies are firmly rooted in the practice of post-democratic politics with its emphasis on elite clients and contacts. They describe their advocacy in these terms:

> We leverage our extensive network to forge partnerships and influence public policy and public awareness. The most effective strategy often depends on getting your message in front of *key individuals who are in a position to act* – with their wallets, their voices or their votes. We have a keen understanding of how public policy is implemented throughout much of the world, and we are proud to engage our network in the name of real results.[12] (emphasis added)

Public policy does not appear to demand a "public" but rather lobbying of "key individuals" who flex financial or political power with their wallets or votes.

Celebrity humanitarians themselves are "elites", key individuals who also become valuable levers that can deliver messages (advocate) to other key individuals. Efficacy is obtained through the strategic use of alliances across politicians, philanthropists, businessmen, and celebrities.

Starting in 2007, williamsworks began the background research towards developing ECI. They take credit for providing ECI with a "creative, rigorous approach, strategic organizational design, extensive networks, expert staffing, advocacy and communications skills, and ability to execute both domestically and on a global stage."[13] The "extensive networks" were drawn in part from williamsworks' own staff and client base. For example, the CEO Whitney Williams is listed as a co-founder of ECI and vice-chair of its board. Williamsworks itself became a donor along with its client Google.org.[14] Similarly, prominent philanthropist Howard G. Buffett (son of business magnate and philanthropist Warren Buffett) is both a donor and a member of ECI's board of directors. More recently, ECI has linked up with the Clinton Global Initiative (another williamsworks client) and the Harvard Humanitarian Initiative.[15] Within the US context, elite networks around humanitarianism appear to overlap and reinforce one another through financial and political ties.

Launching ECI

In March 2010 the ECI was launched as, "the first US based advocacy and grant-making initiative wholly focused on working with and for the people of eastern Congo."[16] The two-pronged approach of ECI straddles political and humanitarian objectives across its two sites of activity: the US and eastern Congo. Here, ECI falls in line with other observers and experts that regard the eastern province as distinct from the West, based on its endemic violence. Critically, Affleck and ECI mediate between the North and its site of Southern activity.

While offering itself as a public charity, there is a general absence of the public on the ECI website for both its advocacy and grant-making activities. The website has no place for the public to get involved in the organization, nor are there any of the usual action tools provided by other advocacy organizations: petitions, talking points, or appeals to call your congressperson. Besides sections furnishing information on the DRC and a simple contact request form, the website offers no interaction. The media offerings are modest: there are the usual features for sharing on social media, a Facebook page, and a Twitter account. In the post-democratic mode, ECI is not seeking to mobilize a mass audience and instead focuses on Affleck as celebrity humanitarian to engage in advocacy on behalf of the public.

There is also little need for fundraising among the public to support ECI's organization and grant-making activities. Through ECI's website it is possible to donate to one of six campaigns with target amounts ranging from US$2,000 (for girls' education) to US$50,000 (for building safe communities). But overall, the impression one gets is that ECI is not relying on a public audience for funding its grant-making activities.

It seems that ECI's access to philanthropists precludes the need for larger fundraising schemes. As a celebrity-led organization with access to williamworks' client base, ECI began an unusually firm financial footing. A multi-million dollar fund was raised from donors who are listed as "investors." These include Lauren Powell Jobs (wife of Apple founder Steve Jobs) and Cindy Hensley McCain (wife of Republican presidential candidate John McCain; she is also described as a co-founder); and the charitable foundation Humanity United (in turn funded by Pierre Omidyar, founder of eBay). These ample funds were collected before ECI had commenced operations, evaluated its programs, and demonstrated effectiveness in the field. In comparison, consider that the DC-based Congo organizations Friends of the Congo and Congo Global Action, Inc. had $66,000 and $50,000 in contributions for 2010, respectively.[17] In 2012 ECI reported contributions and grants amounting to over US $1.8 million.[18]

Meanwhile, the full extent of ECI's finances and its expenditures are unavailable due to the use of a fiscal sponsor. As a registered 501(c)3 nonprofit organization, ECI is considered a public charity as compared to a private foundation.[19] While ECI is incorporated as its own organization, it is managed by the New Venture Fund, itself a 501(c)(3) public charity. The New Venture Fund serves as a fiscal sponsor to ECI, coordinating collaborations with donors and small grant programs.[20] With the use of a fiscal sponsor, it is difficult to track exactly how much ECI is spending on its activities and programs since expenditures are lumped together with the Fund's other activities. The lack of transparency in its financing further reinforces the elite and top-down nature of ECI and Affleck's work. ECI's establishment and operational structure demonstrate how celebrity-led organizations reflect post-democratic politics, based on a private entwining of political and financial interests.

Within a year of its founding, ECI was highlighted by the Chronicle of Philanthropy as "an example of a smart approach."[21] In addition to glowing compliments bestowed by former Secretary of State Hillary Clinton, Affleck was recently awarded the Global Child Advocate Award by the humanitarian agency Save the Children.[22] These endorsements come quite soon after ECI's launch, before its program objectives have been tested and evaluated, suggesting the ability of a celebrity-led organization to transcend "normal" processes of evaluation.

Eastern Congo Initiative mediates between North and South

With costly expert advice, ample funds, and high-level endorsements, it is little surprise that Affleck and ECI gained traction quickly in the political world of Washington DC. ECI engages in advocacy that is centered on shaping foreign policymaking in the US. Positioning itself as a political player in Washington DC, ECI has commissioned White Papers (position papers that document an issue and suggest policy), forged partnerships with government agencies, and sent representatives to testify on Capitol Hill. This advocacy is driven by lobbying of political and philanthropic circles related to humanitarianism and security in the DRC.

To demonstrate, Affleck works extensively with Cindy McCain, businesswoman and wife of former presidential candidate and US Senator, John McCain, whose financial wealth and political ties place her firmly among the elite. Described as "a political odd couple," Affleck and McCain traveled to eastern Congo together, appeared on Capitol Hill to testify before a Senate committee and made the rounds of the news outlets. Affleck has also forged public friendships with other philanthropists and politicians.

The most visible and newsworthy of Affleck's political activities have been invitations to testify before Congress. Within the space of three years Affleck has addressed the House Subcommittee on Africa, Global Health and Human Rights, the House Armed Services Committee, and the Senate's Foreign Relations Committee. That he has spoken before three committees in the two bodies of the US legislature demonstrates the impact of ECI's lobbying efforts. While most other celebrity witnesses speak on domestic issues, Affleck has moved celebrity humanitarianism into the realm of international relations, giving his thoughts about security and the role of the US government in the DRC. Other speakers sitting alongside Affleck have included the US Special Envoy, diplomats, academics, development experts, and other DRC advocates.

Affleck's appearances are not due solely to his status as a celebrity humanitarian, or to ECI's programmatic achievements, but instead are likely the result of lobbying that is coordinated by williamsworks. ECI's fiscal sponsor, New Project Venture, contracts with K&L Gates LLP, a Washington-based international law firm with over $1 billion in yearly revenue.[23] Through lobbying disclosure forms that are filed quarterly, it is possible to learn the amount paid to a lobbyist, issue area, specific issues, and the main branches and agencies targeted.[24] We can determine that the lobbyist K&L Gates lists the New Venture Fund as the client but describes its issues as, "work with the Eastern Congo Initiative."[25] In the three years for which reports were available, K&L Gates earned over $300,000 for its lobbying activities for ECI.[26] Up to 16 employees served as lobbyists for ECI in a given quarter. These lobbyists included former congressmen and government aides. Lobbying reports listed as targets: both Houses of Congress, the US Department of State, the White House, and the USAID.[27] These reports reveal a vast and intricate lobbying campaign targeting multiple political elites to build influence for ECI and its policy proposals.

Besides Affleck's appearances before Congress, ECI has also taken on a leadership role in educating elites in the US by organizing trips for US politicians and philanthropists. In 2012 Affleck personally led a delegation to the DRC that included Howard G. Buffet, Washington Post opinion writer Michael Gerson, USAID representative Eric Naranjo, CBS *This Morning* news correspondent Seth Doane, and Scott Terry, CEO of Tempus Jets.[28] In August 2013, at the invitation of the ECI, the largest ever delegation of US senators traveled to the DRC.[29] ECI's annual report recounted that the politicians met with officials from the UN and the armed forces of the Democratic Republic of Congo (FARDC) and saw "firsthand the remarkable progress of ECI's grantees."[30] In December US Congressman Adam Smith, a Democratic House representative from Washington State (where williamsworks is located), made a five-day trip at a cost of nearly $15,000.

These trips demonstrate the deep ties forged with elites in the US and also show the ways in which ECI mediates US foreign policy towards the DRC. The overall picture gained from the US officials' experience in eastern Congo is circumscribed – a quick survey of the country led by ECI. These visits are not diplomatic meetings with state officials; rather, they are characterized by a focus on the DRC civil society sector. There are some meetings with political officials but the emphasis, drawn from ECI's own work, is on community-based organizations. While political elites in the US are regarded as powerful actors, ECI feels otherwise about the political sphere in the DRC. These visits from the North are without reciprocation – there is no report of Congolese officials traveling to the US to meet their counterparts or lobby for themselves. Media coverage of these trips is also limited.

Grant-making in the South

Through its lobbying, policy proposals and delegation visits, ECI is shaping the North's understanding of the eastern Congo. But through its grant-making, ECI is also influencing how philanthropists and other funding bodies spend their money. For ECI, funding priorities alight on "local, community-based approaches [as] the key to creating a successful society in eastern Congo."[31] ECI's position is not unfamiliar; this strategy is in line with a strategic document drafted by Congolese authorities along with World Bank experts that regards improving access to social services and building community development as priorities.[32] Affleck reinforces this creed: "There are big NGOs that I think do very good work, but when I did research around Congo and other countries, what I saw, what I found, was that the people doing the best work, with the real expertise, who understood what was needed intuitively, just like they would in my neighborhood, who knew who the guy was to talk to, were community-based organizations."[33] Thus, ECI gives grants but claims not to be a direct implementer; "rather we work with Congolese-led organizations to effectively execute locally driven projects."[34] ECI states that its support for social and economic development is undertaken "in a country with historically weak state institutions and virtually nonexistent public services."[35] Again, focus is on supporting the civil society sector, leaving aside the political sphere. One might ask why the civil society sector in the US domestic context appears to remain outside the scope of engagement of ECI.

To determine its grantees and direct the funding priorities of the Global North, ECI has created a database. In partnership with United States Agency for International Development (USAID), ECI conducted a Landscape Analysis of community-based organizations working in the DRC. The report is available as an online, searchable database that "gives policy leaders, investors, and analysts much-needed insight into the workings and nature of work being done to create a sustainable and successful society in eastern Congo."[36] A video about the partnership is available on YouTube and it describes ECI's work in finding "local solutions to local problems."[37] USAID Global Partnerships Division Director Christopher Jurgens explains the rationale: "Through the database and the landscape analysis,

USAID and ECI have laid the groundwork for augmenting foreign assistance in eastern Congo."[38] According to its website, ECI supports 23 Congolese organizations with small grants dispersed by both ECI and the New Venture Fund.[39] ECI is deciding which organizations are eligible to receive direct support and external funding. Nor were any of the granting amounts substantial, in comparison to the hundreds of thousands of dollars spent on lobbying US political circles.

In contract to its entrenchment in US political and philanthropic circles, ECI recommends avoiding similar entities as funding sites in the DRC. In its recommendations the full report of the Landscape Analysis notes, "Funders could also assess the extent to which current patterns of assistance *directly or indirectly support elite networks* that perpetuate instability and *concentrate power and wealth in the hands of a few*" (my italics).[40] Meanwhile, the authority of the report itself is also suspect, due to a lengthy disclaimer included at the beginning of the report which states that the report should not be considered "an endorsement of the organizations described herein," and that neither does it reflect "the views of ECI, its affiliates, or organizations." Additionally, the report does not have the imprimatur of its funder: "This report does not reflect the position or opinions of USAID or the United States Government."[41] As a product of the ECI's independently conducted research, the report does not appear to be the result of consultative practices, or to offer accountability for the content of its findings. Elite networks are appropriate for establishing ECI and supporting its efforts but not in environments like the DRC.

Conclusion

As this chapter has shown, Affleck has expanded the scope of celebrity humanitarianism by establishing his own organization. The particularities of Affleck's "founder's story" as a client of williamsworks suggests a brand of US elite politics where access and influence are the result of elite networks and generous donors. With the ECI as a platform, Affleck gained a platform to promote a unique vision around social and economic development in eastern Congo. The organization raised his credibility, paid for lobbyists, and assured his access to human rights and development circles in the US. While Affleck's status as a celebrity is undoubtedly based on his public appeal and fame, his work as a humanitarian relies on elite consultants and philanthropic supporters. Unlike the public awareness raising of earlier celebrity figures, Affleck's efforts are directed towards a new audience of elite decision-makers and funders in order to shape the North's understanding and approach to the DRC.

Interestingly, Affleck's status as a celebrity abnegates the need for accountability from publics in both the North and South. Rather than join up with another organization, Affleck established his own, an act of entrepreneurship that permits him to play by a different set of rules. In contrast, were he to appear for a host NGO, they would set the terms of his engagement, promote their own mission, and file reports on his activities. Affleck carved out a platform and space to pursue a unique vision for eastern Congo. Yet this vision is untested by traditional means of development delivery, evaluation, and demonstrated efficiency. ECI started with ample funding and political endorsements before making its first grants; Affleck's invitations to address Congress resulted from assiduous lobbying by an international law firm. Affleck's presence muscles out the voices of other Congolese NGOs based in Washington DC, who most likely cannot afford lobbyist fees and therefore do not enjoy such high-level access in US politics.

With his own organization and private backing, Affleck does not have the mass advocacy features to help ECI build influence and raise money. Affleck and ECI rely on endorsements from elite circles rather than bestowed by an adoring public. Nor does ECI engage in significant awareness raising and education around the DRC and its activities. Affleck is playing an elite political game; airing his views at Congressional hearings does not constitute public input or deliberation. As a celebrity humanitarian, Affleck is not accountable to the US public, even less so to the Congolese public. Top-down political processes ensure that American elites decide when and how select individuals are included and supported.

Directed towards political elites, Affleck's statements have the potential to influence foreign policy and financial assistance to the DRC. Celebrities may gain their fame through popular appeal but do not shape their humanitarianism or policy proposals based on public input and deliberation. The DRC remains a recipient of aid, with ECI dictating who should be funded without public deliberation. Political and elite support is absent in the DRC in favor of local community-based organizations. Should projects fail or policies prove miscalculated, Affleck does not lose his job in the next election cycle. Nor would ECI lose its funding from wealthy US sources. Overall, Affleck and ECI reflect a particular set of North–South power relations that are based in a post-democratic context that sustains the elite management of humanitarianism.

Notes

1 United Nations Development Programme 2013, *2013 Human Development Report*. Available at https://data.undp.org/dataset/able-1-Human-Development-Index-and-its-components/wxub-qc5k [accessed on May 30, 2014].
2 International Rescue Committee 2008, *Mortality in the Democratic Republic of Congo: an ongoing crisis*. Available at http://reliefweb.int/report/democratic-republic-congo/mortality-democratic-republic-congo-ongoing-crisis [accessed on October 29, 2014].
3 Boustany, N. 2007. Hollywood stars find an audience for social causes. *The Washington Post*, June 10.
4 Look to the Stars. n.d. *Ben Affleck charity work, events and causes*. Available at http://www.looktothestars.org/celebrity/ben-affleck [accessed on November 26, 2012].
5 OneXOne. n.d. Website. Available at http://www.onexone.org/index.php [accessed on November 26, 2012].
6 Associated Press, 2008. Ben Affleck visits refugee camps in Congo. *The New Zealand Herald*, November 21.
7 B. Affleck. 2008. Turning world's eyes and ears to Congo. *ACB News*, November 26. Available at http://abcnews.go.com/Nightline/story?id=5234555&page=1 [accessed on January 21, 2013].

8 B. Affleck. 2008. Turning world's eyes and ears to Congo. *ACB News* [online]. Available at http://abcnews.go.com/Nightline/story?id=5234555&page=1 [accessed on May 11, 2015].

9 See http://www.friendsofthecongo.org/ and http://www.raisehopeforcongo.org/ [accessed on November 17, 2014].

10 Williamsworks. 2014. Williamsworks turns ten. Available at http://williamsworks.com/news/williamsworks-turns-ten/ [accessed on October 29, 2014].

11 Rapkin, M. 2013. When Ben Affleck wants to change the world, he calls this woman. *Elle*, November 11. Available at http://www.elle.com/life-love/society-career/whitney-williams-profile [accessed on October 29, 2014].

12 Williamsworks. n.d. Practice Areas. Available at http://williamsworks.com/practice-areas/ [accessed on October 29, 2014].

13 Eastern Congo Initiative. n.d. Website. Available at http://www.easterncongo.org/ [accessed on January 21, 2013].

14 Eastern Congo Initiative. n.d. Website.

15 Eastern Congo Initiative. 2013. *Annual Report 2013*. Available at http://www.eastern congo.org/assets/pdf/Eastern_Congo_Initiative_2013_Annual_Report.pdf [accessed on October 29, 2014].

16 Eastern Congo Initiative. n.d. Website.

17 See GuideStar. n.d. Available at http://www.guidestar.org/ [accessed on October 29, 2014].

18 See Eastern Congo Initiative. 2012. Eastern Congo Initiative Forms 990 and Docs. Available from GuideStar at http://www.guidestar.org/organizations/45-4103655/eastern-congo-initiative.aspx [accessed on November 10, 2014].

19 In the US, nonprofit organizations must incorporate themselves with the Internal Revenue Service (IRS), the US tax authority, in order to secure a tax-exempt status. Nonprofits may receive unlimited contributions, but are not required to reveal their funding sources. However, they do have the responsibility to maintain a board of directors, corporate records, and make public expenditures and activities. At this writing, no tax information or list of board of directors is available on the ECI website. Guidestar, which collects publicly available IRS information on registered nonprofits, has one IRS Form 990 for ECI from 2012. The 990 form is typically filed annually with the US Federal Government and reports on finances and operations.

20 In addition, as a 501 (c) (3), ECI is not supposed to influence legislation to any "substantial degree"; lobbying is permitted but limited by amount based on income. See IRS n.d. Exemption Requirements – 501 (c) (3) Organizations. Available at http://www.irs.gov/Charities-&-Non-Profits/Charitable-Organizations/Exemption-Requirements-Section-501%28c%29%283%29-Organizations [accessed on October 29, 2014].

21 C. Preston. 2011. Behind a celebrity's bid to help eastern Congo. *The Chronicle of Philanthropy*, April 20. Available at http://philanthropy.com/blogs/conference/behind-a-celebritys-bid-to-help-eastern-congo/27994 [accessed on November 26, 2012].

22 TV News Desk. 2014. Jennifer Garner, Ben Affleck & more set for 2nd annual Save the Children gala, *tvworld.com*, 15 October. Available at http://www.broadwayworld.com/bwwtv/article/Jennifer-Garner-Ben-Affleck-More-Set-for-2nd-Annual-Save-the-Children-Gala-20141015# [accessed on November 10, 2014].

23 See K&L Gates. n.d. *A guide to political and lobbying activities*. Available at http://www.klgates.com/a-guide-to-political-and-lobbying-activities/ as well as http://www.klgates.com/aboutus/financials/ [accessed on October 29, 2014].

24 Between 2010 and 2012, K&L Gates submitted lobbying reports in accordance with the Lobbying Disclosure Act of 1995 (Section 5). Available at http://disclosures.house.gov/ld/ldsearch.aspx [accessed on October 29, 2014].

25 Clerk of House of Representatives. 2010. Lobbying Registration filed by Organization K&L Gates LLP on behalf of Client New Venture Fund 11/19/2010. Available at http://disclosures.house.gov/ld/ldsearch.aspx [accessed on October 29, 2014].

26 See OpenSecrets.org. n.d. New Venture Fund. Available at http://www.opensecrets.org/lobby/clientsum.php?id=D000064955&year=2012 [accessed on October 29, 2014].

27 In the area of foreign policy, the lobbying issues were listed in varying formulations; one cited "work with Eastern Congo Initiative project to raise awareness regarding US programmatic and funding policy related to Democratic Republic of Congo." Later reports were more detailed, listing pieces of legislation such as Appropriations, specifying "funding for development assistance," or the Defense Authorization Act, specifying "programmatic support."

28 Congo Initiative. n.d. Delegation from Eastern Congo Initiative visits UCBC. Available at http://www.congoinitiative.org/view.cfm?page_id=206 [accessed on November 12, 2014].

29 The delegation was led by Senators Lindsey Graham, the ranking Republican on the Appropriations Subcommittee for State and Foreign Operations, and included Senators Saxby Chambliss, Roy Blunt, John Thune, Mike Johanns and John Barrasso.

30 See Eastern Congo Initiative's *Annual Report 2013*. The delegation visited Goma and attended a briefing by the head of the MONUSCO peacekeeping force. ECI reported that the delegation "discussed the roles that the US and other UN Member States can play in the UN-sponsored Framework for Peace." They also met with the Vice Governor of North Kivu, a notable inclusion of a local politician, and visited ECI grantee Mutaani FM Radio station. *Annual Report 2013* is available for download on the organization's website, http://www.easterncongo.org/ [accessed on November 10, 2014] (p. 7).

31 Eastern Congo Initiative. n.d. "What We Do." Available at http://www.easterncongo.org/about/grantmaking [accessed on October 29, 2014].

32 See, for example, République Démocratique du Congo. *Document de Stratégie de la Croissance et de la Réduction de la Pauvreté*. DSRP-I. Kinshasa, June 2006.

33 T. Murphy. 2013. Want to help Congolese? Give them money – directly, says Ben Affleck. *The Christian Science Monitor*, August 23, 2013. Available at http://www.csmonitor.com/World/Africa/Africa-Monitor/2013/0823/Want-to-help-Congolese-Give-them-money-directly-says-Ben-Affleck [accessed on November 12, 2014].

34 Eastern Congo Initiative. n.d. Grantmaking. Available at http://www.easterncongo.org/about/grantmaking [accessed on October 29, 2014].

35 Eastern Congo Initiative, n.d. Grantmaking: The resurgence of CBOs in eastern Congo. Available at http://www.easterncongo.org/about/grantmaking [accessed on October 29, 2014].

36 Eastern Congo Initiative. n.d. CBO Landscape Analysis Report. Available at http://www.easterncongo.org/about/publications/landscape-analysis [accessed on October 29, 2014].

37 Eastern Congo Initiative. 2013. *USAID and Eastern Congo Initiative partner to conduct landscape analysis of CBOs in DRC*. Available at https://www.youtube.com/watch?v=xJve9XVHWVE [accessed on October 29, 2014].

38 T. Murphy. 2013. Want to help Congolese? Give them money – directly. Says Ben Affleck. *The Christian Science* Monitor. Available at http://www.csmonitor.com/World/Africa/Africa-Monitor/2013/0823/Want-to-help-Congolese-Give-them-money-directly-says-Ben-Affleck [accessed on October 29, 2014].

39 See Eastern Congo Initiative. 2012. Eastern Congo Initiative Forms 990 and Docs or New Venture Fund, 2012. New Venture Fund Form 990 and Docs. Available at http://www.guidestar.org/ [accessed on December 20, 2014].

40 Eastern Congo Initiative, 2011. *Community-based Organization (CBO) Landscape Analysis (Full Report).* p. 11. Available at http://www.easterncongo.org/about/publications/land scape-analysis [accessed on October 29, 2014].
41 Eastern Congo Initiative. 2011. *Community-based Organization (CBO) Landscape Analysis (Full Report).* p. 2.

References

Autesserre, S. 2012. Dangerous tales: dominant narratives on the Congo and their unintended consequences. *African Affairs*, 111 (443), 202–22.

Brockington, D. 2014. *Celebrity Advocacy and International Development.* London and New York: Routledge.

Cooper, A.F. 2008. *Celebrity Diplomacy.* Boulder: Paradigm Publishers.

Crouch, C. 2004. *Post-Democracy.* Cambridge: Polity.

Demaine, L.J. 2009. Navigating policy by the stars: the influence of celebrity entertainers on federal lawmaking. *Journal of Law & Politics*, 25 (2), 83–143.

Eichstaedt, P.H. 2011. *Consuming the Congo: War and Conflict Minerals in the World's Deadliest Place.* Chicago: Lawrence Hill Books.

Goodman, M.K. & Barnes, C. 2011. Star/poverty space: the making of the "development celebrity." *Celebrity Studies*, 2 (1), 69–85.

Hawkins, V. 2011. Creating a groundswell or getting on the bandwagon? Celebrities, the media, and distant conflict. In L. Tsaliki, C.A. Frangonikolopoulos & A. Huliaras (eds), *Transnational Celebrity Activism in Global Politics: Changing the World?* Bristol: Intellect, pp. 85–104.

Huliaras, A. & Tzifakis, N. 2010. Celebrity activism in international relations: in search of a framework for analysis. *Global Society*, 24 (2), 255–74.

Kapoor, I. 2013. *Celebrity Humanitarianism: Ideology of Global Charity.* New York: Routledge.

Paddon, E. 2010. Beyond creed, greed and booty: conflict in the Democratic Republic of Congo, review article. *Africa: The Journal of the International African Institute*, 80 (2), 322–31.

Prunier, G. 2010. *Africa's World War: Congo, The Rwandan Genocide, and the Making of a Continental Catastrophe.* Oxford: Oxford University Press.

Richey, L.A. & Ponte, S. 2011. *Brand Aid: Shopping Well to Save the World.* Minneapolis: University of Minnesota Press.

Street, J. 2012. Do celebrity politics and celebrity politicians matter? *The British Journal of Politics & International Relations*, 14 (3), 346–56.

Thrall, A.T., Lollio-Fakhreddine, J., Berent, J., Donnelly, L., Herrin, W., Paquette, Z., Wenglinski, R. & Wyatt, A. 2008. Star power: Celebrity advocacy and the evolution of the public sphere. *The International Journal of Press/Politics*, 13 (4) (October), 362–85.

Wheeler, M. 2013. *Celebrity Politics.* Cambridge: Polity.

7

HUMANITARIAN RELIEF WORKER SEAN PENN

A contextual story

Annika Bergman Rosamond

I have a little money in my pocket, but I've never been able to do any good with it . . . I've failed at supporting causes with my celebrity. The only positive change that I've ever been able to affect is by getting my own hands dirty in New Orleans.[1]

Introduction

The humanitarianism of Hollywood A-list actor Sean Penn is grounded in a wish to promote the well-being of humanity at large rather than the members of American society alone. A central argument within cosmopolitan international theory is that the human rights of citizens and non-citizens should concern us in equal measure. If we align ourselves with this position we need to consider the cosmopolitan-inspired acts of individuals who seek to further a fairer international society. There is a growing interest in exploring the structure and workings of celebrity humanitarianism and individual stars' advocacy of global justice (Cooper 2008; Brockington 2009, 2014; Kapoor 2013; Chouliaraki 2013; Richey & Ponte 2011, 2008). This chapter focuses on Sean Penn's hands-on approach to humanitarian work and his criticisms of domestic and global poverty, military intervention and structured violence. It argues that his humanitarianism is couched within radical politics and cosmopolitanism. Penn has been willing to break the rules of what is considered appropriate celebrity behavior by criticizing his and other governments' practices. Thus, Penn's activism challenges structural readings of celebrity humanitarianism, which broadly situate it within exploitative capitalist relations and injustices rather than progressive politics (Kapoor 2013). Indeed, an assessment of Penn's humanitarianism can shed light on individual celebrities' involvement in the *actual* conduct of politics, which remains an under-researched area of celebrity studies (Street 2012, pp. 3–4).

Contextually the analysis focuses on Penn's efforts to assist the victims of both Hurricane Katrina in New Orleans in 2005 and the Haitian earthquake in 2010. The two contexts are linked through historical experiences, cultural heritage and embedded practices of racism. Both provide insight into Penn's dual commitment to justice within and beyond US borders. More specifically, my study of Penn's humanitarianism seeks to make three contributions to the wider objectives of this edited volume. First, Penn's activism points to the centrality of assessing celebrity humanitarianism across contexts. The analysis below shows that Penn's commitment to suffering distant others is couched within a consistent ethical value set. Moreover, by locating the analysis within two geographical contexts we can learn more about the ways in which celebrity images and messages are localized in one context, and are then transported into another one.

Second, Penn's efforts to apply himself to humanitarian disaster work across contexts can illustrate the role of actual human agents in seeking to transform global politics in a more equitable and peaceful direction. His story can also bring attention to the practices and discourses of radical celebrity politics grounded in a dual commitment to cosmopolitan values and loyalty to one's own state. Third, Penn's use of his celebrity to offer protection to distant others offers an opportunity to unpack the gendered power relations that surround celebrity politics and popular culture by identifying his situatedness within a context of male privilege (Shepherd 2013).

Structure

I commence by introducing briefly the contexts of New Orleans and Haiti. I then locate the discussion of celebrity activism within wider cosmopolitan international relations (IR) debates. I contend that cosmopolitanism is a fruitful basis for thinking through actual people's ethical contributions to international society. Celebrity studies in turn can substantiate cosmopolitan scholarship by zooming in on the "other-regarding" acts and discourses of individuals in global society. I also argue that Penn's humanitarian story offers insights into the conduct of progressive celebrity politics. Yet, I contend that there are aspects of celebrity humanitarianism that need to be ethically evaluated, in particular the ethical choices that celebrities make in choosing to promote one issue but not another.

This is followed by a discussion of methodology and discourse analysis. I go on to offer a broad discursive analysis of media texts collected from online editions of magazines and newspapers. Through an online ethnography (Bergman Rosamond & Gregoratti 2014) the chapter investigates Penn's self-reflections and those of media in the construction of his relief story. A key analytical question is the extent to which Penn's critical interventions reflect cosmopolitan values and progressive politics and/or his privileged position within gendered power relations. I then provide a historical and political overview of New Orleans, so as to set the scene for the analysis of Sean Penn's rescue work post-Hurricane Katrina. I go on to focus on the distinctiveness of the Haitian context and Penn's commitment to the island. Similarities and significant variations are identified across the two contexts. The conclusion revisits the key contributions of the chapter.

Context

This chapter studies Sean Penn's engagements across two rather different geographical settings. Haiti is a sovereign state located in the global South and New Orleans an urban space situated in the global North. Yet, as Bell notes:[2]

> New Orleans and Haiti were profoundly connected long before their dual disasters. Nowhere else in the US has a longer, deeper relationship with Haiti than New Orleans. Their histories crisscross: Both suffered colonization and enslavement by the Spanish and French . . . they have similar cultures.

New Orleans does not suffer from Haitian levels of abject poverty. Yet the city is characterized by both social inequality and racial discrimination. Haiti is a republic with a proud history rooted in its founding in the context of a slave uprising. However, it is troubled by colonial legacies, poverty and a history of military coups and brutal governments. In different ways Haiti and New Orleans have given Sean Penn an opportunity to engage in hands-on relief work and ethical reflection on structural inequalities and poverty. Sean Penn's relief work in New Orleans was limited to a few days in the aftermath of Hurricane Katrina, while he has always maintained that his presence in Haiti is long-term. This chapter explores Penn's involvement in both contexts against the backdrop of cosmopolitan debates on global obligation and through a deconstruction of a select number of texts.

Theoretical perspectives from cosmopolitanism

This chapter situates Sean Penn's humanitarianism across borders using the insights of cosmopolitan international theory. Cosmopolitanism is a political theory that assumes that all human beings are part of the same universal moral order. It follows that our situatedness within national communities is of secondary significance to our membership of a cosmopolitan-minded world polity. Cosmopolitanism differs significantly from communitarianism though, because the latter contends that our sense of moral obligation should be confined only to the members of our own state (Bergman Rosamond & Phythian 2012). A cosmopolitan-minded actor would be morally obliged to protect the rights and security of all human beings.

Most cosmopolitans do not wish to radically overturn the international order by eradicating national boundaries and governments, but rather seek to rethink moral obligation, rights and political dialogue (Linklater 1998). While the international system of states remains largely intact there are many signs of new non-state actors entering global politics, including celebrities. Most celebrities do not fundamentally challenge statist practices and discourses of sovereign integrity and capitalism (Kapoor 2013), but reproduce these through their privileged position in celebrity society. Yet, there are examples of individual celebrities who do not shy away from loudly criticizing global injustices, colonial practices and unlawful war and intervention (Bergman Rosamond 2011).

While individuals are central to the actual conduct of cosmopolitan politics, there is little research on their role in the progressive transformation of international order. Thus, it is useful to investigate the acts of individuals working towards this goal. Scholarship on celebrity humanitarianism (Kapoor 2013; Chouliaraki 2013), transnationalism (Tsaliki, Huliaras & Frangoonikolopoulos 2011) diplomacy (Cooper 2008) and society (van Krieken 2012) is useful in providing new insights into the cosmopolitan-inspired acts of individual human beings. While individuals of different descriptions make daily contributions to the international community, their humanitarian engagements will not attract the same level of attention as those of celebrities. The conduct of "celebrity diplomacy" by A-listers such as Penn could be viewed as "cosmopolitan activity" which serves to "further the oneness of humanity" (Cooper 2008, p. 91).

Scholars such as Lilie Chouliaraki (2013, p. 79) and Ilan Kapoor (2013) are generally skeptical regarding the merits of celebrity diplomacy and humanitarianism. Kapoor's (2013, p. 1) criticism of celebrity humanitarianism lies in his claim that it is "far from altruistic," but rather "ideological," "self-serving" and promoting the "celebrity brand" and embedding the "very global inequality it seeks to redress." His assessment allows little room for the analysis of celebrity politics as a potential source of cosmopolitan transformation of the prevailing international order. Mark Wheeler's (2013) reading of celebrity politics recognizes the significance of prevailing economic relations, but argues that celebrity interventions are socially contingent and cannot be grouped together without sensitivity to historical and political context.

Chouliaraki (2013, p. 79) posits, "the intensification of the relationship between humanitarian politics and commercial moralism . . . displaces public action in favor of personal diplomacy." Yet, practical expressions of cosmopolitanism are dependent on the ethical acts of individuals. However, Chouliaraki argues that celebrity humanitarianism inspires "narcissistic solidarity obsessed with our own emotions" rather than seriously considering the needs of "suffering others" (2013, p. 79). For the latter to happen, "celebrities need to demonstrate ideological substance and provide clarity in establishing a fixed range of meanings through which people may achieve a real sense of connection with political cause" (Wheeler 2013, p. 171). A word of caution should be sounded here. Studying celebrity cosmopolitanism does not entail accepting its goodness and authenticity at face value (Bergman Rosamond 2011). Rather it involves recognizing celebrity cosmopolitans' role in debates on global justice and radical politics, as well as recognizing the ethical implications of their selection of good causes.

This selection process is tainted by ethical preferences, since by lending his/her voice to a particular cause the celebrity risks excommunicating others (Bergman Rosamond 2011). Here Sean Penn argues that neither "class" nor "nationhood" impact on his humanitarian choices, but rather his commitment to a notional "human family."[3] Further, he limits his statements to areas that he has been a "first-hand witness of."[4] However, his and other celebrities' ethical choices cannot be entirely divorced from the prevailing economic and political structures within domestic and international society.

Methodology

My case study of Sean Penn's activism in New Orleans and Haiti rests on readings of various media texts collected from mainly online editions of magazines and newspapers. This involves recognizing the media's role in constructing disaster narratives, and public perceptions of such disaster discourses (Tierney, Bevc & Kuligowski 2006). I employ discourse analysis, which enables me to identify the semantic markers that inform the Sean Penn story. The key premise here is that discourses confer "meanings to social and physical realities. It is through discourse that individuals . . . and states make sense of themselves, of their ways of living, and of the world around them" (Epstein 2008, p. 2). Here I am interested in the ways in which media and Sean Penn himself attach "meanings to" his acts and discourses, and how these turn into social and physical realities.

Moreover, the analysis is informed by Laclau and Mouffe's (1985, p. 112) discourse theory and its assumption that the most important units of analysis in any given discourse are signifiers composed of: (a) moments that temporarily fix meanings within texts, and/or (b) elements that have several possible meanings within the text. Nodal points in turn are privileged signifiers around which meanings are constructed (Torfing 1999). The texts explored in the analysis section reveal a set of recurrent nodal points in the media and Penn's own construction of his humanitarianism, including a strong belief in the American Constitution, universal human rights and cosmopolitan values, and a clear preference for non-intervention as the guiding principle of global politics.[5]

Penn's celebrity story is told across texts because, "critical to the understanding of the celebrity . . . is the intertextuality of the construction of the celebrity sign. Although a celebrity may be positioned predominantly in one mediated form, that image is informed by the circulation of significant information about the celebrity in newspapers, magazines, interview programs" (Marshall 1997, p. 58). Intertextuality also refers to the assumption that "texts build their arguments and authority through references to other texts: by making direct quotes or by adopting key concepts and catchphrases" (Hansen 2006, p. 9). The humanitarian story about Sean Penn is told across texts through various catchphrases and keywords. However, they are not necessarily spelt out, but at times hidden beyond the word (Kronsell 2006).

Analysis

Sean Penn from bad boy to celebrity aid worker

Sean Penn was long considered the "bad boy" of the US entertainment industry, with a reputation for disregarding authority. He spent 33 days in prison in 1987 for assaulting a photographer. In 1988 he was arrested and charged with domestic assault, having beaten the American pop singer Madonna, his wife at the time. His bad boy and hypermasculine image has seemingly been toned down and skillfully rewritten to fit the humanitarian story about Sean Penn (Parpart & Zalewiski 2008). Penn considers himself a shy and not very social person.[6]

The Sean Penn self-narrative increasingly centers on his hands-on relief work and criticism of war, poverty and neocolonialism. In Haiti and New Orleans he has engaged in practical action by digging trenches and by delivering food and medicine to the needy.[7] Penn does not limit himself to speaking out on behalf of distant others, but participates in heavy-duty rescue and reconstruction work, which adds authenticity, masculinity and radicalism to his story. A key nodal point across texts telling the Penn story is that of "getting one's hands dirty."[8] Penn has adopted the style of an ordinary aid worker who is unafraid of getting his hands dirty. Abundant images of Penn carrying food aid to the needy of Haiti in various media outlets are steeped in masculine assumptions about men as protectors of the needy, most notably women and children (Elshtain 1987).

His ethical stance seems to be that we are all tied together within a "human family"[9] – a nodal point sustaining the Sean Penn cosmopolitan story. His open letter to President George W. Bush in *The Washington Post* in 2002 revealed this position. He emphasized his right to call himself a patriot while opposing unlawful war, thus revealing both a preference for cosmopolitanism and loyalty to the US:

> Like you, I am a father and an American. Like you, I consider myself a patriot. Like you, I was horrified by the events of this past year [. . .] However, I do not believe in a simplistic and inflammatory view of good and evil. I believe this is a big world full of men, women, and children who struggle to eat, to love, to work, to protect their families, their beliefs, and their dreams.[10]

Hence Penn's message here is that it is possible to be both a patriot and a believer in universal rights. Moreover, he argues for an inclusive conception of the US Constitution and the Bill of Rights, which apply "to all Americans who would sacrifice to maintain them and to all human beings as a matter of principle." He asks Bush to "support us, your fellow Americans, and . . . mankind."[11] Penn undertook a three-day trip to Iraq in 2002 to witness the problems facing Iraqi civilians. His position was that war should be avoided and that this would require "enormous commitment on the part of the Iraqi government as well as the United States."[12] He couched his anti-war rhetoric within patriotic discourse by arguing that "I'm here for a simple reason, which is because I'm a patriot and an American who has benefited enormously from being an American, and because I had areas of personal concern and conscience that led me to come to Iraq."[13] Furthermore, "if there's going to be blood on my hands, I'm determined that it's not going to be invisible. That blood is not just Iraqi blood, it's the blood of American soldiers."[14] Penn's dual concern for American soldiers and Iraqi citizens again reveals that cosmopolitanism is a key nodal point in the Penn humanitarian story. In a CNN interview he said, "I am more proud to be an American than ever. And I've always been proud to be an American" – even if some perceive him as a "traitor."[15] In the following extract his cosmopolitan position and respect for cultural and religious difference are set out:

> I wanted to have a full sense of the place. I didn't need to be convinced that people are people anywhere. I had that predisposition. But nonetheless, we were going to blow them up . . . I knew my taxes were going to pay for some of the killing. After the trip, I realized that you don't have to understand people's religion or culture. You can understand people's hearts – and it's the same heart everywhere.[16]

Moreover, he argues that American money "would be better spent on building levees in New Orleans and health care in Africa and care for our veterans,"[17] rather than the military. An assumption here is that Penn's privileged position as a white male within the gendered power relations of American society and the entertainment industry ensures that he can issue such critical statements without facing career-threatening sanctions. This is not a privilege necessarily offered to his female counterparts. His powerful position, moreover, allows him to rather unquestionably engage in gendered discourses of protection beyond borders.

Penn's radical politics has found expression in his friendship with the former President of Venezuela Hugo Chavez and his successor Nicolas Maduro.[18] In 2012 Penn criticized Britain's role in the Falklands during a visit to Argentina, describing the former's sovereign claim to the Falklands as "colonialist, ludicrous and archaic."[19] In sum, Penn's humanitarianism is defined by cosmopolitanism, radical politics and gendered constructions of protection and masculinity. The American Constitution and patriotic sentiments are also key nodal points that occur across multiple texts and contexts. In what follows I will unpack Penn's humanitarian engagements in New Orleans and Haiti.

New Orleans

New Orleans is situated in Louisiana at the mouth of the Mississippi River. The city was founded in 1718 by the French, but the control of the city was shifted to the Spanish empire as a consequence of the Treaty of Paris in 1763. In 1803 it was ceded to the French only to be sold to the United States later the same year. French cultural and linguistic influences were, for long, predominant features of New Orleans. Ethnically, New Orleans is diverse, including French Creoles, and African, Irish, German and Italian immigrants.[20] Of interest here are the people who either fled or decided to move on their own accord to New Orleans in

1804 after the Haitian revolution.[21] In the early 19th century the city was a major center of the slave trade, while being the home of a comparably large number of free people of color (African Americans) who worked in professional trades.[22] The slaves were forced to work on sugar plantations, which were the backbone of the local economy. Racism continued to be a dominant feature of New Orleans post-slavery and beyond.

In this context, a group of US-based social scientists have argued that although the Civil Rights movement brought new rights to the US, New Orleans has remained a city defined by racism and inequalities (Doherty 2013) – these were exacerbated by Hurricane Katrina (Strolovitch, Warren & Frymer 2006, p. 1):

> the hurricane made clear, however . . . the US has not resolved fundamental domestic disparities and inadequacies. Katrina did not create these inequities; it simply added an important reminder that they are deeply embedded and constitutive of American political, economic, and social life.
>
> *(Strolovitch, Warren & Frymer 2006, p. 1)*

The African American community was hit hard by Katrina, with a larger proportion of black households losing their homes. As Strolovitch et al. have observed, "By now, we have all heard the damning statistics about the demographics of New Orleans residents so devastated by Katrina: 67% are African American, 28% live below the poverty line (of whom 84% are black), 100,000 had no car, and therefore had no ability to flee the city when the storm hit" (2006, p. 1). The statistical data cited by the authors point to poverty and racism remaining key issues in New Orleans. In this context, Clarke (2006, pp. 1–2) argues that "the remaining victims of Katrina were poor, and African American to boot, so officials callously turned their backs on those whom they did not care about." An estimated 1,577 people died in Louisiana as a result of Katrina.

Sean Penn's rescue work in New Orleans

Hurricane Katrina attracted a lot of media attention, with New Orleans being represented as a "disaster-stricken city" and a "war zone" (Tierney, Bevc & Kuligowski 2006, pp. 60–61). This disaster narrative prompted several celebrities to offer their support to the inhabitants of New Orleans. John Travolta flew his private jet to the city to distribute relief supplies. George Clooney donated $1 million to the victims of Katrina and other celebrities did the same.[23] CNN journalist Doug Gross discusses the unprecedented levels of celebrity activism post-Katrina by pointing to the city's cultural relevance as the birthplace of jazz.[24] The disaster caused by Hurricane Katrina and the victims' narratives of it have been documented in Spike Lee's film *When the Levees Broke: A Requiem in Four Acts*. This gives voice to the victims, and Sean Penn's account of the events figures in the film. Lee has praised Penn's rescue work in Louisiana (and Haiti) by saying that "Sean . . . was in New Orleans days after, Sean was in Haiti days after the earthquake. He set up a hospital, a women's clinic, was working with the locals."[25] Penn's hands-on approach has also been visually documented in social media showing him in a powerboat around the flooded streets of New Orleans, looking for people to rescue. Penn's own estimate is that his team rescued approximately 40 people, a total sum that seems rather modest, but which has been used by Penn in justifying his presence in New Orleans.[26]

When Penn was asked why he decided to participate in rescue work in New Orleans he answered, "there weren't enough people there . . . it became easy to get out too, for me to get a boat, and get out on the water with some other people, and try to get people out of water."[27] Hence, he wants to "lend a hand" to New Orleans to be able to "live with" himself.[28] In his words, "I was able to lend a hand . . . and that's all I was there to do. People may want to make it more than that, but I don't want to dignify all these talking heads. At the end of the day, you have to do what you think is right."[29] The "lending a hand" nodal point holds together the Penn rescue story. As reported by BBC News in 2005, his activism was also an expression of his distrust in the former Bush administration's ability to help and rescue the sufferers of the disaster:

> "There are people that are dying right now and I mean babies and old people and everybody in between – they're dying," he said . . . "There are people dying and [the US government is] not putting the boats in the water, I think that's criminal negligence."[30]

The quote reveals a radical undertone and anger with the "negligence" of the Bush regime in dealing with the destruction caused by hurricane Katrina. Penn's privileged position within American society offers him opportunities to impact on people's responses to natural disasters. Moreover, his wish to protect innocent civilians is closely linked to his gendered identity as a male white protector. *The Sydney Morning Herald* discursively juxtapositions Sean Penn's rescue work within gendered language and suggests that his approach was not as "emotional" and feminine as that of Celine Dion, for example.[31] The script of Sean Penn's rescue work in New Orleans is thus constituted within gendered binaries that privilege masculine rationality over feminine emotion. The newspaper further reiterates this gendered message by assigning the role of warrior/protector to Penn in describing his efforts in New Orleans as a "personal crusade to save victims"; again employing the gendered language of protection.[32]

Penn did not quite succeed in his mission to protect innocent civilians since his rescue boat started to leak. A *Fox News* reporter wrote in 2005 that the "(m)ovie star and political activist Penn, 45, was in the collapsing city to aid stranded victims of flooding sparked by Hurricane Katrina, but the small boat he was piloting to launch a rescue attempt sprang a leak."[33] Moreover,

> upon hearing the plight of New Orleans . . . political activist Sean Penn sprang into action, flying to the beleaguered city to help in the rescue effort.

But it was Penn who wound up needing to be rescued after the boat he was piled in sprang a leak just seconds after launching. Penn and his entourage, including a personal photographer, were seen frantically bailing the water out of the shrinking vessel with a plastic cup.[34]

The sinking boat episode serves to feminize Penn's persona by identifying gaps in his ability to offer male protection of innocent victims beyond the comforts of his privileged existence.

Such media discourses construct Penn's humanitarianism as an expression of self-promotion and incompetence. *Esquire* journalist Scott Raab wrote in 2007 that Penn "went to New Orleans in the wake of Katrina, found a boat and a rifle, and literally rescued dozens of flood victims; and for his trouble, he has been more vilified than any Tinseltowner since Hanoi Jane."[35] Although seemingly sympathetic to Penn's rescue efforts, the journalist in question likens him to Jane Fonda and her much-ridiculed anti-Vietnam war activism. Penn has defended his rescue work by arguing that "the point was that, out of the benefit of celebrity, I could afford to get on an airplane and get down there. And we got a lot of people out of the water."[36] Furthermore, he argued on CNN's *Larry King Live* that "We went in, a couple of friends of mine, on our own. Certainly we had the attention of some photographers. We tried to do what we could."[37] Penn's ambition, then, seemed to have been to save lives rather than seeking publicity. In a piece written by himself in the *Huffington Post* in 2008 he reiterated this point:

> the mainstream media, in print and on television are, in part, conscious manufacturers of deception . . . It was widely reported that I had commissioned my own photographer to self-promote my involvement among many other volunteers in New Orleans in the aftermath of Katrina. This simply did not happen. Though the notion of self-promotion had not occurred to me, I did later regret that I had not gotten some snaps of the devastation I saw.[38]

Penn's words are interesting for several reasons. First, they raise questions regarding celebrity witnessing and Penn's intended audience. Here mainstream media seems to be the target of his criticism. Second, the text shows how easily the metanarrative of the disaster itself fades away to allow space for the celebrity story to be told. Penn's mere presence in New Orleans supplants stories about the actual sufferers of the disaster. Second, Penn's thoughts reveal irony and self-reflection (Bergman Rosamond 2011; Brassett 2009) as well as anger, which can reinforce his authenticity. He discursively distances himself from the "post-humanitarian" stance (Chouliaraki 2013) which is "self-focused not other-focused" (Brockington 2014, p. 23) by highlighting his commitment and seriousness. His participation in New Orleans could be viewed as an expression of cosmopolitanism within borders by promoting universal values and rights. In what follows we shall turn to Penn's rescue and development work in Haiti.

Haiti

The Republic of Haiti is situated in the Antillean archipelago on the island of Hispaniola. France acquired one-third of Hispaniola in 1697 and soon the sugar plantations were flourishing, sustained by the import of slaves from Africa (Abbot 2010). Towards the end of the 18th century French colonizers made up about 40,000 of the population of Haiti,[39] although they were heavily outnumbered by the African slaves at the time (Abbot 2010). The slaves were treated appallingly and many died just a few years after arrival (Abbot 2010). However, there were also free people of color who were the children of African slave mothers and French fathers and who were granted freedom.[40] The French Revolution inspired a slave uprising and revolution, which led to the establishment of the second Republic of the Americas in 1804 (Dubois 2004). Haiti was not recognized by the US, which feared that it would cause similar uprisings within their colonial dominions.[41] A good number of Haitians left at various points for the US and settled in New Orleans, giving rise to numerous connections being established between the two contexts.

Haiti's contemporary history

Haiti was occupied by the US from 1915 to 1934 and the economy was managed by the US until 1941.[42] A key development was the election of Dr. Francois Duvalier ("Papa Doc") in 1957. Papa Doc enjoyed initial popularity by opting for policies that benefited black Haitians rather than people of color, but proved to be a brutal leader. When he died in 1971 he was replaced by his son Jean-Claude Duvalier ("Baby Doc"), who employed the same measures as his father. Baby Doc was ousted from power in 1986 and several years of unrest and violence followed.[43] In 1990 a former Catholic priest, Jean-Bertrand Aristide, was elected president in a general election. However, he was removed from power in 1991 through a coup. Haiti was subjected to a US-led intervention in 1994 in an effort to establish order and Aristide returned to power.[44] In 2004 another uprising took place, which led to Aristide's forced departure from the island and the establishment of the United Nations Stabilization Mission in Haiti.[45] While the US has been much criticized for its interventionist approach to Haiti, there are also signs of solidarity between the two sovereign entities. However, Jennie M. Smith's (2001) in-depth anthropological study of Haitian peasants indicates that they are skeptical of American democracy and of the Haitian government pushing through "Structural Adjustment" programs. Haiti has been the subject of much international concern and its peasants "are consistently viewed by others as victims in need of rescue or social problems in need of reform" (Smith 2001, p. 2). Abject poverty and social unrest have reinforced this picture as well as the earthquake that struck in 2010.

The 2010 earthquake and Penn's relief work

Haiti was badly hit by the earthquake on 12 January 2010. It caused 220,000 deaths, 300,000 were injured and 1.6 million people lost their homes.[46] The natural disaster has been well documented by the global media, in particular the difficulties in rehousing the homeless people. On 21 January George Clooney and Haitian musician Wyclef Jean, supported by fellow celebrities, organized the world's largest telethon in support of the victims of the earthquake. The event is estimated to have reached 640 million homes across the world.[47] In January 2014 Sean Penn organized a charity gala that featured, among others, U2, and which raised US$6 million for his organization, the S/P Haitian Relief Organization (HRO).[48] Sean Penn tends to favor a more radical, hands-on approach and was one of the first people to turn up in Haiti, a few days after the actual earthquake and remained there for approximately a year. As had been the case in New Orleans, Penn favored a participative approach and allegedly saved two people's lives and hosted them in his house until they had recovered enough to leave.[49]

Penn's activism is constituted within a sense of cosmopolitan obligation to a neighboring state situated "an hour and a half away" from the USA and being the home of "the first major slave revolt."[50] Haiti's proximity to the USA, the historical subordination of its population, as well as its ability to revolt against such practices, provide a normative platform for Penn's activism in Haiti. Penn's dedication to Haiti has been both praised and critiqued by commentators. For example, US Lieutenant General P.K. Keen praised Penn's efforts to bring "international attention and resources to Haiti."[51] "He intuitively knew how to both work with the UN and break its bureaucracy down . . . I applaud all the leadership he has shown. He doesn't have to do this."[52] In 2012 Penn was awarded a Peace Summit Award for his work in Haiti.

FIGURE 7.1   Sean Penn in Haiti 2010 after the earthquake. Photograph by Dan Lundmark. Creative Commons License https://creativecommons.org/licenses/by/2.0/.

Penn's long-term commitment to Haiti and his humanitarian awards

Penn has participated personally in the physical rebuilding of Haitian society by digging trenches, and delivering food and medicine to the needy. He has also undertaken fundraising trips to Washington and the UN.[53] He has maintained that he is in Haiti for the long haul and supports structural development solutions to Haitian economic problems, rather than short-term fixes.[54] Former US President Bill Clinton has praised Penn's long-term dedication, arguing that he is "not a drive-by celebrity . . . he went into those camps and he was actually solving their water problems."[55] Penn himself has observed that the magnitude of the destination was "so bad" that "There's no end point . . . this is where I'll be when I'm not working, for the rest of my life."[56] This led him to fund the HRO in 2010 and to become its chief executive officer and chairperson. Penn describes that decision in rather self-deprecating language: "I started a little NGO. The Haitians that came in and took it over have removed half a million cubic meters of rubble," but he continues to admit that his organization has "got 150 homes fully built and constructed . . . the Haitians that I get credit for that run my organization have taken 58,000 of their own country people out of the tent camp and put them in a sustainable housing situation."[57]

The organization's mission statement is "to save lives and build sustainable programs with the Haitian people quickly and effectively," and its tasks include administering relocation schemes, providing cholera vaccine, sponsoring engineering and structural reinforcement teams, maternity wards and women's clinics as well as providing HIV/Aids testing.[58] On its website, the Penn entertainment narrative is effectively employed to sell the projects of the HRO. This story, which is presumably endorsed by Penn himself, is that of a person who is a critically acclaimed artist, but whose real achievements are within the humanitarian relief sector.[59]

The HRO website lists the awards and appointments that Sean Penn has been given for his contributions to Haitian society.[60] In July 2010, for example, Sean Penn was knighted by former Haitian President René Préval in a ceremony in Port-Au-Prince and, as such, carved out a political and privileged space for himself in Haitian society. On 31 January 2012 Penn was named the "Ambassador at large to the Nation of Haiti" by the country's current president, Michel Martelly. The president said on the occasion that the "only downside" was that he would no longer be able to address the actor by his first name.[61] Penn's efforts in Haiti have also earned him "the Commander's Award for Service (US Army 82nd Airborne Division) . . . for Meritorious Service, the Operation Unified Response JTF Haiti Certificate from Lieutenant General, US Army Commander P.K. Keen." Finally, he has been presented with the "Children's and Families Global Development Fund Humanitarian Award" presented by the Ambassador of the Republic of Haiti, Raymond A. Joseph. The awards are indicative of the local elite and the US Army recognizing Penn's knowledge, authenticity and ethical commitment to Haiti in practice and discourse. However, such awards give Penn access to privileged society and political elites in a fashion somewhat inconsistent with his hands–on approach and radical politics.[62]

Simplicity and privilege

Penn is situated within prevalent development practices and discourses in global politics that are hard to escape. Moreover, his relief work could be considered a privileged representation of global injustices, as read by the actor himself. However, his authorship across texts reveals a desire to question his own and others' privilege.[63] As a mega-star with considerable personal wealth he has been given "access to places, events and people that most of us do not" (Brockington 2014, p. 113). His own description of his role in Haiti is that of a "blan," meaning "that foreign guy who's the boss of the organization working with them in their camps" and as a "potential employer" rather than "a warm and fuzzy humanitarian."[64] In sum, he is a part-time local executive, employer and a friend of the Haitian nation celebrated by the current Haitian leadership.[65] Penn balances his celebrity status and privileged position in US and Haitian societies with a simple lifestyle on the island. His ordinariness and authenticity were strengthened by his decision to take up part-time residence in Haiti in 2011 where he lived in "a tiny plywood cubicle, not wider than a prison cell, in a group home for aid workers in Haiti."[66] While celebrities are often pictured during their trips to war zones or refugee camps, "their input often doesn't extend much beyond hosting fundraisers . . . dinners."[67] Penn's humanitarianism is in many ways quite different. Yet, he cannot escape his celebrity status within privileged white gendered society. As Ella Turenne, an Assistant Dean for Community Engagement at the Occidental College of Haitian Descent, has argued, "so many of Sean Penn's comments about his work in Haiti are always about him . . . There is little talk about how the Haitian people are involved in this, or about how racial politics play into this. Helping, rather than allowing folks to empower themselves, sets up an environment of dependency."[68] In the following, the discursive markers of Penn's Haitian humanitarianism are identified.

Discursive markers

Penn writes in *Rolling Stone* that it took him 30 years to get interested in Haiti and that "It took a fluke of timing and a major fucking earthquake . . . to rattle my cage, while some 230,000 Haitian men, women and children were rattled to a sudden and horrible death for no reason but poverty and neglect."[69] Underlying his current work is his belief in humanity and the economic, social and political rights of the Haitians. He argues that "They need our support . . . for all the children of Haiti," calling upon the world for more generosity and assistance.[70] Sean Penn's dedication to Haiti is situated within cosmopolitan language even if he does not use that label himself (Kronsell 2006). Penn's ethical commitment to distant other sufferers, in particular displaced people, resembles his activities in

New Orleans because it is constituted within discourses and practices of hands-on activism. His hands-on celebrity image is thus transported across geographical and textual contexts. In a testimony before the Senate Foreign Relations Committee, Penn reflected on how he personally "rode in the back of the ambulance while the patient was refused from several hospitals because the 15-year-old boy . . . was diagnosed with a disease for which those hospitals had no treatment capability."[71] Lending a hand to distant others could be seen as an actual other-regarding cosmopolitan act. Key to Sean Penn's ethical self-narrative is his wish to be near the people he is seeking to help and as such deploring the tendency to gather in "conference rooms" since in his opinion it is not enough to deliberate. Rather it is "time to act in support of, and on behalf of, the Haitian people and their government."[72] Yet Penn's cosmopolitanism and pursuit of on the ground radical politics are coupled with his patriotic celebration of the ability of the USA to engage in altruistic acts. In his words, "the compassionate and no nonsense posture of our military has been moving and inspiring."[73] By praising the US military for its relief work in post-earthquake Haiti, and by arguing that the "mission was not only performed with great humanism" but was also an "emergency-relief success,"[74] he reinforces militarizing practices and discourses of protection that are situated within global gendered binaries and the North–South divide. His patriotism is also visible in his praise for President Obama's efforts to put Haiti on the global agenda. Penn is both a bastion of radical celebrity politics and a defender of US foreign policy. His privileged and gendered statesmanlike position in US society enables him to say and do things that others might not be able to.

However, Penn's support for Haiti is also an outflow of his commitment to the long-term development of the island.[75] He has stated across texts that the reconstruction and eradication of poverty cannot happen overnight and that long-term structural solutions are key to future success stories.[76] He has pointed to the tendency on the part of the media to construct an overly negative Haitian story. Penn writes in *Newsweek*, "the people of Haiti have come a long way, which may shock those who watch the news. Headlines continue to spin Haiti as a dark, poverty-entrenched no man's land. Even on the left, efforts at economic development have been portrayed as colonization by corporations or occupation by a foreign force."[77] He warns against overstating the colonial or imperial message as it deters foreign investment, despite being opposed to such colonial practices himself. However, he promotes the empowerment of Haitians by arguing that structural development projects ought to be led by and benefit Haitians rather than "enlisting help from other countries and peoples,"[78] thus committing himself to localized knowledge and experience. Moreover, Penn argues that "coverage scares away would-be investors, hindering economic development and reinforcing prejudices that Haiti is beyond help," and removes attention from remaining development issues.[79]

In sum, the Sean Penn story in Haiti is held together by numerous discursive nodal points that are intertextually linked across texts (Hansen 2006). This story is invested with a good deal of optimism and Penn's belief in economic progress. He couches his celebrity humanitarianism within broad cosmopolitan language while resorting to statist rhetoric by celebrating the efforts of the US military and government. His own location within intersectional and gendered privilege is not fully problematized by Penn himself, or the media and here there is room for more exploration of his ideological preference and motives (Wheeler 2013; Street 2012). Yet, his humanitarianism can begin to tell us something about the actual conduct of a celebrity politics that allows room for personal engagement rather than being entirely structurally determined (Wheeler 2013).

Conclusion

I started the chapter by exploring the benefits of combining cosmopolitanism and celebrity studies. In so doing I argued that progressive transformations of global society cannot be fully captured unless we consider the ethical contributions of individuals, whether celebrities or not. In turn, cosmopolitanism can equip celebrity scholars with a deeper understanding of the boundaries of ethical obligation. I also discursively unpacked Sean Penn's ethical stance on a range of global issues including military interventionism. A set of key nodal points was identified, including his commitment to humanity at large, patriotism and his opposition to war and colonialism. I also observed that Penn's masculinity and privileged position within Western society give him opportunities to divert from expected celebrity behavior by, for example, voicing loud criticism against American interventionism. I then surveyed Sean Penn's humanitarian involvements in post-Katrina New Orleans and post-earthquake Haiti. In contrast to Penn's involvement in Haiti, his relief work in New Orleans was temporally limited to the immediate aftermath of the disaster. Moreover, his hands-on approach was mocked by the media. He has countered this media construction by arguing that his hands-on approach was not an act of self-promotion, but an effort to help and protect civilians in need. However, this could be viewed as a gendered undertaking that reinforces his role as the white male protector of distant others.

Penn's Haitian activism is also discursively marked by his preference for a hands-on approach. Media images of him employing his physical masculine strength when carrying food to the needy are not innocent, but contribute to the gendering of his celebrity activism. However, his moral authority and authenticity are discursively strengthened through his long-term commitment to Haiti and concern for humanity at large. Penn's Haitian activism has been criticized though, as we have seen above. Moreover, his radical politics can be discursively challenged by his simultaneous celebration of the roles of the US president and military in the rebuilding of the island.

So what broad insights does this chapter bring to the volume? First, Sean Penn's humanitarian work in New Orleans and Haiti draws attention to the relevance of exploring relief activism within and beyond borders. In particular, it provides new insights into the ways in which his messages of humanity are locally constituted within borders (New Orleans) and then translated into other settings (Haiti). Penn's hands-on approach and conception of the human race as a "family" are present in both contexts. Yet, Penn also professes to be a believer in patriotism and US-led progressive change. Second, Penn's humanitarian disaster work across contexts can offer new insights into the role of actual human beings in furthering the cosmopolitan agenda of peace, protection and rights. While Penn has attracted a fair measure of negative attention for his humanitarianism, his story has simultaneously brought attention to the practice of radical celebrity politics and this personalized form of cosmopolitanism within and beyond borders. Third, by studying Penn's relief work we can unpack the gendered power relations that surround celebrity politics by identifying specific actors' situatedness within male privileged societies, and by problematizing their employment of discourses of protection.

Notes

1 JamBase, undated, Dirty hands: Sean Penn's trip to Nola, p. 1, http://www.jambase.com/Articles/14175/Dirty-Hands-Sean-Penn's-Trip-to-NOLA [accessed on June 23, 2014].
2 B. Bell. 2012. The Creole connection: New Orleans, Haiti and catastrophe, http://www.huffingtonpost.com/beverly-bell/new-orleans-haiti_b_1841502.html [accessed on October 12, 2014].
3 Al Jazeera. 2014. Sean Penn: actor and activist – talk to Al Jazeera, 12 April, www.aljazeera.com/.../sean-penn-actor-activist-2014411155423327970.htm [accessed on December 12, 2014].
4 Ibid.
5 Sean Penn is not a passive observer in the writing of his own story – he has written several pieces in magazines and newspapers and takes part in newspaper and TV interviews.
6 The Oprah Magazine. 2005. Oprah talks to Sean Penn, p. 5, http://www.oprah.com/omagazine/Oprah-Interviews-Sean-Penn [accessed on July 12, 2014].
7 The Independent, 2012. Sean Penn; rebel with a cause, February 18, http://www.independent.co.uk/news/people/profiles/sean-penn-rebel-with-a-cause-7079713.html [accessed on December 19, 2014].
8 JamBase, undated.
9 Al Jazeera (2014).
10 S. Penn. 2002. An Open Letter to the President of the United States of America, *Washington Post*, October 19, http://www.peace.ca/seanpenn.htm [accessed on April 20, 2013].
11 Ibid.
12 A. Lyon. 2002. Sean Penn says war in Iraq is avoidable, *Common Dreams*, http://www.commondreams.org/headlines02/1215-10.htm [accessed on April 20, 2013].
13 Ibid.
14 Ibid.
15 CNN. 2011. Piers Morgan live interview with Sean Penn, October 14, http://transcripts.cnn.com/TRANSCRIPTS/1110/14/pmt.01.html [accessed on June 16, 2014].
16 The Oprah Magazine. 2005, p. 5.
17 Fox News 2007. Sean Penn leads California Town Hall against Iraq war, March 26, 2007, http://wwww.foxnews.com/story/0,2933,261145,00.html [accessed on November 1, 2012].
18 The Hollywood Reporter. 2013. Sean Penn on Hugo Chavez's death: I lost a friend, http://www.hollywoodreporter.com/news/hugo-chavez-dead-sean-penn-426205 [accessed on September 14, 2014].

19 The Telegraph. 2012. Sean Penn accuses Britain of "colonialism" over Falklands, February, 24, www.telegraph.co.uk/.../Sean-Penn-accuses-Britain-of-colonialism-over-Falklands.html [accessed on December 19, 2014].

20 A. Hirsch & J. Logsdon. undated. The people and culture of New Orleans, New Orleans, http://www.neworleansonline.com/neworleans/history/people.html [accessed on August 15, 2014].

21 Ibid.

22 Ibid.

23 D. Gross. 2009. Celebrities keep spotlight on New Orleans 4 years after Katrina, CNN, August 27, http://edition.cnn.com/2009/SHOWBIZ/08/25/katrina.new.orleans.celebrities/index.html?iref=newssearch [accessed on July 17, 2014].

24 Ibid.

25 GQ, 2010. Spike Lee is still doing the right thing, September issue, http://www.gq.com/news-politics/big-issues/201009/spike-lee-new-orleans-katrina-bp-oil-obama-da-creek-dont-rise [accessed on July 16, 2014].

26 Gross. 2009.

27 CNN. 2005. Larry King Live, September 7, http://transcripts.cnn.com/TRANSCRIPTS/0509/07/lkl.01.html [accessed on September 11, 2014].

28 S. Bowles. 2006. Sean Penn plays politics, USA Today, September 18, http://usatoday30.usatoday.com/life/movies/news/2006-09-18-sean-penn_x.htm [accessed on September 16, 2014].

29 Ibid.

30 BBC News. 2005. Travolta jets for Katrina effort, September 6, http://news.bbc.co.uk/2/hi/entertainment/4218450.stm BBC [accessed on September 16, 2014].

31 The Sydney Morning Herald, 5 September 2005, Penn's rescue attempt springs a leak, http://www.smh.com.au/news/world/penns-rescue-attempt-springs-a-leak/2005/09/05/1125772436185.html [accessed on June 15, 2014].

32 Ibid.

33 B.Hume. 2005. Who's to blame and who isn't to blame?, Fox News, September 6, http://www.foxnews.com/story/2005/09/06/who-to-blame-and-who-isnt-to-blame/ [accessed on June 16, 2014].

34 Ibid.

35 S. Raab. 2007. Penn, the Esquire, http://www.esquire.com/features/seanpenn0907 [accessed on September 16, 2014].

36 Gross. 2009.

37 CNN, 2005. The Larry King Show, September 7, http://transcripts.cnn.com/TRANSCRIPTS/0509/07/lkl.01.html [accessed on July 7, 2014].

38 S. Penn. 2008. Mountain of snakes, The Huffington Post, http://www.huffingtonpost.com/sean-penn/mountain-of-snakes_b_146765.html Penn [accessed on July 16, 2014].

39 BlackPast.Org, undated, Haitian Revolution 1791–1804, http://www.blackpast.org/gah/haitian-revolution-1791-1804 [accessed on September 7, 2014].

40 Ibid.

41 US Department of State Office of The Historian, undated, The United States and the Haitian Revolution, 1791–1804, https://history.state.gov/milestones/1784-1800/haitian-rev [accessed on September 14, 2014].

42 BBC News. 2010. The long history of troubled ties between Haiti and the US, http://news.bbc.co.uk/2/hi/americas/8460185.stm [accessed on September 11, 2014].

43 Ibid.

44 Ibid.

45 Ibid.

46 Oxfam International. 2014. Haiti earthquake: 4 years later, http://www.oxfam.org/haitiquake [accessed on September 15, 2014].

47 The Independent. 2010. Haiti telethon gathers huge all-star lineup, http://www.independent.co.uk/incoming/haiti-telethon-gathers-huge-allstar-lineup-1874467.html [accessed on September 14, 2014].

48 The Hollywood Reporter. 2014. U2 Surprises at Sean Penn's Haiti Benefit Gala 12 January, http://www.hollywoodreporter.com/news/u2-surprises-at-sean-penns-670129 [accessed on September 15, 2014].

49 The Huffington Post. 2010. Sean Penn saving lives in Haiti, http://www.huffingtonpost.com/2010/02/26/sean-penn-saving-lives-in_n_477912.html [accessed on September 14, 2014].

50 CNN. 2011.

51 The Lieutenant General is the Military Deputy Commander of US Southern Command, Miami, Florida. As such, he has been in charge of US-led military operations and rescue missions in the Caribbean, including Haiti, US Southern Command, undated, Biography Lieutenant General P.K. (Ken) Keen, Military Deputy Commander USSOUTHCOM, http://usacac.army.mil/cac2/AOKM/aokm2009/bio/Keen_PK_LTG_Bio.pdf [accessed on November 30, 2014].

52 The Huffington Post. 2010b, Sean Penn: Robin Wright "Is A Ghost To me Now," June 3, http://www.huffingtonpost.com/2010/06/03/sean-penn-robin-wright-is_n_599028 [accessed on September 19, 2014].

53 C. Rosen. 2012. Sean Penn at Cannes: Haiti was abandoned by whole F—king world, *The Huffington Post*, May 18, http://www.huffingtonpost.com/2012/05/18/sean-penn-at-canne [accessed on September 18, 2014]. The Hollywood Reporter. 2014. U2 surprises at Sean Penn's Haiti Benefit Gala, http://www.hollywoodreporter.com/news/u2-surprises-at-sean-penns-670129 [accessed on December 19, 2014].

54 Rosen. 2012.

55 Ibid.

56 The Huffington Post. 2011. Sean Penn: In Haiti "For the rest of my life," January 6, http://www.huffingtonpost.com/2011/01/06/sean-penn-in-haiti-for-the-rest-of-my-life_n_805137.html [accessed on July 16, 2014].

57 CNN. 2013. Piers Morgan Live: interview with Sean Penn, October 28, http://transcripts.cnn.com/TRANSCRIPTS/1310/28/pmt.01.html CNN 2013 [accessed on August 16, 2014].

58 S/P Haitian Relief Organization. 2014. About us, http://jphro.org/about.html [accessed on September 16, 2014].

59 Ibid.

60 Ibid.

61 CBS News. 2012a. Haiti names Sean Penn "ambassador at large," February 1, 2012, http://www.cbsnews.com/news/haiti-names-sean-penn-ambassador-at-large/ [accessed on June 17, 2014].

62 Rolling Stone has criticized the HRO for its controversial relocation policy. The dispute concerned the relocation of internally displaced persons in Haiti who had been living in a camp site managed by HRO. Some 5,000 people on that site were persuaded to move to another site as the United Nations had predicted that the original one could be hit by flooding. However, the 5,000 people who were relocated ended up remaining in the temporary location permanently with few prospects of employment (Penn 2011).

63 S. Penn. 2011. Sean Penn responds to Rolling Stone's Haiti Story, Rolling Stone, September, 30, http://www.rollingstone.com/politics/news/sean-penn-responds-to-rolling-stone-s-haiti-story-20110930 [accessed on August 7, 2014]. S. Penn. 2014. We've

turned the corner in Haiti, Newsweek, June 18, http://www.newsweek.com/sean-penn-weve-turned-corner-haiti-255490 [accessed on June 19, 2014].
64 Penn. 2011. p. 5.
65 M. Garrahan. 2013. Sean Penn on rebuilding Haiti, Financial Times, December 6, 2013.
66 CBC News. 2012b. Person to person: Sean Penn's mission to rebuild, http://www.cbsnews.com/news/person-to-person-sean-penns-mission-to-rebuild-haiti/ [accessed on September 16, 2014].
67 Garrahan. 2013, p. 1.
68 E. Turenne. 2011. Who's a hero? Haitians can help themselves, too, The Huffington Post, August 15, http://www.huffingtonpost.com/ella-turenne/whos-a-hero-haitians-can-_b_925493.html [accessed on October 19, 2014].
69 Penn. 2011.
70 Ibid.
71 S. Penn. 2010. My Senate Foreign Relations Committee Testimony on rebuilding Haiti, The Huffington Post, May 19, http://www.huffingtonpost.com/sean-penn/my-senate-foreign-relatio_b_582320.html [accessed on June 15, 2014].
72 Penn. 2011.
73 Penn. 2010.
74 Penn. 2011.
75 HRO. 2014.
76 Penn. 2011.
77 Penn. 2014.
78 P. Ferrari. 2012. Help us help Haitians learn to fish, and more, The Huffington Post, 23 May, http://www.huffingtonpost.com/pierre-ferrari/sean-penn-haiti_b_1540412.html [accessed on September 11, 2014].
79 Penn. 2014.

References

Abbot, E. 2010. *Sugar a Bittersweet History*. New York: The Duckworth Overlook Press.
Bergman Rosamond, A. 2011. The cosmopolitan–communitarian divide and celebrity anti-war activism. In L. Tsaliki, A. Huliaras & C.A. Frangonikolopoulos (eds) *Transnational Celebrity Activism In Global Politics Changing the World*? Chicago: Chicago University Press.
Bergman Rosamond, A. & Gregoratti, C. 2014. Empowering commodities and celebrities, paper presented at *The Celebrity–Business–Development Nexus Symposium*, Copenhagen Business School, May 8.
Bergman Rosamond, A. & Phythian, M. 2012. *War, Ethics and Justice: New Perspectives on a Post-9/11 World*. Oxford: Routledge.
Brassett, J. 2009. British irony, global justice: a pragmatic reading of Chris Brown, Banksy and Ricky Gervais. *Review of International Studies*, 35 (1), 219–245.
Brockington, D. 2009. *Celebrity and the Environment: Fame, Wealth and Power in Conversation*. London: Zed Books.
Brockington, D. 2014. *Celebrity Advocacy and International Development*. London and New York: Routledge.
Chouliaraki, L. 2013. *The Ironic Spectator – Solidarity in the Age of Post-humanitarianism*. Cambridge: Polity Press.
Clarke, L. 2006. *Worst Case Katrina Understanding Katrina Perspectives from the Social Sciences*, http://understandingkatrina.ssrc.org/Clarke/ [accessed on August 14, 2014].

Cooper, A.F. 2008. *Celebrity Diplomacy*. London: Paradigm.

Doherty, D. 2013. Remembering Katrina: wide racial divide over government's response. Pew Research Center 28 August, http://www.pewresearch.org/fact-tank/2013/08/28/remembering-katrina-wide-racial-divide-over-governments-response/ [accessed on September 15, 2014].

Dubois, L. 2004. *Avengers of the New World: The Story of the Haitian Revolution*. Cambridge: Harvard University Press.

Elshtain, J.B. 1987. *Women and War*. Chicago: University of Chicago Press.

Epstein, C. 2008. *The Power of Words in International Relations: Birth of an Anti-whaling Discourse*. London: the MIT Press.

Hansen, L. 2006. *Security as Practice*. London: Routledge.

Kapoor, I. 2013. *Celebrity Humanitarianism: the Ideology of Global Charity*. London: Routledge.

Kronsell, A. 2006. Methods for studying silences: gender analysis in institutions of hegemonic masculinity. In B.A. Ackerly, M. Stern & J. True (eds) *Feminist Methodologies for International Relations*. Cambridge: Cambridge University Press.

Laclau, E. & Mouffe, C. 1985. *Hegemony and Socialist Strategy: Towards a Radical Democratic Politics*. London: Verso.

Linklater, A. 1998. *The Transformation of Political Community*. Cambridge: Polity Press.

Marshall, D.P. 1997. *Celebrity and Power: Fame in Contemporary Culture*. Minneapolis: University of Minnesota Press.

Parpart, J. & Zalewiski, M. 2008. *Rethinking the Man Question: Sex, Gender and Violence in International Relations*. London: Zed Books.

Richey, L.A. & Ponte, S. 2008. Better (Red)™ than dead? Celebrities, consumption and international aid. *Third World Quarterly*, 29 (4), 711–29.

Richey, L.A. & Ponte, S. 2011. *Brand Aid Shopping Well to Save the World*. Minneapolis: Minnesota University Press.

Shepherd, L.J. 2013. *Gender, Violence and Popular Culture: Telling Stories*. Oxford: Routledge.

Smith, J. 2001. *When the Hands are Many: Community Organization and Social Change in Rural Haiti*. New York: Cornell University Press.

Street, J. 2012. Do celebrity politics and celebrity politicians matter? *The British Journal of Politics and International Relations*, 14 (3), 345–56.

Strolovitch, D., Warren, D. & Frymer, P. 2006. Katrina's political roots and divisions: race, class, and federalism in American Politics 11, *Understanding Katrina Perspectives from the Social Sciences*, http://understandingkatrina.ssrc.org/FrymerStrolovitchWarren [accessed on July 10, 2014].

Tierney, K., Bevc, C. & Kuligowski, E. 2006. Metaphors matter: disaster myths, media frames, and their consequences in Hurricane Katrina. *The Annals of the American Academy of Political and Social Science*, 604 (1), 57–81.

Tsaliki, L., Huliaras, A., & Frangonikolopoulos, C.A. 2011. *Transnational Celebrity Activism in Global Politics – Changing the World?* Chicago: Chicago University Press.

Torfing, J. 1999. *New Theories of Discourse: Laclau, Mouffe, and Žižek*. Oxford: Blackwell.

van Krieken, R. 2012. *Celebrity Society*. Oxford: Routledge.

Wheeler, M. 2013. *Celebrity Politics*. Cambridge: Polity Press.

8

IRONY AND POLITICALLY INCORRECT HUMANITARIANISM

Danish celebrity-led benefit events

Mette Fog Olwig and Lene Bull Christiansen

Introduction

> I don't mean any harm by it at all, but I do hear it myself, when I say that "we
> are out collecting for the *negroes*," it does not sound very nice. But we have to
> remember one thing: I love the Africans, and I love all the people in the world.[1]
> *(Linse Kessler (Danish reality TV star) speaking at
> Danish benefit event[2])*

Recent literature on the role of celebrities and so-called philanthrocapitalists in
the aid industry (e.g. Farrell 2012; McGoey 2012; Nickel 2012) has largely taken
its point of departure in the mainstream Anglo-American setting where celebrity philanthropy has been promoted in the context of a highly commercialized
and hierarchical celebrity culture (e.g. Richey & Ponte 2011, p. 90). "Celebrity,"
however, is a culturally loaded word reflecting the values that are celebrated in a
given society (see Richey, in this volume). In the following we will broaden the
understanding of celebrity by focusing on Danish examples. We will argue that
celebrity involvement in aid campaigning in Denmark is situated in a different
political economy and culture of celebrity, in which anti-elitist sentiments must be
inscribed into celebrity performances in order to place them in local national cultural norms and in accordance with varying social codes. These codes and norms
are based in understandings of democratic inclusion and equality by being for and
of the people, often through an ostensibly politically incorrect, unassuming and
underplayed, irony. It is because of the existence of such norms that celebritization
places development aid in a depoliticized broad popular narrative, rather than in a
politically correct elitist narrative, as exemplified by the introductory quote. While

our examples are Danish, the politically incorrect philanthropy that they reveal might well be found in other cultures or subcultures where standardized, politically correct, popular Anglo-American culture is less influential.

Within the Nordic countries, development aid has traditionally enjoyed popular support and high levels of state funding (Bach et al. 2008; Brunbech et al. 2008). Yet, over the last decade, critical discourses concerning the feasibility and long-term consequences of development aid have begun to take hold of both public opinion and state policies.[3] In the Danish aid industry, this shift has been met by two communication strategies: firstly, a strategy of increasingly aggressive fundraising, and secondly, a strategy aimed at depicting positive outcomes of development aid.[4] Following mainstream Anglo-American trends, celebrity activists are central to both these communication strategies, functioning as witnesses, mediators and "guarantors" in the aid-positive campaigns (Richey & Ponte 2011, p. 20; Christiansen 2013).

As Ilan Kapoor (2013) argues, this celebritization not only shifts attention to more "sellable" issues, but also functions to depoliticize global inequalities into a question of aid and charity. These tendencies thus function to underpin a global order of inequality, in which human suffering is depicted as exceptional cases of misfortune that therefore call for individual moral (rather than political) engagement (Kapoor 2013, pp. 2–3, 96, 112–114). "Selling" humanitarianism through celebritization thus involves difficult compromises, or what Michael K. Goodman (2010), in the context of celebritized fair trade, has referred to as "Faustian bargains." Goodman argues that celebrities may attract more money for poor and marginalized farmers, but there is the risk that consumers purchase fair-trade products only to copy their favorite celebrities at the cost of building connections between consumers and producers. This is a consequence of marketing space – in the media and on the products – being increasingly overtaken by celebrities and their fair-trade experiences, thus eclipsing stories about the producers. Goodman laments that "to lose one of fair trade's key sources of its difference – the construction of distance-crossing moral economy and possibilities of more conscious and politicized consumers [. . .] seems not only problematic but a rather substantial reversal of its original intent as an alternative way of doing development" (Goodman 2010, p. 115).

Lilie Chouliaraki similarly discusses a "deep ambivalence" in relation to aid concerts: "Whereas the positive argument emphasizes the power of rock concerts to mobilize a global economy of genuine commitment that can make a real difference to vulnerable others, the skeptical argument draws attention to the profound inauthenticity of media events [. . .] in that they commercialize, rather than enhance, commitments to solidarity and reproduce, rather than challenge, colonial stereotypes of vulnerable others" (2013, pp. 108–9). Chouliaraki, however, goes on to suggest that in order to move beyond this impasse we should "turn towards empirical analysis" (2013, p. 113). Taking Chouliaraki's proposition as our point of departure, we here present an empirically grounded analysis of the inherent compromises introduced with celebrity activism and at the intersection of culture and political economy.

By focusing on a case that differs from the dominant Anglo-American standard we illustrate how Danish celebritized benefit events promote humanitarianism by drawing on a combination of international trends while referring to national sets of cultural norms. The Danish case, we posit, can thereby shed light on the inter-play between the local and the global contexts, and thus also inform studies of mainstream celebrity activism with regard to potential localized particularities. This chapter thus argues that contextualizing celebrity-led benefit events with regard to local cultural norms is of pivotal importance to understanding the rationales behind their execution and potential impact in terms of local perceptions and practices of humanitarianism. We will therefore begin by briefly introducing the Danish con-text in which celebrities must navigate.

The Danish context: humility and humor

As Michelle R. Nelson and Sharon Shavitt explain: "benevolent policies toward the least fortunate in society, coupled with a social modesty code that frowns on showing off, characterize Danish society" (2002, p. 439). The importance of humility in contemporary Danish society is, as we will further discuss below, strongly linked to anti-elitism and anti-intellectualism. The Danish-Norwegian author Aksel Sandemose formulated *Janteloven* (the law of Jante) as a satirical rendi-tion of this social modesty code. He describes the "who-do-you-think-you-are?" mentality of a small community called "Jante," in his novel *A Fugitive Crosses his Tracks* (Sandemose 1936).[5] *Janteloven*'s "ten commandments" begin with the overall statement: "Thou shalt not believe thou art something" (Sandemose 1936, p. 77). *Janteloven* can thus be described as the antithesis of "the American dream" – those who strive for something "higher" should be kept down. Sandemose employs irony and sarcasm in order to depict the damaging social consequences of anti-elitism and anti-intellectualism. While there is, of course, more to Denmark than *Janteloven* it has become a national trope. In our context, we understand this cultural code as a normative rejection of intellectualism, political correctness and critical distance – everything and anyone who oversteps the norms of modesty by claiming an intellectually informed "moral critique."

The rules of *Janteloven* are often handled through an extensive use of ironic humor, as indicated by the event, "The Jante Law and irony," hosted by an inde-pendent nonprofit company offering classes in Danish. On its website the company describes *Janteloven* as a "hidden social code" that is "closely knitted into Danish behavior" and frequently "combined with irony that can be confusing to under-stand."[6] Irony as a mainstay of "Danishness" has important literary roots in the work of two key Danish literary figures, Søren Kierkegaard (Kierkegaard 1989) and H.C. Andersen (Bredsdorff 2011), and is mentioned on numerous websites seeking to explain Danish culture. The website of *The Association of Folk High Schools in Denmark*,[7] for example, states:

To many Danes, humour and irony are closely linked. Understanding this irony is an important part of understanding the Danish mentality. You might sometimes find that it is easy to misunderstand Danes during a conversation due to the excessive use of irony. In those situations you should not be afraid to ask. Self-irony is also a big part of the Danish mentality, so if you feel that a Danish person might be trying to make fun of you, it is most likely not the case at all. In these situations you also should not be afraid to ask either, and hopefully, you will be able to laugh at the situation.[8]

Danish celebrities in many ways go against the social modesty code of *Janteloven* just by being famous. When they promote humanitarianism, they therefore often downplay their fame through ironic humor and their elitism by being politically incorrect – a task that is not always easy to achieve. Underplayed ironic humor thus can be very difficult to identify and when combining irony with the use of politically incorrect sentiments, for example racist stereotypes, it can be almost impossible to know whether the humor is racist or ironic – at the expense of racists. In the following we will discuss the concept of irony and how it can lead to political incorrectness, counterintuitively through notions of enlightenment and democracy.

Theoretical framework: irony, enlightenment and democracy

According to Thomas Bredsdorff, irony can mean many things, but its most fundamental purpose is "to say something else than what you mean, in such a way that your real meaning is understood. This is easy in theory, but quite difficult in praxis"[9] (2011, p. 11). Bredsdorff elaborates that there are several reasons for wishing to avoid saying directly what one means, and he views irony as a weapon: "The one who masters the power of language can use it against the one who has the physical and economic power" (2011, p. 18),[10] for example in the case of dictatorships or occupations. Traditionally, irony has thus been depicted as an important democratic form of expression, particularly in contexts of oppression, where political satire and irony can "speak truth to power" through the means of humor (Colletta 2009). Discussing a different use of "the critical power of irony" James Brassett notes that: "irony can be playful: chiding us to drop the straight faced moral seriousness that sometimes freezes ethical (self-) critique" (2009, p. 223). While powerful, irony is, however, hard to pull off in practice, as Bredsdorff points out. On the one hand, when people use irony, it is difficult to know what their opinion really is, and they therefore do not have to take responsibility for what they say – perhaps it was only meant in jest. Through irony it becomes possible to say and do things that would otherwise be off-limits, for example under a dictatorship. On the other hand, one does so at the risk of it being misunderstood – the intended meaning may be lost. It may, furthermore, be unclear whether ironic critique constitutes an actual critique, or merely serves as an "illusion (and enjoyment) of critique" (Kapoor 2013,

p. 25; see also Littler (2008) on the use of ironic distance by celebrities involved in humanitarianism).

In the field of British aid celebrity studies, Brassett has connected irony to notions of global justice, contending "that irony is one of the greatest ethical resources on offer to (perhaps from) the British: an abject collective sense of ethical limits" (2009, p. 221). He concludes that it is "through the prism of British irony, [that we can] highlight some ways in which the limits of global ethics might be understood and contested" (2009, p. 221). As illustrated above, Danes, not unlike the British, often emphasize that Danish ironic humor is key to understanding Danes. The Danish use of irony, however, differs from the British. In the Danish context irony is often combined with anti-elitism and used to excuse or blur politically incorrect statements. This, we argue, can be linked to the history of enlightenment and democracy in Denmark.

N.F.S. Grundtvig, who lived from 1783 to 1872, is an important figure in shaping the democratic norms of Danish society. Grundtvig has had a strong influence on Danish culture through his work as an author, poet, bishop, historian, educator and Enlightenment theologian (de Certeau 1984). Grundtvig's Enlightenment ideology of *folkeoplysning* – education for the people, including peasants and the working classes – saw universal lifelong enlightenment as a prerequisite for democratic participation. These ideals have shaped Danish perceptions of the roots of the welfare state to this day (Damsholt 2003; Pedersen 1989). Grundtvig's legacy is also acknowledged internationally for having pioneered a movement of education for the people in Scandinavia and beyond and for contributing to the introduction of parliamentary government in Denmark in 1849.[11]

The ideology of inclusive education for the people is closely linked with the concept *folkelighed*. *Folk* translates most correctly into "the people" (Damsholt 1995, p. 5), and *folkelighed* into "what belongs to the people" (de Certeau 1984, p. 131). *Folkelig* is an adjective, which depicts something as qualitatively rooted in popular appeal. It also indicates an unassuming character and is positioned in opposition to narrow elitist aesthetics and intellectuality. Thus, Grundtvig's Enlightenment democratic ideals are today connected to the democratic notions of the all-inclusive welfare state, to cultural roots in rural farming communities and to working-class culture (Hvenegaard-Lassen 2006; Kristiansen & Jørgensen 2003). In contemporary Danish society these roots have come to stand for an inclusive notion of *folkelighed,* where not excluding anyone also means not excluding any points of view. Thus (ironically), inclusiveness and anti-elitism, which for Grundtvig was intended to be a means of enlightening the common people, has come to mean that even an "unenlightened" point of view is seen as a valid standpoint in political debate, social commentary and cultural critique.

We will show in our analysis that *folkelighed* enframes the benefit events serving democratizing and inclusionary functions. In other words, everyone is welcome at the event, even members of the elite, such as celebrities, as long as they act like one of the people and put aside intellectual critique and instruction – often through the use of politically incorrect and ironic humor.

Methodology: two case studies

This chapter is based on studies of two Danish benefit events: the annual national telethon and week-long media event *Danmarks Indsamling* (Denmark's Fundraiser), which is the largest fundraising event in Denmark; and an annual one-day fair-trade benefit concert, which we will refer to as the *Fairtrade Concert*. This chapter focuses on the data collected during participant observation conducted at the 2012 fundraiser and the 2013 concert as well as from the media output and online debates directly connected with the 2012 and 2013 telethons and the 2013 concert. We have also participated in, and followed, the media coverage of *Danmarks Indsamling* since 2010 and the *Fairtrade Concert* since 2008. The study of events has been an important methodological approach in anthropology. As Michael Jackson puts it: "many of the classic and enduring works of ethnography are essentially descriptions of single events" (2005, p. xxvi). Such events have included the opening of a bridge (Gluckman 1940), rites of initiation (Turner 1967) and a Balinese cock fight (Geertz 1973). According to Jackson, "an ethnography of events seeks to explore the interplay of the singular and shared, the private and public, as well as the relationship between personal 'reasons' and impersonal 'causes' in the constitution of events" (ibid. xxvii). By studying both one of Denmark's largest and one of its smallest fundraising events, this study encompasses the possible scope and scale of celebrity-laden development interventions in contemporary Denmark, enabling us to investigate the important common features that cut across scale and place.

Danmarks Indsamling is organized by 12 leading NGOs and the dominant, national non-commercial public broadcaster Danmarks Radio (DR). It is a wide-ranging multi-platform media event, comparable to, for example, the annual media event around Hollywood's Academy Awards (Compton 2004, p. 134). The main TV and radio channels provide week-long run-up coverage and the children's TV channel *Ramasjang* promotes the telethon via a partnership with the multi-national Danish toy manufacturer LEGO. A broad spectrum of private initiatives and organization-driven local and national initiatives add to the event, including lower secondary-school students competing to raise money through posting fund-raising videos on YouTube, childcare workers organizing cupcake bake sales, and local sports clubs giving proceeds from matches and athletic events to *Danmarks Indsamling*. Collection boxes are distributed to local businesses across the country and corporate sponsors are featured throughout the telethon.

The *Fairtrade Concert* is organized by a non-commercial fair-trade company and takes place in a Danish province that is a popular tourist destination. The concert is widely advertised locally, is promoted on the local TV channel and draws more than 1,000 volunteers and between 7,000 and 10,000 visitors. Danish celebrities host the concert, which includes a number of well-known bands, mostly Danish, but also a few international artists, including African ones. There is a wide variety of music genres, targeting audiences of all ages. In 2013, the two celebrity hosts performed a "new Africa song"[12] entitled *Medaase for kaffe*,[13] which they had produced in collaboration with the fair-trade company organizing the concert and with support from the Information Fund of the Danish International Development Agency (Danida). At the concert, various organizations run stalls promoting "good causes" and selling products such as Ghanaian fair-trade baskets and glass bead jewelry. The concert proceeds support projects in Ghana, directly benefitting the bead makers and basket weavers. Major commercial organizations were also present, such as Denmark's largest retail supermarket COOP that promotes a range of Sub-Saharan products. There are also several food stalls and an extensive children's area with pony rides and games. While the two events were clearly different in size and scope, they also shared important characteristics, which we will further elaborate below.

Targeting a Danish audience through politically incorrect *folkelighed*

Every day during the week leading up to the 2013 *Danmarks Indsamling*, two celebrities competed to raise the most funds. On DR1's primetime daily talk show *Aftenshowet* the viewers could follow how the two celebrities, during the day, collected money in their local neighborhoods, and during the talk show continued to solicit support via text messages from the TV audience. Throughout the week the show featured two politicians (from opposite ends of the political spectrum), a celebrity couple and two of the show's hosts. On the day before the telethon, and thus forming the grand finale of *Aftenshowet*'s collection, two "TV personalities" were set to compete. One was the TV presenter Camilla Ottesen, well known for hosting popular shows and for a documentary series about her life in South Africa, where she lived for a few years. The other was the reality TV star Linse Kessler, whose brother was formerly the middleweight boxing world champion. Her celebrity persona is based on a distinct look: large (implanted) breasts, platinum blond hair, manifold tattoos and a frank working-class Copenhagen manner. Her success is based on depicting her working-class lifestyle in its sexualized excesses, both in defiance of "proper middle-class femininity" (Skeggs 1997) and against intellectual critiques of the sexualization of women in public. Kessler portrays herself as a happy former stripper who is proud of her working-class roots.

The *Danmarks Indsamling* segment kicks off by pitting the two celebrities against each other in "a battle between brunettes and blondes," but also between Ottesen's upper-middle-class Copenhagen neighborhood and Kessler's working-class neighborhood. They are shown walking around their home neighborhoods, and Kessler is depicted talking to shopkeepers about her collection for "negro children and negro people."[14] After the reportage has been shown, the talk show host confronts Kessler about her particular use of language: "There might be people out there who are thinking: 'she is saying *negroes* – that is a little denigrating, isn't it!?'" In response, Kessler continues explaining as she elaborates on the quotation with which we started this chapter:

I have no problem with them whether they be dark or yellow or whatever they are. But I'm so old, that when I was little, the term was "negro!" [. . .] they were not called Africans or Afro-Americans [. . .] and [negro] was not a bad word to say, and I mean no harm by that. I can hear that it sounds wrong, but . . .

Here the host, in an attempt to lend support, or perhaps to interrupt this speech, chimes in encouragingly: "it did not seem that way to me either"; Kessler, however, continues: "I don't mean it that way at all, I have a friend in Ghana, her name is Mercy, so they are my friends too!"

In the context of the otherwise streamlined media campaign, this interlude is somewhat embarrassing. Debates over the problematic nature of the term "negro"[15] have been raging over the last 20 years in Denmark (Schack 1995). Kessler's reference to the stereotypical figure of "the negro," which in the early 19th century functioned pedagogically to discipline the "lower class Others" into the national biopolitics of health and progress (Andreassen & Henningsen 2011; Hvenegaard-Lassen 2006), in this context becomes an embarrassing marker of lack of sophistication. Thus, the host, Ottesen (who had depicted her experiences in South Africa), and Kessler herself both appear embarrassed by the use of the term. However, the producers of the show could, of course, easily have removed the embarrassing scenes from the reportage or instructed Kessler during the takes, that she was using "taboo language." They chose not to, which leads us to analyze the segment as an illustration of the construction of *folkelighed* in the overall media campaign.

Kessler's hypersexualized persona and her self-identification as from the working class places her at the periphery of social acceptability – indeed, the success of her TV show is partly based on "lower-class freak show" trends in contemporary media (Faber et al. 2012, p. 9). Displaying commitment to the cause of development aid is not expected of someone with Kessler's gender performance and class position. Therefore, allowances are made for her to enter into the politically correct realm of "speaking for the cause." Conversely, silencing Kessler's politically incorrect attitude to the fundraising, would, in keeping with *Janteloven*'s democratic ideology, be a breach of the cultural norms of *folkelighed*. Kessler's voice is an important one – she is the token working-class representative. We argue that a mirroring is meant to occur between parts of the audience and Kessler as she represents TV viewers who would employ this type of language and resort to the same style of arguments in defense of the term. In the overall context of *Danmarks Indsamling*, the politically incorrect terminology underscores *Danmarks Indsamling*'s attempt to appear inclusive (and, by extension, the inclusive appeal of the cause of development aid).

The presence of politically incorrect and taboo elements ensures that viewers do not feel that they are being told what to do or think by "know-it-all" experts and people who use fancy, politically correct, language; rather, they are being included.

Seen in this context the host's questioning of the language served as a "highbrow killjoy" moment where Kessler was admonished for her use of what could be viewed as an offensive term, and which the host (possibly) tried to downplay by conceding to Kessler, that "it did not seem that way to me either." The importance that this Danish event be *folkelig* (that is, for and of the people) and avoid critical intellectualism allows for the inclusion of politically incorrect sentiments, meaning that objections to the denigrating legacy of the term "negro" are overridden.

The difficulties involved in combining politically incorrect sentiments with irony can be illustrated by the ways in which the 2013 *Fairtrade Concert* was hosted by the Danish celebrities Martin Brygman (comedian, musician and actor) and Anette Heick (singer and TV host), as recorded in the following fieldnotes:

> Nabiha, a singer-songwriter with both Danish and northwest African roots, has opened the show on the main stage and we join the crowd, which is mostly sitting on the grass enjoying the music – picnic style. As soon as

FIGURE 8.1 Politically incorrect forms of expression were also present at the *Fairtrade Concert*. The most eye-catching example was a booth where guests could shoot rifles at oversized playing cards featuring naked pin-up girls. Photograph by Mette Fog Olwig.

Nabiha has concluded her show with her hit *Mind the gap*, the two Danish celebrity hosts, Martin Brygman and Anette Heick, enter the stage to fill out the time between bands. Heick is wearing a white Afro explaining that she was jealous that Brygman had something in common with Nabiha – a large space between the front teeth – and therefore she put on the Afro so that she would also share something with her. [. . . Later in the show] Heick steps out onto the stage again, this time wearing a zebra outfit, or rather a dress with zebra print. She explains that she is planning on getting increasingly "wild" during the show.

When Heick wears an Afro (see Figure 8.2), it is not clear whether she is employing an ethnic stereotype in order to be funny at the expense of Nabiha, or whether she is being ironic about Danes' use of stereotypes. If she is being ironic, one could argue that she is not being racist, and poking fun at someone who is a racist, rather than Nabiha. However, if she is not being ironic (and how do we really know?), then she is either naïve and ignorant or employing ethnic stereotypes and arguably being racist. The ambiguity of employing this kind of humor is further illustrated by the official music video of the new "Africa song." On the *Fairtrade Concert*'s website it is explained that the music video project was intended to provide a tribute to Africa's cultural and economic contribution to the world and thereby

FIGURE 8.2 Brygman and Heick wearing a white Afro. Photograph by Mette Fog Olwig.

to offer a positive perspective on the many opportunities on the African continent and a sense of community across borders. In this way, the concert organizers hoped to draw attention to the difference fair trade can make. These explanations thereby clearly link up with the overall strategy by the aid industry discussed earlier to depict positive outcomes of development aid. Furthermore, there is an emphasis on the importance of fair trade getting "attention."

The music video begins with two girls of African descent leafing through a photo album containing pictures from Ghana. The camera zooms in on a photo that comes alive with Ghanaian sights and sounds. Then drumming starts. A group of schoolchildren begin singing *medaase*. Quickly, we cut to four women also singing *medaase* and dancing. The music is rather catchy, with a good beat. An appropriately adorable little girl has learned the dance and the camera shifts between the schoolchildren, the four women and the little girl. The video returns to the two girls who are turning the pages of the photo album to a picture of Heick and Brygman posing in a savanna landscape wearing remarkable outfits: Brygman in batik trousers, naked torso and leather suspenders while Heick is sporting a grass skirt and coconut bra. The outfits are arguably playing on both racial and gender stereotypes. Brygman starts singing with a comic facial expression while Heick makes her way through the tall grass with dramatic movements. The two perform in a silly manner while the lyrics ask what we would do without coffee, timber, chocolate, gold and tuna. This is followed by several *medaases* as well as a call to "shake your booty and give it a slap."[16] Brygman and Heick continue singing and dancing, intermittently slapping each other's behinds and making funny faces, and Brygman eats an imaginary nut from Heick's coconut bra and then uses the coconut bra as a drum. This playful sexualized silliness is intercut with scenes of the schoolchildren, the four dancing women and the little girl as well as a few other generic African scenes, including men opening cocoa pods with big knives and people dancing in colorful clothes. Two-thirds of the way through the video Heick and Brygman are joined by Sellasi Dewornu (a Ghanaian musician), who is wearing an outfit similar to Brygman's. His entrance intersects with lyrics which depict "Africa's music," and their interplay underlines his musical talents. At the high point of the video, Heick and Brygman are seen performing in the village at what seems to be a large celebration (here not in the grass–skirt costumes). Several shots depict the villagers, from children to elders, "having a blast" while Heick and Brygman are performing with their Ghanaian band and dancers. The video concludes with Heick and Brygman, surrounded by Ghanaians, looking up and waving at the camera that slowly zooms out until the photo album is closed.

In order to draw attention, and to have a positive vibe, the music video uses self-deprecating humor, yet it does so by playing ironically with stereotypes. Despite the fact that the two performers are not in "actual blackface," their outfits are so similar to stereotypical historical racist references that they can be read as equivalent to "blackface." Yet this reading must be nuanced by incorporating the fact that Sellasi, the Ghanaian musician, also participates in the interplay, but is not included in the sexual innuendo. His presence adds to a comical reading of Brygman. While Brygman looks goofy and not sexually appealing in his outfit, Sellasi can carry off this outfit. In fact, it appears as if the costumes Brygman and Heick are wearing have been modeled on his performance dress as well as similar female performance dress styles.[17] As both Brygman and Heick look comical in this attire compared to Sellasi, this can be read as an attempt at ironic humor and distance. That is, wearing "blackface" in a Danish cultural context is normatively permitted if you simultaneously open yourself up for ridicule – a point to which we will return.

Avoiding the use of sophisticated humor, and instead using folksy, inclusive humor, may in part be an attempt to counter a global trend in the promotion of fair trade "to develop fair trade as a set of 'quality' branded products of distinction and 'good' taste" (Goodman 2010, p. 110). In this music video, by contrast, fair trade is shown to be not about spending money on expensive, exotic, high-quality products from the Global South, nor is it about being political, showing off, or being part of the elite. When this is performed by celebrity figures, who are often considered part of the elite, a double articulation occurs. On the one hand, these figures would not have been chosen to perform were it not for their celebrity status, thus status *is* ascribed to the fair-trade products via their involvement. On the other hand, the celebrity position in a Danish cultural context does not function to elevate the celebrity above the democratic ideals inscribed in *Janteloven*. Rather, it falls to celebrity figures to perform their celebrity personas in such a way as to signal – if not ordinariness – then equality; and the self-deprecating humor of the video serves well in this respect. By association, the fair-trade products are then re-inscribed into a normative framework of anti-elitism and equality.

The use of self-deprecating *folkelig* humor, which involves sexual innuendo, is a widespread and popular form of entertainment in Denmark, which was also employed in *Danmarks Indsamling*. We will here dwell on an example from the 2012 telethon. During a competition for donations, Søren Rasted (a member of the internationally successful pop group *Aqua*) pledged to "damage his career" if a target number of donations was made. This "damage" involved performing a sketch (authored by Martin Brygman) with three fellow celebrities: Lars Brygman (actor), Anders Breinholt (journalist/comedian) and Martin Buch (actor/comedian). The four men dressed up as respectively two testicles, a penis and an anus. During the sketch the men read from a manuscript, apparently for the first time (something which is a popular party trick in Denmark). The storyline depicted four men gathering for a meeting in their housing association, and the comical content consisted of sexual innuendo and double meanings throughout their interactions. This was, obviously, underlined by their costumes. Rasted expressly prefaced the sketch by saying, "Now, I hope that most kids have been sent to bed at home in the TV-living rooms."[18] Nevertheless, the performance generated extensive criticism from viewers, primarily because many children *had* seen the show.

For our purposes, the debates that followed the performance shed light on the normative negotiations involved in "Danish humor" – and will help us understand the mechanisms involved in employing lurid humor in an attempt to establish *folke-lighed*. First of all, fieldnotes from observing the show on site describe the mood among the live audience as mixed – many people laughed, while others shifted uncomfortably in their seats, or simply looked bored. So, while TV audiences did hear a background of laughter, this was coming from only half of the audience. The divided on-site audience perhaps functioned as a warning for the performers on stage that something was awry. The performers seemed affected by the uneasy atmosphere in the concert hall. Instead of keeping to the format, where performers are meant to break down laughing because they "cannot help themselves," they ran through the sketch professionally and then got quickly off-stage.

In the "audience storm" which followed, three main claims were laid at the door of DR. Firstly (and predominantly) since the show had explicitly targeted an audience of children, it was seen as either distasteful (in the mild critiques) or perverse (in the harsh critiques) to expose children to such imagery and language. Secondly (and much less prominently), some viewers argued that given the chosen cause of *Danmarks Indsamling 2012* "Child Refugees," such a lurid sketch was not appropriate. Thirdly, a few complaints were made as to the quality of the comedy – it was seen as not funny enough and therefore embarrassing.[19] This caused the DR spokesperson Jakob Mollerup to respond by admitting: "We can air such a sketch late in the evening. There is nothing wrong in that. But five minutes of half-corny penis-sketch in the middle of a telethon appealing to a wide demographic is not ingenious timing. If only it had at least been hilariously funny."[20] In other words, there was nothing wrong in principle with the sketch in terms of content, but its timing and placement in the context of *Danmarks Indsamling* were misjudged. His last comment suggests, however, that criticism would have been avoided if the sketch had been truly funny. This echoes a number of the 280 comments that were posted on DR's website.[21]

In the absence of laughter, reflection set in, and in the cold sharp light of "not funny enough" a "half-corny penis-sketch" revealed itself to be inappropriate. While Heick and Brygman, in their performance in the fair-trade music video, were able to impose the normative framework of *Janteloven* onto the fair-trade products via their self-deprecating performance, the celebrity personae in *Danmarks Indsamling* came to be interpreted as inappropriately self-indulgent via the "not funny enough penis sketch." They were seen to have had a laugh at the expense of the cause – that is, thinking that their celebrity status allowed them to act outside the moral parameters of the show. The logic of the debates that ensued after the show reveals how the celebrity sign functions in the Danish context. If the celebrity cannot deliver on the promise of being "funny enough" then the mere fact that they have celebrity status is deemed irrelevant to their attractiveness as ambassadors for the cause.

In the online debates on *Danmarks Indsamling* two camps quickly formed. Firstly, the people who complained about the sketch on the grounds depicted above, and secondly, those who took issue with what they saw as petty small-mindedness and overzealous moralizing. One commentator, identifying herself as Trine Møller, wrote: "Now, should we not take care not to become too narrow-minded?! It is as if American conditions are coming closer, and that is a crying shame. We may soon also experience beeping noises if there is swearing on screen. Hopefully not! And why is it always the children, who are used as a reason for adults to sit and get prudish and offended. Most children know the expressions we were 'exposed' to last Friday, and they probably use them quite often amongst themselves when adults are not within earshot."[22] This commentator outlines a dichotomy between Danish humor and "American conditions," which Danes should take care to avoid. Prudishness and narrow-mindedness are not what Danes want to convey to children. A lurid joke or swearing is something that Danish children are well accustomed to, the commentator argues, and this is not problematic – rather the opposite. Here, as in the majority of comments on the website, there is a disconnection between the issue of *Danmarks Indsamling*'s purpose – collecting funding for development aid – and the moral debates over the sketch. The "larger issue" at hand seems to be whether or not the skit complied with Danish cultural norms.

While we argue that the execution of the music video and the penis sketch are shaped by Danish cultural norms, this does not mean they necessarily *succeed* in terms of Danish public approval. Whereas the penis sketch caused an "audience storm," the fair-trade music video, being linked to a much smaller-scale event, has not received as much attention.[23] In order to gauge the reaction of a Danish audience we therefore showed the music video to a small focus group of five Danes, two men and three women. Four had advanced social science university degrees. One of the participants was very familiar with Brygman's work and began laughing as soon as his face appeared. She thought it was a funny music video and commented, "I like the farts-are-funny kind of humor that he represents, I love him." Another participant also liked the video, being a fan of the humor used by Brygman and similar Danish comedians because of its absurdity. Two participants did not find the video at all funny whereas the last participant was undecided as to whether or not it was funny. When they were told that the music video was funded by Danida's Information Fund, however, they all agreed that the "information" relayed was very unclear and one even stated that she felt "her tax money had been wasted."

In connection with a verbal presentation of an earlier version of this chapter, we also showed the music video at an international conference. Here the audience expressed shock and bewilderment, one person stating that he had never before seen a short video straddling so many negative stereotypes at once, covering both gender and racial stereotypes. The Danish focus group, despite disagreeing on whether the video was funny, was surprised to hear about this very harsh reaction toward the video. When told that the video was perceived as politically incorrect and inappropriate, several reacted by commenting: "but if we cannot make fun of these kinds of issues (like gender and racial stereotypes), where will we be?" This statement reflects the idea that resisting political correctness is interconnected with democratic ideals in Denmark, an idea that has been connected to a national narrative, particularly over the last 20 years.

On the one hand, Danish anti-elitist and politically incorrect sentiments have been supported by juxtaposing Danish and Swedish approaches to multicultural-ism. The Swedish approach is often presented in the Danish media as one in which one cannot make fun of issues linked to race and gender through politically incor-rect stereotypes, and this, it is claimed, can lead to violence. This argument was presented, for example, by the political commentator Ralf Pittelkow in *Jyllands Posten*, the newspaper that originally printed the cartoons that led to the so-called "Muhammad Cartoon Crisis" (Hansen 2011; Hervik 2012; Yılmaz 2011). The headline of the article was "Sweden as a nightmare scenario," and in the article it was explained that this scenario is caused by the fact that "the politically cor-rect elite has thrown their society into a multicultural experiment" with extreme violence as a result.[24] Pittelkow thus points to Sweden as the country in the EU with the highest levels of violent crime such as fatal arson and rape. Here again, we see politically incorrect sentiments used to demarcate "Danishness" as opposed to either the moralizing discourses of "American conditions" (as in the debate over the penis sketch), or in this case against multiculturalist Sweden. On the other hand, the politically incorrect approach to race is shaped by a collective amnesia in relation to Danish colonial history and ignorance of Danish structural racism (e.g. Christiansen et al. 2006). This is illustrated by a quote from Per Durst-Andersen, professor at Copenhagen Business School, in the official Danish science blog vid-enskab.dk: "calling [the word negro] politically incorrect in a Danish context is untenable. In Denmark we have not seen the same racial discrimination as has the US. As I see it, it is far worse to call a person 'black'"[25] Race is thus conceptual-ized in terms of a particular historical situation, which supposedly does not apply to Denmark.

Conclusion

In this chapter we have aimed to explain why celebrity performances, that in many other contexts would be considered counterproductive to open-mindedness and disrespectful of "others," are supported with Danish development funds, and pro-moted as pro-development aid and fair trade. We show how in the Danish cultural context these celebrity performances, in fact, become points of demarcation for in- and exclusion in relation to the democratic body of the nation. We argue that this is partially a result of the anti-elitist Danish social code, as embodied in *Janteloven*, that one must not be superior nor preach morals and ethics (thereby presuming to be more moral or ethical than others). Instead, every voice is considered equal, including the unenlightened voices. The tensions entailed in the resulting form of humanitarianism lead to several compromises and ambiguities through which Danish celebrities must navigate, and have specific implications in terms of local Danish understandings and practices of humanitarianism.

First, though the celebritization of aid takes its inspiration from global trends, we have shown how celebrity aid can, in a local national setting, develop in ways that are contrary to the political correctness characteristic of global celebrity humanitarianism. A particularly Danish normative code of anti-elitism thus runs through both the events and the celebrity performances that characterize them. In order to establish the benefit events as *folkelige* (i.e. for the people) politically incorrect language use, attitudes and humor are deployed. This, we argue, is a bargain, whereby intellectual criticism of the world order that produces inequality is sidelined in order to make room for the *folkelige*, sellable "good time" event, where elitist critique and highbrow political debates would be considered a "killjoy." Where the politically incorrect sentiments are central in attempts at popularizing a cause (fair trade or development aid) which is normally associated with political correctness, the ironic use of stereotypes nevertheless runs the risk of using the intended messages of the campaign to legitimate a willful blindness to Danish structural racism and colonial history.

While our examples have been Danish, the compromises and ambiguities the Danish celebrity humanitarians face may well be relevant elsewhere, beyond the sanitized confines of globalized elite celebrity humanitarianism. Our case of the music video in which the Danish celebrities Brygman and Heick promote fair trade illustrates a general problem with ironic humor, especially underplayed irony, namely that it easily remains unclear whether a statement is meant to be ironic or not. Following Brassett (2009), by approaching racism and sexism through irony Brygman and Heick attempted to unfreeze ethical self-critique and thereby speak the cause of development and fair trade while avoiding the cultural taboo of moralizing. One can, however, just as well perceive Brygman and Heick as being simply sexist and racist, just as one can view them as merely trying to get attention by doing something they are not supposed to do.

There is a risk that Danish-style ironic humanitarianism can be perceived as endorsing callous ignorance through the use of politically incorrect, underplayed and unassuming irony. On the other hand, it is a highly inclusive ignorance. Consequently, we argue, Danish humanitarianism can become non-elite and inclusive and, perhaps as a result, enjoy a comparatively high level of popular support and state funding. The downside of this, however, is that there is something condescending about packaging humanitarianism within a coating of ironic political incorrectness. Though Denmark is a democracy, it reveals itself here as being an *unenlightened* democracy, unaware of those it excludes – that is, the Other who is kept invisible through the legacies of colonial history and the unequal power relations between the Other and Us.

Notes

1 Translated from Danish.
2 Aftenshowet. July 2, 2013. Danmarks Radio: DR1.
3 N.B. Petersen. 2013, June 8. V vil skære i ulandsbistanden – men sende flere penge til Afrika. www.b.dk/politiko/v-vil-skaere-i-ulandsbistanden-men-sende-flere-penge-til-afrika [accessed on March 6, 2014]; A. Sokoler [accessed on September 26, 2013]. Danskerne vil skære i ulandsbistanden, www.jyllands-posten.dk/protected/premium/indland/ECE6009538/danskerne-vil-skaere-i-ulandsbistanden/ [accessed on March 6, 2014];

Udenrigsministeriet. 2000. *Strategi for dansk støtte til civilsamfundet i udviklingslandene – herunder samarbejdet med de danske NGO'er* (Analysedokument og Strategi). Copenhagen.

4 Danmarks Indsamling – det nytter (2013, January 29). Danmarks Radio: DR1; www.verdensbedstenyheder.dk [accessed on March 6, 2014]; Udenrigsministeriet.

5 The 1936 version is a translation of the 1933 Norwegian version (Sandemose 1933).

6 http://www.clavis.org/en/for-students/courses-in-danish/events-at-clavis/saturday-mornings-at-clavis/the-jante-law-and-irony/ [accessed on February 3, 2014].

7 A folk high school offers adult education in the spirit of Grundtvig's promotion of education for the people (see discussion below).

8 www.danishfolkhighschools.com/faq/what-is-danish-culture [accessed on February 3, 2014].

9 Translated from Danish.

10 Translated from Danish.

11 Britannica Online Encyclopedia. (n.d.). N.F.S. Grundtvig (Danish bishop and poet). www.britannica.com/EBchecked/topic/247414/NFS-Grundtvig/ [accessed on March 6, 2014].

12 As explained by Christiansen and Richey, referring to the original Africa song; "celebrity engagement in and the popular appeal of development aid has arguably had its largest impact on pop-culture representations of Africa via the song 'Afrika', which, not unlike *Do they know it's Christmas*, has become a modern classic in Danish music history" (Christiansen & Richey, 2015).

13 The title is a mix of Twi, a language spoken in many parts of Ghana, and Danish. *Medaase* means "thank you" in Twi, and *for kaffe* means "for coffee" in Danish. The title has a double meaning; firstly the straightforward "thank you for coffee," and secondly the Danish turn of phrase *tak for kaffe!* This is an expression, used to signify something as intense or overwhelming – here the phrase is employed to comical effect, because of its double meaning.

14 Aftenshowet. (2013, July 2). Danmarks Radio: DR1. Translated from Danish.

15 The Danish word "neger" is derived from Spanish and Portuguese "negro" and has entered Danish through German and French. Historically, the term was used to denote people of African descent, but is today associated with the history of slavery and colonialism. It therefore shares the same negative connotations as the English term "negro."

16 www.youtube.com/watch?v=2ZWHxx9bE3s [accessed on February 3, 2014].

17 Selassi grew up in Ghana and now lives in Denmark, where he is a professional drummer and dancer. He performed at the 2013 *Fairtrade Concert* and here, and on his website (www.sellasi.com), he wears similar outfits to that worn in the music video.

18 Danmarks Indsamling – Børn på flugt. 2012, January 30. Danmarks Radio: DR1. Translated from Danish.

19 N.Vestergaard. 2012, February 4. Kritik af DR: Penis-sketch var langt under bæltestedet, http://www.dr.dk/Nyheder/Indland/2012/02/04/155302.htm [accessed on March 2, 2012]; N.Vestergaard. 2012, February 6. DR's seerredaktør: Penis-sketch var ikke genial timing, http://www.dr.dk/Nyheder/Indland/2012/02/05/233711.htm [accessed on June 2, 2012].

20 N.Vestergaard. 2012, February 6. DR's seerredaktør: Penis-sketch var ikke genial timing, http://www.dr.dk/Nyheder/Indland/2012/02/05/233711.htm [accessed on June 2, 2012].

21 http://www.dr.dk/Nyheder/Indland/2012/02/04/155302.htm [accessed on April 2, 2012].

22 http://www.dr.dk/Nyheder/Indland/2012/02/04/155302.htm [accessed on February 4, 2012].

23 As of February 2014, nine months after it was first uploaded, the music video had received almost 25,000 views on YouTube.
24 R. Pittelkow. 2009. November 10. Sverige som skrækeksempel. *Jyllands-Posten*, p. 16. Aarhus.
25 Translated from Danish, http://videnskab.dk/sporg-videnskaben/hvorfor-ma-man-ikke-sige-neger [accessed on March 7, 2014].

References

Andreassen, R. & Henningsen, A.F. 2011. *Menneske Udstilling. Fremvisninger af eksotiske mennesker i Zoologisk Have og Tivoli*. København: Tiderne Skifter.
Bach, C.F., Due-Nielsen, C., Feldbæk, O. & Petersen, N. (eds). 2008. *Idealer og realiteter*. Copenhagen: Gyldendal.
Brassett, J. 2009. British irony, global justice: a pragmatic reading of Chris Brown, Banksy and Ricky Gervais. *Review of International Studies*, 35 (1), 219–45.
Bredsdorff, T. 2011. *Ironiens pris: fire store ironikere-og et begreb*. Copenhagen: Gyldendal.
Brunbech, E., Hansen, A.S. & Midtgaard, K. 2008. Historier om dansk udviklingsbistand. *Den Jyske Historiker*, Special Issue (120).
Chouliaraki, L. 2013. *The Ironic Spectator: Solidarity in the Age of Post-Humanitarianism*. Cambridge: Polity.
Christiansen, L.B. 2013. "Kærlig hilsen fra Danmark": Kendisser og forestillinger om udviklingshjælp i Danmarks Indsamling. *Internasjonal Politikk*, 71 (4), 601–610.
Christiansen, L.B., Hansen, T.B., Jensen, L., Johansen, P., Kok, S., De Palo, A., . . . Poulsen, S. (eds). 2006. *Jagten på det eksotiske* (vol. 2006). Roskilde: Institut for Kultur og Identitet, Roskilde Universitet.
Christiansen, L.B. & Richey, L.A. (2015). Celebrity-black: the meanings of race and performances of aid celebrity outside the mainstream Hollywood–UK circuit. *Celebrity Studies*.
Colletta, L. 2009. Political satire and postmodern irony in the age of Stephen Colbert and Jon Stewart. *The Journal of Popular Culture*, 42 (5), 856–874.
Compton, J.R. 2004. *The Integrated News Spectacle: A Political Economy of Cultural Performance* (vol. 6). New York: Peter Lang.
Damsholt, T. 1995. On the Concept of the "Folk." *Ethnologia Scandinavia: A Journal for Nordic Ethnology*, 1995 (25), 5–24.
Damsholt, T. 2003. Grundtvig og de ansvarlige borgere. En diskussion af Grundtvigs politiske ideer om demokrati, frihed og ansvarligehed set som udgryk for moderne ledelsesrationaler. In H. Sanders & O. Vind, *Grundtvig – Nyckeln till det danska?* Göteborg: Makdam Förlag, pp. 28–59.
de Certeau, M. 1984. *The Practice of Everyday Life*. Berkeley: University of California Press.
Faber, S.T., Prieur, A., Rosenlund, L. & Skjøtt-Larsen, J. 2012. *Det Nye Klassesamfund*. Århus: Århus Universitetsforlag.
Farrell, N. 2012. Celebrity politics: Bono, product (RED) and the legitimising of philanthrocapitalism. *The British Journal of Politics & International Relations*, 14 (3), 392–406.
Geertz, C. 1973. *The Interpretation of Cultures*. New York: Basic Books.
Gluckman, M. 1940. Analysis of a social situation in Modern Zululand. *Bantu Studies*, 14 (1), 1–30.
Goodman, M.K. 2010. The mirror of consumption: celebritization, developmental consumption and the shifting cultural politics of fair trade. *Geoforum*, 41 (1), 104–16.
Hansen, L. 2011. Theorizing the image for security studies – visual securitization and the Muhammad cartoon crisis. *European Journal of International Relations*, 17 (1), 51–74.

Hervik, P. 2012. *The Danish Muhammad Cartoon Conflict*. Malmö: Malmö University.

Hvenegaard-Lassen, K. 2006. Velfærdsstatens Andre: in- og eksklusion af mennesker i den moderne danske stat. 1800–1980. *Tidsskrift for Velferdsforskning*, (4), 198–209.

Jackson, M. 2005. *Existential Anthropology: Events, Exigencies, and Effects*. Oxford: Berghahn.

Kapoor, I. 2013. *Celebrity Humanitarianism: The Ideology of Global Charity*. New York: Routledge.

Kierkegaard, S. 1989. *The Concept of Irony, with Continual Reference to Socrates: Together with Notes of Schelling's Berlin Lectures*, trans. H.V. Hong & E.H. Hong. Princeton, NJ: Princeton University Press.

Kristiansen, T. & Jørgensen, J.N. 2003. The sociolinguistics of Danish. *International Journal of the Sociology of Language*, (159), 1–7.

Littler, J. 2008. "I feel your pain": cosmopolitan charity and the public fashioning of the celebrity soul. *Social Semiotics*, 18 (2), 237–251.

McGoey, L. 2012. Philanthrocapitalism and its critics. *Poetics*, 40 (2), 185–199.

Nelson, M.R. & Shavitt, S. 2002. Horizontal and vertical individualism and achievement values: a multimethod examination of Denmark and the United States. *Journal of Cross-Cultural Psychology*, 33 (5), 439–458.

Nickel, P.M. 2012. Philanthromentality: celebrity parables as technologies of transfer. *Celebrity Studies*, 3 (2), 164–182.

Pedersen, P. 1989. Grundtvig i verdenshistorien og blandt fremmede folk. In *Dansk Mental Geografi. Danskernes syn på verden – og på sig selv*. Aarhus: Aarhus Universitetsforlag, pp. 26–34.

Richey, L.A. & Ponte, S. 2011. *Brand Aid: Shopping Well to Save the World*. Minneapolis: University of Minnesota Press.

Sandemose, A. 1933. *En flyktning krysser sitt spor: fortelling om en morders barndom*. Copenhagen: Gyldendal.

Sandemose, A. 1936. *A Fugitive Crosses His Tracks*. New York: Knopf.

Schack, J. 1995. Om ordet neger. *Nyt fra Sprognævnet*, 1995 (4), 1–5.

Skeggs, B. 1997. *Formations of Class & Gender: Becoming Respectable*. London: Sage.

Turner, V. 1967. *The Forest of Symbols: Aspects of Ndembu Ritual*. Ithaca, NY: Cornell University Press.

Yılmaz, F. 2011. The politics of the Danish cartoon affair: hegemonic intervention by the extreme right. *Communication Studies*, 62 (1), 5–22.

9

CELEBRITY, HUMANITARIANISM AND SETTLER-COLONIALISM

G.A. Robinson and the Aborigines of Van Diemen's Land

Robert van Krieken

FIGURE 9.1 Benjamin Duterrau, *The Conciliation*, 1840. Tasmanian Museum and Art Gallery.

> I did well to engage with the government for the capture of all the natives, for if I had been restricted to their first offer, I should not have seen any natives and they would have been dissatisfied and would have withheld from me their reward. By taking the whole I gain not only the reward but celebrity.
>
> *(George Augustus Robinson, 3 September 1832; Plomley 1966, p. 647)*

Critical portrayals of celebrity humanitarianism (Kapoor 2013; Littler 2008; Chouliaraki 2012; Daley 2013; Richey & Ponte 2011; Yrjölä 2009, 2012; Goodman 2010; Goodman & Barnes 2011; Browne 2013; Rojek 2013) usually make the following sorts of observations: that it benefits the celebrities themselves and the dominant groups in their own societies far more than recipients of their charity; that it disguises the real causes of the poverty, disasters or health problems their charity is meant to be alleviating; that it turns political action into a pale consumerist shadow of anything remotely capable of effecting genuine change, and that it mobilizes a politics of pity which displaces any politics of justice (Arendt 1963, pp. 70–1; Boltanski 1999, pp. 3–6). One recent critique of the 2014 Band Aid production argues that its portrayal of Africa is "a grotesque recycling of patronizing and offensive clichés about Africa as a place of darkness and perpetual suffering," which ignores the legacy of "300 years of empire," and that the time has now come for respect as well as pity.[1]

A stronger version of this argument appears in the work of writers like Riina Yrjölä (2012, p. 362), who suggests that it is not just a matter of legacies, but one of the ongoing colonial relationship between North and South, rendering the South "merely" the recipient of the North's charity. Bono can be seen as a modern version of 19th-century humanitarian Christian missionaries, intent on saving bodies and souls, but only in ways that are compatible with the North's economic interests (Duvall 2009). Robert Clarke (2009) develops the concept of "celebrity colonialism," pointing to the ways in which colonial settings operated as an important stage for celebrity production, and to roles played by celebrities in colonial governance, arguing that "the examination of celebrity promises to enrich our understanding of what colonialism was and, more significantly, what it has become" (2009, p. 4). Yrjölä argues along similar lines that celebrity humanitarianism displays "the re-actualisation of Western colonialism through images of the celebrity – as opposed to the soldier, the merchant or the priest, which were the icons of the older colonial culture" (2009, p. 17).

These analyses suggest that it is important to give more thought to the linkages between the concepts of "celebrity humanitarianism" and "celebrity colonialism," placing the critique of celebrity humanitarianism as an exercise in contemporary colonialism in the context of the history of colonialism itself, drawing out the connections between humanitarianism in earlier historical periods and the more contemporary expressions in what Barnett (2011) refers to as the "empire of humanity." Celebrity colonialism in its current form can only be understood in relation to its history, in order to grasp the underlying logic of humanitarianism as an essential, if always contested, element of the colonial project. Thinking in terms of a contemporary "empire of humanity" only makes sense if one understands the logic of imperialism and colonialism as it has unfolded over time, so that one can perceive both the continuities and the breaks between past and present manifestations of celebrity colonialism. For example, it is important to see the roots of the concept of "humanity" in the anti-slavery movement's anchorage in the Christian concept of "one blood," as well as the overall missionary project's conception of the essential unity of humankind under Christ (Harris 1990).

The roots of the humanitarian sensibility – the "passion for compassion" (Arendt 1963) – reach deep into the heart of colonialism and imperialism, having emerged at precisely the point where Europeans were reflecting on their relationships with vulnerable, non-European "Others" – slaves and indigenous peoples – whose vulnerability and suffering were precisely the result of Europeans' own actions. Didier Fassin (2011, p. xii) describes "humanitarian reason" as pursuing "the fantasy of the global moral community," an aspiration which creates the illusion that the world's contradictions have been resolved, and which "makes the intolerableness of its injustices somewhat bearable." In describing this "imaginary of communion and redemption" as "secular" Fassin has already drawn attention, if only implicitly, to the need to understand the roots of this imaginary, for Europeans at least, in Christian-inspired endeavors to make the injustices of empire and settler-colonialism somewhat more bearable. This makes it useful to look more closely at those imperial roots in order to understand how and why contemporary humanitarianism can be understood as an "empire of humanity" (Barnett 2011). Settler-colonialism and humanitarianism were bound at the hip, with the latter the product of the awareness that people with any concept of "humanity" were more or less obliged to make some attempt to soften the impact of European expansion on the human beings they were encountering beyond Europe.

The core initial concerns of humanitarians were slavery and the treatment of indigenous peoples. Most accounts present the second as having emerged from the first (Barnett 2011), but Peter Stamatov (2013) has argued that one can see the earliest forms of humanitarian concerns already at the beginnings of colonial expansion in the 16th century, with colonization the central original driver of shifts in the "boundaries of moral responsibility" (Haskell 1985, p. 359) that underpinned a humanitarian ethos. For Stamatov, the prehistory of the 18th-century anti-slavery movement lay in the response to the harsh and inhuman treatment of the inhabitants of the New World with, from 1511 onwards, various Spanish and Portuguese clerics developing a range of long-distance advocacy practices and "action technologies" to bring about greater recognition of the shared humanity of all peoples regardless of race, and to argue for their ethical treatment, if only as potential recruits to the Christian faith (2013, p. 177). Against that background, the concern with slavery did then introduce something quite new in becoming a "movement" which "involved for the first time a critical mass of lay supporters for a distant cause – that of ending the colonial slave trade" (Stamatov 2013, p. 2), and it was this need to attract popular support that added the element of celebrity production to humanitarian practices. Equally important was the influence of the emergence of mass market dynamics themselves which, as Thomas Haskell (1985) has argued, underpinned the shifts in cognitive orientations and perceptions of causal connections that made it possible for at least some Europeans to feel a connection with the suffering of "distant strangers," including the indigenous peoples being dispossessed and eliminated by the expansion of their own colonial empires.

When one looks at the colonial origins of humanitarianism, one encounters a particular kind of celebrity humanitarianism, one where the significant personalities are humanitarians first and celebrities second.[2] An important 19th-century celebrity humanitarian – in the sense of a humanitarian who became a celebrity – was George Augustus Robinson (1791–1866), through his attempts to prevent the complete annihilation of the indigenous population by the settlers in Van Diemen's Land, as Tasmania was then called. Robinson was a builder by trade, but with a humanitarian sensibility, and became famous in British humanitarian circles as the developer of a workable model for saving indigenous peoples from the worst excesses of British colonial expansion, and as the first official Protector of Aborigines in Australia. As Alan Lester emphasizes, he was a significant player in the ongoing "propaganda war" between humanitarians and colonial settlers in Australia, South Africa, the West Indies, New Zealand, North America and India about how indigenous peoples could and should be treated as settler-colonialism explosively expanded (2008, pp. 27–8). For the conceptual concern with the relationship between the global North and South, settler-colonial settings like Australia are an especially interesting example, constituting a complex mixture of North–South relations. The confrontation between settler frontier violence and educated humanitarians focused on the "civilized" metropole was also a manifestation of how the North relates to itself in the South.

For Robinson to acquire international recognition as "The Conciliator" was only possible through careful management of his public profile, his relations with powerful local figures as well as with influential humanitarian networks and networks of patronage; mastered with a view to how his ideas and actions would fit within broader international discourse about humanitarian problems created by European colonial expansion and settler-colonialism. Some commentators even suggest that ultimately he was more concerned with his own fame than he was with the fate of the Aborigines (Ryan 2004; Rae-Ellis 1988; Dowling 1967). Johnston, for example, describes Robinson as "an incredibly self-regarding, self-important man who used his engagement with the Tasmanian aboriginal population to further his own ambitions."[3] Without coming to a definitive view on that question, it is certainly true that Robinson's humanitarianism should be understood as intimately bound up with a concern for celebrity status, both driven by and driving a concern for public recognition within local and global humanitarian networks. Robinson was a key figure in the early stages of the development of the networking, media-savvy humanitarian, linking ambitions for personal advancement with the pursuit of a particular humanitarian issue, and this chapter reflects on how his career illuminates a number of important aspects of the logic of contemporary celebrity humanitarianism (Johnston 2009), in particular its relationship to colonialism and empire.

My argument will be that a closer analysis of the history of the relationship between celebrity, humanitarianism and colonialism helps us to see how the critiques of celebrity humanitarianism are fundamentally critiques of humanitarianism in all its forms over time; that the failures and moral ambiguities of contemporary celebrity humanitarianism have characterized colonial relations with non-European peoples from the beginnings of European expansion, and are expressions of how contemporary celebrity humanitarianism is anchored in ongoing relations of power between North and South. It also helps understand the ways in which humanitarianism – including the specific form taken by celebrity humanitarianism – should be understood as a mode of global governance, because that is how it has always operated. As Skinner and Lester observe, "the long-distance webs of concern spun by humanitarians within empire have always been intrinsic to the politics both of empire itself and of nation-state formation" (2012, p. 731).

George Augustus Robinson – "The Conciliator"

When George Augustus Robinson boarded a ship in Edinburgh bound for Australia in 1823, he was not emigrating with a view to becoming a famous humanitarian who would do his best to save the Aborigines in Van Diemen's Land. Although he had been doing quite well as a builder, brickmaker and bricklayer, he had suffered "a reverse of fortune," so he chose to "migrate to this remote appendage of his magesty's empire" (quoted in D'Arcy 2010, p. 55.7) primarily to improve his income, build up his assets and make his wife and five children "comfortable" (Plomley 1966, p. 14). But he was of a humanitarian sensibility, having been active in the Church Missionary Society in London, and after arriving in early 1824 became active in religious and charitable work, coming to be known in Hobart as "hard-working and public-spirited" (Plomley 1966, p. 14).

Robinson's arrival was followed a few months later by that of the new Lieutenant-Governor George Arthur. Arthur's previous posting had been as Lieutenant-Colonel of Honduras, where he had acquired a reputation both for his efficiency and for his anti-slavery policies, attracting the attention of William Wilberforce, who in turn helped him secure the appointment in Van Diemen's Land (Shaw 2004). His time in Honduras had sensitized him to the question of responsible governance of the indigenous population. Arthur was an evangelical Calvinist Anglican, also supportive of the work of the Church Missionary Society, a concern that would facilitate a close connection between the two men.

One of the issues demanding much of Arthur's attention was the heightening violence and tension between the settlers and the Aborigines. Relations between the two groups had never been especially good: Aboriginal women and children were frequently abducted and enslaved, and the convicts, stockmen and settlers didn't hesitate to torture, maim and kill any Aborigines they encountered, both in response to their retaliatory attacks, but also just to clear them from land they desired, regarding them as so primitive as to be subhuman. Robinson described the treatment of Aborigines around the island as "a refinement of cruelty not to be met with in the present day . . . parallel only with those cruelties practised upon the South American Indians by the blood-thirsty Spaniards" (Plomley 1966, p. 566, 26 December 1831). Robinson gives this account as an example:

The stockmen used to shoot and hunt the natives. One of them boasted that he had thrown a woman upon the fire and burned her to death. Another, named Carrot, having killed a native in his attempt to carry off his wife, cut off the dead man's head, and obliged the woman to go with him, carrying it suspended round her neck. Another, named Ibbens, had killed half the eastern tribe, by creeping amongst them, and firing amongst them with his double barrelled gun. It was stated to the committee that the worst characters were the best to send after them. Lemon and Brown, the bushrangers, committed every species of cruelty upon the natives; they used to stick them, and fire at them as marks while alive.

(Robinson 1839)

The brutality of the contact between Europeans and Aborigines was regarded as shockingly repellent by educated townsfolk, administrators, visitors and inhabitants of the metropole – in *The Voyage of the Beagle* Charles Darwin (1839) attributed the violence to "infamous conduct of some of our countrymen" – but for those living in fear for their own lives in the dangerous and insecure conditions of the frontier, like all frontier situations, it was seen as the only possible way of life.

After 1818 the island was opened up for new settlers, who were given grants of land according to the capital they brought with them (Plomley 1966, p. 25). The colony was still a penal settlement, so all labor was done by convicts hardened to the exercise of violence. As the European population grew, with more and more livestock requiring grazing land, the violence between the two groups intensified, making it entirely reasonable to describe the relationship as one of ongoing warfare (Plomley 1966, p. 28). The brutality went in both directions, emphasizes Henry Reynolds, so that although the Europeans were generally the original instigators of violence, "by the 1820s the Aborigines gave as good as they got" (2004, p. 73). By 1824 the Aboriginal population had been reduced from roughly 4,000 to 1,000, with diseases like venereal disease, influenza, pneumonia and tuberculosis resulting from European contact proving even more deadly than muskets and poisoned flour. But those that remained were not going to go down without a fight; they were determined to defend themselves and their country, and to retaliate against the atrocities they were being subjected to by stockmen, sealers, convicts and settlers, not to mention the theft of their land.

In response to the continuing attacks on settlers, the *Colonial Times* declared in 1826 that there were only two alternatives: either kill all the Aborigines, or remove them somehow from the territories desired by the settlers, specifically to King Island in the Bass Strait. The settler position could not have been clearer: "THE GOVERNMENT MUST REMOVE THE NATIVES – IF NOT, THEY WILL BE HUNTED DOWN LIKE WILD BEASTS, AND DESTROYED!" (Plomley 1987, p. 7). The Aborigines who attacked settlers found it relatively easy to evade the police and the legal system, so settlers took matters into their own hands, and Arthur and his executive council feared that the Aborigines would simply be annihilated. Arthur's declaration of martial law in 1828, beginning the Black War, was meant to impose some order on the exercise of violence, but it simply meant that settlers felt even freer to kill the Aborigines, and the attacks from both sides intensified. This was indeed a serious humanitarian crisis – there was not much time left before the island would have been cleared of all Aborigines – maimed, raped, tortured, knifed, shot, and burned to death.

Arthur was in an unfortunate position, partly because of his own moral qualms about overseeing wholesale massacre and slaughter, but also because of the growing humanitarian spirit (it was at the midst of the anti-slavery campaign) of the instructions he was receiving from Sir George Murray in the London Colonial Office (Reynolds 2004, p. 115). To pursue policies and permit practices aiming either explicitly or implicitly at the extinction of an indigenous population would only "leave an indelible stain upon the British Government", as it was expressed in 1837 in the *Report from the Select Committee on Aborigines (British Settlement)* (quoted in Lester 2008, p. 35). That moral stain could only be avoided if at least some effort were made to ensure that, if the Aborigines did become extinct, it was not at the hands of British colonists, or in the absence of some humanitarian efforts to prevent their disappearance. The thorny problem facing Arthur, as it did all other colonial administrators at the time, was how to make ongoing settler-colonial expansion "compatible with both the protection and salvation of indigenous peoples" (Lester & Dussart 2014, p. 4).

The Colonial Office was insisting that anyone causing the death of a native was to be subjected to criminal prosecution, but Arthur and his executive council thought this would make the settlers' lives impossible and drive most of them to abandon their farms. The colony's administrators were also concerned, as Lester and Dussart note, to do their best to monopolize the means of violence (2014, p. 20), to shape the moral habitus of settlers by seeking to deprive them of the opportunity to torture and maim other human beings. But Arthur's capacity to achieve this was non-existent while he was unable to control the Aborigines' retaliatory action, which was why the closest he could get to this aim was to try and put the Aborigines out of the settlers' reach, and transform them from warriors defending their stolen land into mendicant supplicants.

The first solution to the dilemma, then, remaining true to a humanitarian concern to avoid the extermination of the Aborigines, was an attempt at a knock-out blow in 1830: the organization of 2,200 men to move in a line across the island to corral all the Aborigines into the Tasman Peninsula, southeast of Hobart, known as the "Black Line." The Aborigines had no difficulty evading the Black Line, being so much more familiar with the territory, and the expensive venture failed miserably, capturing only two Aborigines, and killing another three.

But Arthur was pursuing a dual strategy, because alongside the military action he also supported other endeavors aiming at conciliation. In British Honduras he had encountered the concepts of the "amelioration" of recently freed slaves and of a "protectorate" for former slaves, both designed to address a very similar problem: how to prepare a population of former slaves for assimilation into European society without endangering the interests of European settlers (Lester & Dussart 2008)? Gilbert Robertson, another settler concerned about the suffering of the Aborigines, had had some success in capturing potentially influential Aborigines in 1828, and he hoped he would be able to work with them to effect an amicable relationship with the tribes remaining in conflict with the settlers, if they could be persuaded to put themselves under government protection. But Robertson was unable to repeat his success in later expeditions. His view of Aborigines as worthy of respect as warriors and deserving of a formal treaty was also out of step with Arthur's own conception of them as, although deserving of Christian charity, nonetheless inferior beings with no legitimate claims to land. Arthur translated the Caribbean concept of amelioration and a protectorate to Van Diemen's Land through supporting, from 1824, the "humanitarian experiment" (Lester 2012, p. 1478) of a potential "model community" on Bruny Island (Reynolds 2004, p. 130), and in 1829 he sought to appoint a superintendent to take charge there.

Robinson's humanitarian sensibility was rooted in his familiarity with, and commitment to, the arguments for the abolition of slavery through his involvement with the Church Missionary Society, co-founded by the leading anti-slavery campaigner, William Wilberforce. Robinson found a new outlet for that sensibility when he read the advertisement that Arthur placed in the *Hobart Town Gazette* in March 1829, seeking "in furtherance of the Lieutenant-Governor's anxious desire to ameliorate the condition of the aboriginal inhabitants of this territory . . . a steady person of good character . . . who will take an interest in effecting an intercourse with this unfortunate race . . . taking charge of the provisions supplied for the use of the natives" (Plomley 1966, p. 51). Robinson replied, writing that he felt a strong desire to devote himself to this cause, and agreed that Arthur's plan was "the only one whereby this unfortunate race can be ameliorated" — note his use of the concept of amelioration, drawing Arthur's attention to his familiarity with that discourse. Developing this theme, Robinson wrote that just as the Hottentot had been "raised in the scale of being" and the Tahitians "made an industrious and intelligent race," the same results could be achieved in Van Diemen's Land with similar efforts. Robinson underscored his understanding of the condition of the Aborigines by using terms central to the humanitarian discourse to which he knew Arthur would be committed. He wrote that under slavery: "Might overcame right and the original possessors of the soil became, not free men, but slaves under the force of war; but in many cases without the advantage of slaves, of being cared for" (Plomley 1966, p. 52; Brantlinger 2008). The Aborigines were treated like animals ("brutes"), thought Robinson, but they were in fact men "made after the express image of God," and he "felt persuaded that by kindness these poor creatures could be brought to a sense of the obligations and be made useful members of society" (Plomley 1966, p. 52). Robinson had already indicated in previous correspondence with Arthur about his land grant, that he shared both his involvement in the CMS and some degree of connection, albeit fleeting, with a significant imperial military network from his time working on military fortifications, which he was careful to highlight (D'Arcy 2010, p. 55.5). As Jacqueline D'Arcy observes, not only did Robinson draw on the same humanitarian imperial discourse that Arthur was already familiar with, he also had the wit to secure the endorsement of a friend who was also a CMS missionary – the Reverend James Norman – and D'Arcy suggests that "it was Norman's confirmation of Robinson's own personal links with the CMS network that helped him secure the post" (2010, p. 55.11).

Robinson said later, looking back, that his friends thought he was rash, being prepared "to live among savages for £50 a year" (Plomley 1966, p. 53). But, he said, "there were other things worth living for besides money making." And Robinson had been good at making money – by this stage he owned several houses that he was renting out (Pybus 2008, p. 102). However, it is also unlikely that evangelical zeal was his only motivation, or enough to persuade his wife it was good idea. He would also have understood that humanitarianism had become an important route to status and social recognition beyond what he could achieve as a builder. Hence, as Pybus notes, "the careful self-massaging of his image – in the journal he kept for future publication, as well in his public utterances – as the sole protector and father figure of the Aborigines" (2008, p. 102). As Dan Brockington has emphasized (2014, p. 56), in the 19th century the pursuit of humanitarian causes in exotic parts of the world was an important driver of celebrity, generating many of the widely-known figures of the time – William Wilberforce, Florence Nightingale, and Thomas Barnardo – supported by the emerging industrialization of the celebrity production process (van Krieken 2012, pp. 40–50). Many of the period's celebrity humanitarians:

> were able to thrive because of the mass-circulating commodities they could create. Explorers' books, and the prestige of speakers at the Royal Geographical Society, bought money and fame. The potter Josiah Wedgewood produced one of the first mass-circulated commodities in support of a humanitarian cause overseas . . . The commodity making commerce that fuelled early forms of celebrity also drove the renown of early forms of celebrity advocacy.
>
> *(Brockington 2014, p. 57; see also Morgan 2013 and Johnston 2009)*

Anna Johnston (2005) gives the examples of the explorer David Livingstone and the missionary John Williams, both of whom were skilled at the creation and nourishment of their celebrity status through self-promotion, management of extended networks through organizations like the London Missionary Society, organized publicity campaigns, and exploitation of the print media's thirst for narratives that would capture the attention of the ever-expanding mass audience of the emerging public sphere. It is worth noting how recognizable as a contemporary celebrity David Livingstone was: Henry Morton Stanley's supposed "discovery" of Livingstone, engraved on popular consciousness with the phrase "Dr Livingstone, I presume?," was a media event planned by the editor of the *New York Herald*, James Gordon Bennett. African expeditions were media events, organized by metropolitan magazines and their sponsors, who manufactured Stanley's celebrity identity as a "distinguished gentleman out to build an Empire" (Richards 1990, p. 135). Like any celebrity today, Stanley made sure he turned his activities into a bestselling and widely-translated book, *In Darkest Africa*. He became the star of banquets, balls, receptions and parades – it "became 'Stanley season' in high society" (Richards 1990, p. 136), a Stanley medallion was struck, and he did his share of product endorsements – Pears soap, pipes, tea, Bovril and tents (Richards 1990, p. 136). Celebrity explorers like Stanley and missionaries like Williams embodied key elements of Empire – exploration, that is appropriation, of ever-more new territory, and Christianization, the transformation of the inhabitants of those territories into more or less governable subjects. Stanley and Williams were key examples of the cognitive reference points for the emerging mass media's construction of their readership, an imagined community (Anderson 1983) whose interests needed to be shaped around shared narratives, emotional orientations and values in order to become a mass market, both for the print publications themselves and the rapidly expanding range of consumer products they advertised.

Robinson would have been well aware of that aspect of what it could mean to become famous as a traveller and a humanitarian concerned with building the right kind of British Empire, as the savior of the suffering Aborigines, and his later conduct indicates that it was indeed central to his motivations. For example, he was already giving thought to converting his endeavors into a book, no doubt hoping from the outset to thereby secure his status and fame in the broader "Aborigine Protection" field and to "accumulate 'honour' and political capital as a humanitarian inclined colonial settler" (Lester & Dussart 2014, p. 77). Duterreau's painting was originally intended for the book (Plomley 1966, p. 927). When he undertook his "Friendly Mission" expeditions around the island, he "cast himself in the role of imperial explorers and adventurers and was very proud of himself for being the first white man to walk up the west coast of Tasmania."[4] He was also anticipating a nice boost to his wealth – part of the deal with Arthur was additional cash and land if he succeeded in bringing in the Aboriginal tribes peacefully.

The Friendly Mission

The Bruny Island settlement contained a small number of Aborigines, mostly originating from other parts of Tasmania, made homeless by conflicts with settlers. The group included 18-year-old Truganini, a member of the Nuenonne tribe who had been born on Bruny Island, and was later to become famous as the last surviving full-blood Aborigine, whom Robinson befriended.[5] Robinson's plan was to establish a village with a school, along European lines, so that the adults would be "acquiring the habits of industry" and the children instructed "in the principles of Christianity" (Plomley 1966, p. 56). This plan never got far: only two months later Robinson decided that he needed to know more about Aboriginal culture and beliefs, but also to make active contact with the Aborigines of Tasmania – they were not going to come to Bruny Island of their own accord. One of the women there had herself walked from the west coast to visit friends on Bruny Island, indicating to Robinson that a walk in the other direction was also possible.[6] He put a plan to Arthur to travel around Tasmania, beginning with the west coast, in a more systematic way than Robertson had, taking the Aborigines he had befriended on Bruny Island with him as translators, guides and facilitators. The aim of this conciliatory or "friendly" mission would be to negotiate with the independent tribes and persuade them to surrender and allow themselves to be removed to somewhere safe from the settlers' murderous violence. As Lester put it:

> Through Robinson, Arthur found a way to bridge the crucial differences between an established discourse of amelioration, based on the protection and reform of captive, enslaved people, and the conciliation and protection of a defiant indigenous population. Even as all of the remaining Aboriginal people on the island (and not just those involved in conflict) were finally rounded up and exiled, the deterritorialization of amelioration in Van Diemen's Land and its reterritorialization as protection provided salvation for Arthur's reputation as a humanitarian governor.
>
> *(Lester 2008, p. 1478)*

Robinson's Friendly Mission should be placed in the context of the nine-year tour of two leading members of the Quakers, James Backhouse and George Washington Walker, of British colonies between 1832 and 1840, including three years in Van Diemen's Land. They epitomized the way in which early humanitarianism was organized around travelling to sites of humanitarian concern, combined with in-depth reports of those travels detailing the relevant humanitarian abuses, indicating the lines of responsibility and accountability, and above all the connections back to the British elite audience demanding particular actions and interventions on their part. As Edmonds puts it:

> With their elite connections, extensive networks of correspondents and multi-reform agenda, Backhouse and Walker were fundamental to the creation and expansion of humanitarian networks in the antipodes, where they made major humanitarian interventions in matters concerning Aboriginal peoples, penal reform, slavery and education. This foundational trans-colonial journey had a significant impact upon colonial and imperial policy concerning empire's management of Aboriginal and enslaved peoples, convicted felons and indentured labourers alike.
>
> *(Edmonds 2012, p. 770)*

The concept of "travelling under concern," emphasizes Edmonds, was an established Quaker tradition, "part of an emergent global mission to proselytise, witness and testify to the sufferings of others" (Edmonds 2012, p. 773), and to harvest information which would be mobilized back home – in lectures, submissions to government commissions of inquiry, popular books, pamphlets and magazine articles – to inform political action aiming to remedy the relevant abuses. Although Robinson's Friendly Mission was of much more limited scope and had a more practical aim – persuading the Aborigines to surrender themselves – and although he was not a Quaker, it was certainly had a lot in common with "travelling under concern." Edmonds observes that the Backhouse and Walker tour should be viewed in relation to, and in part an extension of, Robinson's efforts (2014, p. 27). I would argue that the two projects are better understood as both stemming from similar sources of humanitarian sensibility. Backhouse and Walker were much more firmly located at the center of the global humanitarian networks that Robinson was attempting to break into, and in that sense they were more an expression of the context of Robinson's endeavors than the other way around. Robinson himself clearly understood the broader significance of the exercise, particularly its potential as a model of protection of indigenous people that could be mobilized across the British Empire: "I trust the time is not far distant when the same humane policy will be adopted towards the aboriginal inhabitants of every colony throughout the British empire" (Letter to Arthur 1833, in Lawson 2014, p. 87).

The Black Line had failed, but it did have an impact by indicating how seriously the Aborigines were outnumbered, and how unlikely it was that they would be able to retain their freedom (Rae-Ellis 1988, p. 66). This, together with the efforts of Robinson's Aboriginal companions, especially Truganini and her partner, Woorraddy, and Robinson's willingness to learn the languages and travel to the tribes' own homelands, underpinned his spectacular success in persuading the various tribes during his six expeditions between 1830 and 1834 to surrender themselves to European "protection." Robinson made all sorts of promises that he had no intention of keeping – that the removal to an island would be temporary, that it would be possible for the Aborigines to return to their homeland, that their customs would be respected, and that all their wants and needs would be provided. On this basis the last of the tribes agreed to accompany Robinson peacefully to Hobart. Perhaps they were unaware of the trap they were entering, or perhaps they had an inkling but felt they had no option other than to place all their hopes in the possibility that the Europeans might honor their promises after all.

The Establishment for Aborigines, Flinders Island

After some early attempts at settlements on smaller islands in the Bass Strait, the "Establishment for Aborigines" to which all the Aborigines were taken, given the name "Wybalenna" (Johnston 2004), was located on the larger, Flinders Island, also in the Bass Strait. The Establishment was a complete disaster, an "endless saga of sickness, death and mourning" (Reynolds 2001, p. 83). The Aborigines died at a rapid rate, primarily of respiratory diseases, dropping from 220 in 1833 to 54 by 1842, with only 44 remaining in 1847 when Flinders Island was closed and the survivors moved to Oyster Bay, clearly no longer a danger to anyone. The Oyster Bay camp was closed in 1874, and Truganini was taken in by a Hobart family until her death in 1876. As a humanitarian exercise, Flinders Island was a dismal failure, and in many respects it was understood by the global Aborigines Protection Movement as a warning about how destructive contact with Europeans was (Heartfield 2011, p. 18). But Robinson made every effort to put a more positive spin on his model, attributing its failure to other factors beyond his control, invoking the concept of a "doomed race," arguing that at least their journey to Heaven had been facilitated by becoming Christians. At one point he declared that the "only thing to be deplored" about the settlement was the "mortality" of its inhabitants (Robinson 1839, p. 6). Robinson could only say that their demise was more civilized, in the sense of being pacified and Christian, than it would have been had they fought to the last in the Tasmanian countryside.

Robinson achieved much of the celebrity he sought. His reports were circulated widely throughout the British Empire, Charles Darwin would refer to his fearlessness and "intrepid exertions" (1839, p. 536), Backhouse's reports ensured his name was circulated back in London, and Arthur and his successor, John Franklin, also lent their support to the circulation of his name. His report was published by the British House of Commons in a parliamentary paper in 1839, to lend authority to the view that it was possible to effect a compromise between humanitarian principles and continued economic progress, and to establish that one could protect indigenous populations without halting or even slowing the advancement of settler-colonialism (Heartfield 2011, p. 95). Robinson's official reports on the orderliness of Wybalenna were largely fiction, but he wasn't inclined to let the facts get in the way of a good story, just as contemporary accounts of the success of humanitarian interventions are often at odds with the descriptions of those directly affected by them (Lawson 2014, p. 107). The Colonial Office bought the story, he was acknowledged by many, although not all, commentators as an expert on the concept of aboriginal protection, and Robinson's approach was accepted as the best way to halt or at least slow the extermination of the Aboriginal race. The Colonial Secretary, Lord Glenelg, agreed to create the post of Chief Protector of Aborigines with Robinson as its first incumbent, having shown himself to be "eminently qualified for such an office" (Heartfield 2011, p. 98). As Alan Lester has noted, Robinson's narratives about his model "were read by many as powerful support for a trans-imperial, humanitarian campaign against settlers' brutal dispossession of indigenous peoples" (2008, p. 28). Like all celebrity, though, there was an economic dimension to the story as well.

For the European settlers, the success of the Friendly Mission's removal of the remaining Aborigines to Flinders Island had a very positive economic impact. Once the island was pacified, the value of land rose between 50 and 100 percent, and the Crown earned 13 times more from the sale of land in 1836 than it had in 1831 (Lawson 2014, p. 88). Arthur himself profited, both from his mortgage loans to settlers and officials and from the "enormous rise in land values" (Shaw 2004). There was lots more room for sheep too – 200,000 more in 1836 than in 1831. For all the official wringing of hands about the disappearance of the Tasmanian Aborigines, there was clearly an economic upside. As Charles Darwin noted in 1839, the island now "enjoys the great advantage of being free from a native population" [p. 533]. Robinson was very aware of these financial dimensions to the outcome of his Friendly Mission, and he claimed a matching reward for the economic benefits he felt he had been instrumental in bringing to the colony. Every Aborigine he persuaded to come to Hobart attracted a bounty of £5.00 so the more he rounded up, the better his earnings. His celebrity status as the sole architect of the solution to the Aboriginal problem was an important vehicle for the pursuit of that reward; he was keen to secure "subscriptions" or donations from settlers grateful for all he had done for them in managing "hostile blacks," but that meant of course that he had to be known for his efforts.

An important feature of Robinson's humanitarianism, then, as Duncan Andrews (2012) points out, is the extent to which it fitted with Arthurs' and the settlers' concerns, rather than challenging them in any way, as the abolitionist movement had. For Backhouse and Walker the underlying structural problem was clearly the violent theft of Aboriginal land, and in their report to Arthur they argued that greater respect for Aborigines' "natural and indefeasible rights" would have made it possible to avoid "the misery, and waste of human life, that have ensued in this Colony" (quoted in Johnston 2003, p. 102). This was a position far too distant from the concerns of the British settlers for Robinson, who focused instead on "improving" the Aborigines by bringing them the benefits of Christianity and the discipline of industry. It is hard not to notice the tidy profit that this approach generated for Arthur as well as Robinson, which was to make both men very comfortable.

There are a number of aspects of Robinson's humanitarian efforts that are especially important for an understanding of his role as a celebrity humanitarian, including the position of his distinct, particular intervention in Van Diemen's Land in the context of wider networks of humanitarian concern about what "being human" actually means and what implications that understanding has for the ethical conduct of European expansion, as well as the role of his efforts in preventing the suffering of the Aborigines within the overall formation of settler-colonialism and empire.

Humanitarianism and the networks of empire

Robinson was a significant pioneer in an emerging global humanitarian network (Laidlaw 2005) engaging with the condition of indigenous populations, manifested in bodies like the Aborigines' Protection Society (Heartfield 2011, p. 23). The anti-slavery movement had created a set of organizational forms and practices, drawing on existing forms of evangelical Calvinist church organizations, which linked witnessing the suffering of distant strangers with effective political action. Robinson's Friendly Mission was part and parcel of the extension of the anti-slavery movement into the development of policy and practices concerning the treatment of indigenous peoples around the world, in an attempt to make that treatment consistent with humanitarian principles in a variety of ways. Robinson was positioned precisely at the juncture between the anti-slavery movement and the mobilization of its humanitarian principles in an equally important arena, the governance of a period of enormous settler-colonial expansion so as to contain its impact on indigenous peoples within sufficiently humane boundaries (Lester & Dussart 2014, p. 77). Alan Lester remarks that the networks put in place by the anti-slavery movement, organized around "books, pamphlets, prints and artifacts, using all the resources that modern print capitalism, the 'birth of consumer society' and the growth of the 'public sphere' put at its disposal" (Lester 2002, p. 26), were subsequently "redeployed and extended" with respect to indigenous peoples across the empire.

All forms of celebrity were being industrialized in the 19th century with the development of a "public sphere" and the enormous expansion of all forms of printed communication – newspapers, books, pamphlets, etc. – which constituted the waves upon which global celebrity was carried, and Robinson's own celebrity was yet another example of that (Johnston 2009, p. 155). Lester and Dussart (2008) point out that Robinson was in many respects functioning as one of the promoters and vehicles for a particular idea and technology, that of the "Protectorate of Aborigines," which originated in Trinidad, developed in Van Diemen's Land, was refined in London with reference to South Africa, was re-exported to New South Wales, finally ending up in New Zealand.

Elizabeth Elbourne notes the connections between discussions about the treatment of indigenous people in different parts of the British Empire, in particular Van Diemen's Land and the Cape Colony, which were "used as mutually reinforcing examples to argue for the necessity of civilisation as a means to save indigenous peoples from destruction" (2008, p. 90; see also Laidlaw 2012; Ford 2014). Elbourne argues that one can see an emerging class of "experts in indigenous affairs" aiming to "make a career of giving advice" (2008, p. 91), giving the example of Saxe Bannister, the NSW Attorney-General at the time (1824–6), who wrote numerous pamphlets on the rights of indigenous peoples, as well as many letters to wealthy individuals seeking their financial support, "presenting himself as an expert for hire who could advise the government and others on the best road to living in peace with indigenous people" (2008, p. 91). An "international language about 'Aborigines' and a nascent world of would-be policy experts" was slowly forming and, as Elbourne observes, "Robinson was at least in part trying to appeal to this international audience" (2008, p. 93).

Robinson wasn't just addressing a local audience, even though persuading Arthur was the most important immediate practical concern. Hooking up with Arthur's own ambitions, there was an anxiety to persuade officials in London and other parts of the British Empire of the efficacy of his "model" of how to manage indigenous populations in a settler-colonial office, hoping to influence the "center" in ways that would then be mobilized in other peripheral colonial contexts. He was positioning himself alongside figures like Backhouse and Walker, Arthur and other critics of settler-colonial violence as "discussants and interlocutors of empire, colonial morality and of the indigenous peoples dispossessed by empire" (Edmonds 2012, p. 782). He was attempting to produce a "standardized and reproducible script of action" (Stamatov 2013, p. 12) that he hoped could be mobilized throughout the British Empire, accompanied, of course, by a corresponding increase in his celebrity and thus his income. A " . . . product of extensive trans-imperial networking among humanitarians" (Lester 2008, p. 35), his 1837 report to the House of Commons Select Committee on Aborigines (British Settlements) was both an expression of and a vehicle for Robinson's emerging celebrity as "The Conciliator."

The tour of the British colonies – the Cape Colony, Mauritius and Australia – by Backhouse and Walker was an important vehicle for the enhancement of Robinson's profile. The Quakers were pioneers of "long-distance advocacy," generating a celebrity logic in the sense of needing to attract the attention of a large-enough public audience, and of acting as the point of contact or envoy between that audience and powerful policymaking individuals and organizations, vehicles for the message that was being delivered. By the middle of the 1830s, writes Lester, Robinson had gone beyond simply drawing on the existing human-itarianism to inform his endeavors; he was in a position to "shape it by gaining a trans-imperial reputation as an innovative and humane expert on Aborigines" (Lester 2008, p. 35).

Networks need nodes, so long-distance advocacy (Stamatov 2013) or "trans-national advocacy networks" (David 2007; Keck & Sikkink 1998) such as the Quakers or the Church Missionary Society rely heavily on particular individuals to constitute the focal points of a global network pursuing particular humanitarian objectives, and these "nodal individuals" can be understood as the celebrities of the network (Morgan 2013). For individuals who already have a celebrity status in other fields, this explains their role in contemporary humanitarian projects – they have a particular ready-made network of other celebrities and an audience that they can bring to the project in useful ways. But in these early examples (or more recent ones like the New Left in the US in the 1960s [Gitlin 1980]), the price to be paid for this was an amplification of the nodal celebrity's concerns, at the expense of the supposed recipients of humanitarian assistance. In Robinson's case, this took the form of the steady advancement of his own wealth and career, while the Aborigines on Flinders Island died of pneumonia and respiratory diseases.

Conclusion

Robinson is a particularly important example of celebrity humanitarianism because he was dealing precisely with the destructive impact of the expansion of European society itself, rather than some natural disaster, catastrophe or emergency for which Europeans, or Northerners, could not be held responsible. He was part of, and an important contributor to, a global discourse and movement critical of the destructive impact of colonialism on indigenous populations, aiming to counter the barbaric aspects of the expansion of European civilization around the world, to "civilize the civilizers" in effect. Humanitarianism is today generally understood as the provision of aid to the victims not of the humanitarians themselves, but of something or someone else. Here, however, the impact of colonialism was the direct result of actions by Europeans, so in this context humanitarian intervention was very closely tied up with the self-image of Europeans in a way that is less clear and obvious for, say, interventions in relation to the outbreak of Ebola.

This is precisely one of the central critiques of contemporary humanitarianism, perhaps especially with the involvement of celebrities because of the heightened moral claims that are made, and the circularity of the relationship: the aid being provided is made necessary, to a large extent, precisely by key aspects of everyday life in the world of the givers of aid, to which they refuse to give any thought, and which they certainly have no intention of changing. Humanitarian aid is in that sense primarily a salve to their consciences, and it helps to understand the logic of that relationship by looking closely at earlier and more transparent examples of it.

The following four points can be identified as particularly important aspects of Robinson's career as a celebrity humanitarian. First, his example shows that it is important to see celebrity humanitarianism in the context of humanitarianism more broadly, itself in turn deeply rooted in the colonial beginnings of modernity. In this respect any "colonial" or "post-colonial" aspects of contemporary celebrity humanitarianism need to be approached as having developed from that original connection between humanitarianism and the colonization of indigenous peoples. This makes an important difference to exactly how the critique of celebrity humanitarianism is framed, to the extent that it overlaps with the critique of *all* forms of humanitarianism, not just those that happen to be fronted by celebrities.

Second, the trajectory taken by Robinson's endeavors also illustrates the importance of understanding the ways in which all humanitarian action becomes driven by the concerns of the givers, while putting those of the receivers into the background (Barnett 2011, p. 223). The fantasy element of Robinson's account of Flinders Island and how successful it was, contrary to the reality on the ground, captures an important aspect of many forms of humanitarian intervention, accentuated by the role of the celebrity figure, because their positioning within a communicative network, the narrative that is being constructed, becomes the most important issue, not the accuracy of the portrayal of any particular problem or set of actions. "Humanitarianism," writes Barnett, "is the answer when the devout worry about the moral character of society" (2011, p. 227), but this means that establishing the moral character of society takes on a life of its own, overshadowing the sorts of social, economic and political issues underpinning the problems being addressed.

Third, the Flinders Island story displays in a particularly dramatic way the disjunction between the aims of humanitarian action and its actual outcomes. It also illustrates how this contrast is the result precisely of the refusal to question key aspects of the provider of humanitarian assistance's way of life. Edmonds draws our attention to Jenkins and Klandermans' (1995, p. 3) concept of "institutional opponents" – critics of a system or regime who mobilize their critique from within, and remain within the system's overall framework. Humanitarian actors, by definition, are required to leave certain issues out of bounds, no matter how central those issues are to the production of the very problems being addressed, because going beyond these boundaries turns humanitarianism into something completely different – politics. The concept of the Aboriginal protectorate failed because it was conceived solely in terms of assimilation without allowing for indigenous self-determination, making it an impossible route for Aborigines themselves to follow, and then nourishing complaints that it was not a workable model. Together with the settlers' counter-mobilization, this ensured that the concept of Protection was doomed to failure (Lester 2008, p. 28).

Finally, Robinson usefully illustrates the close connections between empire, humanitarianism, and celebrity, as well as why the figure of the "celebrity humanitarian" emerged during the 19th century. As the European empires expanded, the contact between Europeans and indigenous populations intensified, provoking increasing violence and abuse, stimulating greater concern among those with a particular Christian morality about the treatment of other human beings, in turn requiring the mechanisms of celebrity to influence public opinion and official policymakers. Historical figures like Robinson are important in understanding the current configuration of celebrity humanitarianism as the outcome of long and complex historical processes. Colonial and settler-colonial examples of humanitarian projects constitute the foundation of a particular model of "long-distance advocacy" (Stamatov 2013) that underpins all contemporary humanitarian efforts. Humanitarian action has from its origins been organized around global networks of actors, which in turn require celebrities as key nodal points and points of reference for the mass media, putting a face and a body to the humanitarian idea. Celebrities thus play a particular role within all humanitarian projects that can only be properly grasped when one understands the logic of humanitarianism as it has evolved over time, with Robinson an important example displaying early versions of many of its key features.

As an exercise in humanitarian intervention, Robinson's removal of the Aborigines of Van Diemen's Land to Flinders Island was a failure that could hardly have been more spectacular, perfectly fine except for the fact that everybody died. His pursuit of his own personal advancement and celebrity played an important role in that failure, helping to frame the issues in ways that made it much harder, if not impossible, to see how inadequate the intervention actually was. When he was not busy massaging his public image, Robinson could be entirely frank about the outcome of his humanitarian endeavors. It was "an appalling sight," he wrote on Christmas Day 1839, to view all the burial mounds of the Aborigines who had died on Flinders Island. "Look back," he said, "and weep in silence" (Plomley 1987, p. 329). It was a salutary reminder of what can happen when humanitarians get too caught up in their own passion for compassion.

Notes

1 Ekow Eshun, November 21, 2014, BBC One *This Week*, https://www.youtube.com/watch?v=EbVcbdk2G-M [accessed on December 23, 2014].
2 Although we can correctly speak of "celebrity humanitarianism," it is a misnomer to refer to individuals like Bono, Geldof, and Jolie as "celebrity humanitarians," because their primary identity is that of a celebrity, with their humanitarianism coming second, making them "humanitarian celebrities."

3 Anna Johnson interview, ABC RN, The Book Show, June 9, 2009, http://www.abc.net.au/radionational/programs/bookshow/the-tasmanian-journals-of-george-augustus-robinson/3141954 [accessed on December 23, 2014].

4 Idem.

5 The female figure in Duterrau's painting persuading one of the men to approach Robinson is understood to represent Truganini.

6 Anna Johnson interview, see note 3.

References

Anderson, B. 1983. *Imagined Communities: Reflections on the Origin and Spread of Nationalism.* London: Verso.

Andrews, D. 2012. Was the Friendly Mission to the Aboriginal people of Van Dieman's Land in the 1830s an evangelical enterprise? *Integrity: A Journal of Australian Church History,* 1, 57–80.

Arendt, H. 1963. *On Revolution.* London: Faber.

Barnett, M. 2011. *Empire of Humanity: A History of Humanitarianism.* Ithaca, NY: Cornell University Press.

Boltanski, L. 1999. *Distant Suffering: Morality, Media and Politics.* Cambridge: Cambridge University Press.

Brantlinger, P. 2008. King Billy's bones: colonial knowledge production in nineteenth-century Tasmania. In Anna Johnston & Mitchell Rolls (eds) *Reading Robinson: Companion Essays to Friendly Mission.* Hobart: Quintus, pp. 45–57.

Brockington, D. 2014. *Celebrity Advocacy and International Development.* London: Routledge.

Browne, H. 2013. *The Frontman: Bono (In the Name of Power).* London: Verso.

Chouliaraki, L. 2012. The theatricality of humanitarianism: a critique of celebrity advocacy. *Communication & Critical/Cultural Studies,* 9 (1), 1–21.

Clarke, R. 2009. The idea of celebrity colonialism: an introduction. In Robert Clarke (ed.), *Celebrity Colonialism: Fame, Power and Representation in Colonial and Postcolonial Cultures,* pp. 1–12. Newcastle: Cambridge Scholars Publishing.

Daley, P. (2013). Rescuing African bodies: celebrities, consumerism and neoliberal humanitarianism, *Review of African Political Economy,* 40 (137), 375–93.

D'Arcy, J. 2010. Child of the metropolis: George Augustus Robinson in London. *History Australia,* 7 (3), 55.1–55.18.

Darwin, C.R. 1839. *Narrative of the surveying voyages of His Majesty's Ships Adventure and Beagle between the years 1826 and 1836, describing their examination of the southern shores of South America, and the Beagle's circumnavigation of the globe. Journal and remarks. 1832–1836.* London: Henry Colburn.

David, H.T. 2007. Transnational advocacy in the eighteenth century: transatlantic activism and the anti-slavery movement. *Global Networks,* 7 (3), 367–82.

Dowling, W.P. (1967), Robinson, George Augustus (1791–1866). In National Centre of Biography, ANU (ed.), *Australian Dictionary of Biography,* Canberra: National Centre of Biography, Australian National University.

Duvall, S.-S. 2009. Dying for our sins: Christian salvation rhetoric in celebrity colonialism. In Robert Clarke (ed.), *Celebrity Colonialism: Fame, Power and Representation in Colonial and Postcolonial Cultures.* Newcastle: Cambridge Scholars Publishing, pp. 91–106.

Edmonds, P. 2012. Travelling 'Under Concern': Quakers James Backhouse and George Washington Walker tour the Antipodean colonies, 1832–41. *Journal of Imperial & Commonwealth History,* 40(5): 769–88.

Edmonds, P. 2014. Collecting Looerryminer's "Testimony": Aboriginal women, sealers, and Quaker humanitarian anti-slavery thought and action in the Bass Strait Islands. *Australian Historical Studies*, 45 (1), 13–33.

Elbourne, E. 2008. Between Van Diemen's Land and the Cape Colony. In Anna Johnston & Mitchell Rolls (eds) *Reading Robinson: Companion Essays to Friendly Mission*. Hobart: Quintus, pp. 77–94.

Fassin, D. 2011. *Humanitarian Reason: A Moral History of the Present*. Berkeley: University of California Press.

Ford, L. 2014. Anti-slavery and the reconstitution of empire. *Australian Historical Studies,* 45 (1), 71–86.

Gitlin, T. 1980. *The Whole World is Watching: Mass Media in the Making and Unmaking of the New Left*. Berkeley: University of California Press.

Goodman, M.K. 2010. The mirror of consumption: celebritisation, developmental consumption and the shifting cultural politics of fair trade. *Geoforum*, 41 (1), 104–16.

Goodman, M.K. & C. Barnes. 2011. Star/poverty space: the making of the "development celebrity." *Celebrity Studies*, 2 (1), 69–85.

Harris, J. (1990), *One Blood – 200 Years of Aboriginal Encounter with Christianity: A Story of Hope*. Sydney: Albatross Books.

Haskell, T.L. (1985). Capitalism and the origins of the humanitarian sensibility, Parts 1 and 2, *American Historical Review*, 90(2 & 3), 339–61 and 547–66.

Heartfield, J. 2011. *Aborigines' Protection Society: Humanitarian Imperialism in Australia, New Zealand, Fiji, Canada, South Africa, and the Congo, 1837–1909*. New York: Columbia University Press.

Jenkins, J.C. & B. Klandermans (eds.) 1995. *The Politics of Social Protest: Comparative Perspectives on States and Social Movements*. Minneapolis: University of Minnesota Press.

Johnston, A. 2003. The well-intentioned imperialists: missionary textuality and (post) colonial politics. In Bruce Bennett, Susan Cowan, Satendra Nandan, & Jennifer Webb (eds) *Resistance and Reconciliation: Writing in the Commonwealth*. Canberra: Association for Commonwealth Literature & Language Studies, pp. 102–13.

Johnston, A. 2004. The "little empire of Wybalenna": Becoming colonial in Australia. *Journal of Australian Studies,* 81, 17–31.

Johnston, A. 2005. British missionary publishing, missionary celebrity, and empire. *Nineteenth-Century Prose*, 32 (2), 20–47.

Johnston, A. 2009. George Augustus Robinson, the "Great Conciliator": colonial celebrity and its postcolonial aftermath. *Postcolonial Studies*, 12 (2), 153–72.

Kapoor, I. 2013. *Celebrity Humanitarianism: The Ideology of Global Charity*. London: Routledge.

Keck, M.E. & K. Sikkink. 1998. *Activists Beyond Borders: Advocacy Networks in International Politics*. New York: Cornell University Press.

Laidlaw, Z. 2005. *Colonial Connections, 1815–45: Patronage, the Information Revolution and Colonial Government*. Manchester: Manchester University Press.

Laidlaw, Z. 2012. Investigating empire: humanitarians, reform and the Commission of Eastern Inquiry. *Journal of Imperial & Commonwealth History*, 5, 749–68.

Lawson, T. 2014. *The Last Man: A British Genocide in Tasmania*. London: IB Tauris.

Lester, A. 2002. British settler discourse and the circuits of empire. *History Workshop Journal*, 54 (1), 27–50.

Lester, A. 2008. George Augustus Robinson and imperial networks. In Anna Johnston & Mitchell Rolls (eds) *Reading Robinson: Companion Essays to Friendly Mission*. Hobart: Quintus, pp. 27–43.

Lester, A. 2012. Personifying colonial governance: George Arthur and the transition from humanitarian to development discourse. *Annals of the Association of American Geographers*, 102 (6), 1468–88.

Lester, A. & F. Dussart. 2008. Trajectories of protection: Protectorates of Aborigines in early 19th century Australia and Aotearoa New Zealand. *The New Zealand Geographer*, 64 (3), 205–20.

Lester, A. & F. Dussart. 2014. *Colonization and the Origins of Humanitarian Governance: Protecting Aborigines across the Nineteenth-Century British Empire*. Cambridge: Cambridge University Press.

Littler, J. 2008. "I feel your pain": cosmopolitan charity and the public fashioning of the celebrity soul. *Social Semiotics*, 18 (2), 237–51.

Morgan, S. 2013. The Political as Personal: Transatlantic Abolitionism c. 1833–67. In William Mulligan & Maurice Bric (eds) *A Global History of Anti-Slavery Politics in the Nineteenth Century*. Basingstoke: Palgrave Macmillan, pp. 78–96.

Plomley, N.J.B. (ed.). 1966. *Friendly Mission: The Tasmanian Journals and Papers of George Augustus Robinson, 1829–1834*, edited by N.J.B. Plomley. Hobart: Tasmanian Historical Research Association.

Plomley, N.J.B. (ed.). 1987. *Weep in Silence: a History of the Flinders Island Aboriginal Settlement; with the Flinders Island Journal of George Augustus Robinson, 1835–1839*. Hobart: Blubber Head Press.

Pybus, C. 2008. A self-made man. In Anna Johnston & Mitchell Rolls (eds) *Reading Robinson: Companion Essays to Friendly Mission*. Hobart: Quintus.

Rojek, C. (2013). "Big citizen" celanthropy and its discontents. *International Journal of Cultural Studies*, 17(2).

Rae-Ellis, V. 1988. *Black Robinson, Protector of Aborigines*. Melbourne: Melbourne University Press.

Reynolds, H. 2001. *An Indelible Stain? The Question of Genocide in Australia's History*. Melbourne: Viking.

Reynolds, H. 2004 [1995]. *Fate of a Free People*. Melbourne: Penguin.

Richards, T. 1990. *The Commodity Culture of Victorian England: Advertising and Spectacle, 1851–1914*. Stanford: Stanford University Press.

Richey, L.A. & S. Ponte. 2011. *Brand Aid: Shopping Well to Save the World*. Minneapolis: University of Minnesota Press.

Robinson, G.A. 1839. Report on the Aboriginal Establishment at Flinders Island, in *British Parliamentary Paper Commons Australian Aborigines: Copies or Extracts of Despatches Relative to the Massacre of Various Aborigines in the Year 1838, and Respecting the Trial of their Murderers*, pp. 6–19.

Ryan, L. 2004. Robinson, George Augustus (1791–1866). In National Centre of Biography, ANU (ed.) *Oxford Dictionary of National Biography*. Oxford: Oxford University Press.

Shaw, A.G.L. 2004. Arthur, Sir George, first baronet (1784–1854). In *Oxford Dictionary of National Biography*. Oxford: Oxford University Press.

Skinner, R. & A. Lester. 2012. Humanitarianism and empire: new research agendas. *Journal of Imperial & Commonwealth History*, 40 (5), 729–47.

Stamatov, P. 2013. *The Origins of Global Humanitarianism: Religion, Empires, and Advocacy*. Cambridge: Cambridge University Press.

van Krieken, R. 2012. *Celebrity Society*: Routledge.

Yrjölä, R. 2009. The invisible violence of celebrity humanitarianism: soft images and hard words in the making and unmaking of Africa. *World Political Science Review*, 5(1).

Yrjölä, R. 2009. 2012. From street into the world: towards a politicised reading of celebrity humanitarianism. *British Journal of Politics & International Relations*, 14 (3), 357–74.

EPILOGUE

The politics of celebrity humanitarianism

Dan Brockington

> Radical Chic after all, is only radical in style; in its heart it is part of Society and its traditions. Politics, like Rock, Pop and Camp, has its uses; but to put one's whole status on the line for *nostalgie de la boue* in any of its forms would be unprincipled.
>
> *(Wolfe 1970, p. 79)*

> Just so you know, we're on the good side with y'all. We do not want this war, this violence, and we're ashamed that the president of the United States is from Texas.
>
> *(Natalie Maines, singer from the Dixie Chicks, in concert in London in 2003)*

Let me put the statements above in context. The first comes from Tom Wolfe's famous satirical essay *Radical Chic* which was inspired by a moment in the 1960s when wealthy New York socialites invited Black Panther activists for a soirée at their home. The guests mingled to discuss violent revolution over champagne and canapés, while fighting (and, in the Panthers' case, winning) battles as to who could be most stylishly dressed and coiffured *and* radical. The second was an off-the-cuff remark by a singer from the Texan band, the Dixie Chicks, during a concert in London. Its unpatriotic stance triggered a widespread backlash and plummeting sales of their work. It also marked a new political awakening for the band, and a change to their substance, as well as their image.

There is an obvious tension in these statements. One suggests that the radical and the privileged cannot mix with any authenticity. Indeed, the powerful in society will actively co-opt and silence voices which too outrageously, and especially too effectively, challenge their authority. By extension, therefore, celebrity humanitarianism is flawed from the start, because it will be unable to propose any foundational change. The second demonstrates that for all the co-optation and careful PR work, that politics, people and celebrity are simply too unruly to be easily contained.

It is a tension which is actively policed by the systems that produce celebrity humanitarianism. When Jessica Lange (an actress) went on a trip with UNICEF to the Democratic Republic of Congo (DRC) in 2003, she was asked by Ann McFerran (the journalist covering the story) why she was doing this trip. Jessica replied that she was there because she was so ashamed to be an American living under President George Bush because of the damage his foreign policies were causing. Later that evening the UNICEF advisors on the visit told Ann that if she ran that story then it would "destroy" UNICEF's relationship with Lange.[1]

It is a tension which seems to sum up many of the issues that plague celebrity humanitarianism. For, if it is too well organized, celebrity humanitarianism entails bringing highly visible mediagenic people to places which need attention, but then requires them not to speak out on important political matters, and particularly not on some of the root structures and politics that underpin injustice, want and inequality. They can draw attention to causes only so long as those causes do not threaten those in power, even though those in power ultimately hold responsibility for so many of the problems celebrities are trying to highlight. It matters a great deal, therefore, how vigorous and vital this tension is, and how frequently it surfaces. It matters too whether or not this unruliness effects any change.

We can put this problem more generally, simply by asking "what are the politics of celebrity humanitarianism?" There are several aspects to this enquiry. First, what contests over different resources (financial, symbolic, discursive, representational space) are they associated with? What disputes do they make possible, what do they stymie, what do they cultivate? Is it the case that celebrity humanitarianism obliterates the radical, and moreover intentionally and systematically tries to do so? This appears to be the case with UNICEF's engagements, as described above. But if that is the case, then under what conditions might celebrity humanitarians be freer, and attempt to accomplish more?

Second, what actually happens as a result of these contestations? What changes, how quickly and directly, and who notices, benefits and suffers from these changes? Are the only consequences felt in the realm of media text and image? Do they spread to other realms, to policy changes? Do the policies effect any other change? Do they affect urgent development issues such as refugee flows, nutrition, education, capabilities and capacities? This is perhaps the most important aspect. And so, therefore, we must ask too what changes do not happen as a result of these interventions? If celebrity humanitarianism for development causes is ultimately about reducing poverty, alleviating its effects, empowerment, and promoting prosperity, then the persistence of these issues, the lack of change following interventions, is problematic.

In both cases, with respect to contests and consequences, it is useful to explore the contradictions entailed. Contradictions expose the weaknesses of the authentic relationships carefully cultivated over many years between non-governmental organizations (NGOs) and celebrity patrons. They expose the hypocrisies entailed (as we have seen in Affleck cultivating elite politics in the US, but shunning them for their corrupt tendencies in the DRC). They raise awkward questions about the wealth of rich humanitarians, and their tax contributions. The contradictions, and their resolutions and persistence, make clear all the changes, voices and disputes that are silenced or ruled out by celebrity humanitarianism.

And underpinning all these questions lurks a more normative agenda: what politics do we want from celebrity humanitarianism? We can learn a great deal from describing what the actually existing politics of celebrity humanitarianism are – what sorts of contests they constitute, and what sorts of changes they produce. But it is important also to hold in mind a more idealistic agenda.

This agenda, most obviously, might want to makes demands based on the obscenity of continued inequality, poverty and structural violence. But, less obviously, we might be more expansive. Human needs, capabilities and capacities are not simply issues of poverty, hunger and so forth. A richer agenda is possible. Curiously this agenda, expanded fully and including needs for joy, fun and entertainment, would be likely to include celebrity, though perhaps not necessarily celebrity humanitarianism. However far one extends them, my point here is simply that normative mandates need not be restricted to "bare" lives, as Agamben (1998) has argued. Indeed as normative agendas they should not be.

It is worthwhile revisiting the standard texts that Richey cited in her introduction to examine their view about the politics of celebrity humanitarianism (Kapoor, Wheeler, Chouliaraki and my own). For these four capture the general range of responses available thus far, and in particular they capture the general anxiety about these politics in the academic literature. They also make clear the significance and contributions of this volume.

Ilan Kapoor takes a reductionist approach, reading off the politics from the unjust exploitative capitalist relations that must underpin celebrity, and what he feels could quite possibly be the sadistic personalities of public figures themselves (Kapoor 2013). Celebrity humanitarianism for Kapoor is simply about maintaining hegemony and injustice, all cloaked in a repugnant veneer of doing good. Not surprisingly he will have none of it.

Mark Wheeler (and others like John Street whose frameworks Wheeler finds so useful) is more tolerant and pragmatic (Street 2004; Wheeler 2013). For Wheeler celebrity politics cannot be read off from economic relations, but rather are historically specific, contingent and varied. They require, as Wheeler exemplifies, a solid grasp of the detail and the history of their particularities (in Wheeler's case relations between Hollywood and Washington). They reflect both structural and personal forces, but can only be understood, as Wheeler puts it, through "a more intellectually curious critique of celebrity politics" (Wheeler 2013, p. 171).

Chouliaraki's concern is to identify the zeitgeist underpinning what she describes as "an epistemic shift in the communication of solidarity" (Chouliaraki 2013, p. 3). Humanitarianism now focuses on the self, not the other. We are humanitarians because of the self-fulfillment or lifestyles that makes possible. Chouliaraki insists that we have to recognize the narcissism of this move; but this is the starting point, in her analysis, for seeking a more progressive politics. This lies in the fact that humanitarianism has to be *theatrical*; it portrays and represents others' need to stimulate action and empathy. Her analysis of diverse humanitarian events (celebrity visits, rock concerts and news) is concerned with seeking the possibilities of a politics of justice that recognizes the inevitability of theatricality, but not the narcissism.

My own approach (Brockington 2014a) is best summed up by a statement that was uttered to me by a highly seasoned campaigner with many years' experience of working in international development NGOs based in Britain. When commenting about the effectiveness of different campaigning strategies my interviewee said: "If we could do all that [campaigning] without the bother of reaching out to millions of people we would do so. It's cheaper and easier." This person was commenting on the value of celebrity-based campaigning and the importance of getting access to key decision-makers in order to influence their work and change their minds. My source noted the importance of populism to acquire a mandate, but beyond that felt that celebrity-based campaigning was simply much more straightforward.

Another way, however, of expressing this sentiment, is that celebrity humanitarianism is cheaper and easier *because* it is elitist. Because it involves a select few, because it can cultivate and deal with informed, educated opinions. Because its politics and transaction costs involve fewer people, this refined, untainted campaigning can move more easily in its rarefied atmosphere. Elite-led decision-making is easier, clearer and simpler.

As Brendon Cox's analysis of twenty years of celebrity-based campaigning for development causes (and my own work) makes clear, there is a deception involved here (Cox 2011). Celebrity humanitarianism provides a mandate because celebrities signify the public. They act as a proxy for public involvement. They simulate the public to politicians even if, as Cox notes in pretty much all cases they, the public, were not engaged initially.[2] The politics of celebrity humanitarianism is a *post-democratic* politics, privileging the lobbyists and undemocratic corporate influence (Crouch 2004). It is also a necessary politics that NGOs attempting to influence policy have to engage with.

These four authors are quite different, variously despairing, hopeful and wary. But they all share one common trait. For all are rooted in the politics of the global North. They are about northern publics, northern politicians, northern corporations, northern celebrities, media, NGOs, networks, and northern responses. They are based on work undertaken in the global North. They help northerners understand better their lives and their societies.

The contradiction should be obvious. For celebrity humanitarianism is so often concerned with the South, and the relationships that constitute and create it. It is concerned with Southern publics, politicians, celebrities, media, and business interests. It is about the economic, cultural and financial relations within the South, and between the South and North. These are the voices which have been too muted in the academic literature on this topic thus far.

The "South," as Richey has made clear, is not simply a geographical designation. Indeed, the more one explores the category, the more blurred it becomes,
and the greater the diversity it contains. But this just makes the omission, thus
far, all the more glaring. For there is so much going on which has yet to feature
adequately in the current literature.

A central contribution of this collection is that it takes on the challenge of
exploring the diversity of Southern politics that surround celebrity humanitarianism. It thoroughly broadens, deepens and challenges what our notions of the politics of celebrity humanitarianism encompass. For by exploring politics in the South
it both explodes and brings into new relief the categories, ideas and questions that
the politics of celebrity humanitarianism entails.

In the chapters we have seen how Jolie's visits to refugee camps in Thailand
create hope and expectations among Burmese refugees – at the same time as these
same refugees have abandoned hope that the UN organizations for whom Jolie
appears might do anything for them. We have seen how Madonna's charitable
ventures in Malawi have resulted in impoverishment for particular villagers, and
how that poverty is disconnected from the political debates nationally. We have
seen how the grant-making practices and political engagements of Affleck's work
in eastern DRC, dedicated to not cultivating elite politics, throws into stark relief
his thoroughly elitist strategy of political engagements in Washington. We have
seen how South African consumer politics are served and wage disputes constituted, through local celebrity humanitarianism.

In all these cases too we have seen what does not happen. The UN organizations are locally reviled for their inactivity; Afflek's organization tries to evade
particular forms of local politics, and Malawian villagers have become poorer, and
remained poorer as a result of celebrity intervention. The lacunae around celebrity
humanitarians can speak louder than their words.

In exploring Southern politics and specific contexts the book also furthers a second important agenda, which is taking hold within celebrity and media studies. For
it is increasingly acknowledged that the study of celebrity needs to better recognize
the diversity of celebrity industries and cultures in different places. In highlighting the variety of responses to celebrity humanitarianism in Burma, South Africa,
Australia, China and elsewhere, this collection strengthens that agenda. Indeed it is
essential for the South–North program that is central to the enquiry that animates
this book. For understanding North–South relations hinges upon understanding
some of that diversity. Thus the boorishness and insensitivities of populist Danish
culture matter because of what they imply for cosmopolitan agendas of a deep and
rigorous concern for others. They are constitutive of North–South relations. There
is here too a welcome editorial steer that has successfully provincialized each case,
whether it is about Copenhagen, Washington or Johannesburg. At no point have
the authors assumed that their world, their place or even their celebrities, are so
centrally important that all readers will have heard about them.

A further key contribution is the way different chapters have explored the
tensions between structure (system) and agency (personality) at work in celebrity

humanitarianism. Olwig and Christiansen show how politically incorrect celebrity humanitarianism in Denmark stems not just from the minds of the scriptwriters, organizers and celebrities involved. It is a product of Danish audiences, and their expectations and desires. The celebrities are delivering performances that come easily to them given their backgrounds, and which they anticipate will generate the most favorable responses. Similarly Sean Penn's freedom to speak out on Iraq needs to be contrasted to the unfreedom constraining, for example, female stars such as the Dixie Chicks, whose milder outspokenness produced a much more hostile reaction and vilification. Penn's freedom, as Rosamond argues, has to be understood in the context of the construction of his masculinity that US society makes possible, and that Penn's audiences demand. Likewise the Dixie Chicks suffered from not being the sort of women (and, worse still, Texan women) their fans wanted them to be.

At the same time, as I have argued elsewhere (Brockington 2014b), once we pay due attention to structure and system then the role and space for individuality and personality become much clearer. It is hard to argue, for example, that Martin Buch's appearance as an anus in a Danish fundraising telethon was structurally determined. This was not, we hope, a logically necessary expression of the Danish public's will. He and his colleagues invented the role, and indeed their ingenuity provoked much anger from many of their compatriots. Likewise what Sean Penn said (as opposed to its response) owes much to his own views, as do his unusual decisions to spend far more time and money in Haiti than is normally the case. Schwittay's work on Yunus is particularly provocative here. For it is not clear at all to what extent this charismatic approach was necessary for microfinance (and the poor families microfinance is meant to serve) or whether it was necessary for Yunus himself.

And does any emancipatory politics emerge from the celebrity humanitarianism that these cases have examined? Presuming that emancipatory politics are the norm we seek, then the possibilities here seem limited. Perhaps the strongest effects are visible in microfinance, which has affected the lives of millions of people across Asia, Latin America and, more recently, Africa. How beneficial those changes are to the borrowers, and how much they actually owe to the personality of its advocates, are moot points.

But does this expect too much of celebrity humanitarians? If Sean Penn's, Jessica Lange's, and the Dixie Chicks' outrage did nothing to stop violent American foreign policy, should we hold that against them? What if they had been able to succeed? This implies that a similarly unaccountable but strong-willed individual might be able to *start* a war. Perhaps the worst nightmare is that so elitist and unaccountable a politics might actually start to work.

This takes us back to the dilemmas of post-democracy. As Robert van Krieken has pointed out to me, the idea that democracy is elitist is not new. In the late 1960s and early 1970s, with the horrors of fascism still fresh in people's minds, democracy that was excessively populist was feared (Pateman 1970). As Carol Patemen wrote later, "[c]itizen apathy was functional for the democratic system" (Pateman 2012, p. 7).

Rather, the purpose of democracy was to provide genial elites with a mandate that would prevent the fascist tendencies of the public from taking control. Rule of the people by the people for the people could not be trusted to the people.

But there is something new in post-democracy. First, the economic context is completely different. As Tomas Piketty's extraordinary corpus demonstrates, the 1960s and 1970s were a time when the social contract between corporations, electorates and governments produced a different distribution of the benefits of capitalism (Piketty 2014). Tensions between labor and capital were resolved in ways which substantially improved the lives of many laborers. Key measures of inequality, which had dramatically shifted during the world wars, continued to decline. Citizens became apathetic in part because their elites were sharing out the gains of their work more equally than ever before.

Now, however, the climate is completely different. Measures of inequality are rising sharply. There are expectations and "cultures" of huge rewards taking over boardrooms and political leaders that have seen the income, assets and opportunities of the very richest rise far more than those of their lowly fellow citizens, as Piketty's data demonstrate. Hence Colin Crouch's fear of the corporate lobby, because as he puts it "one of the core political objectives of corporate elites is clearly to combat egalitarianism" (Crouch 2004, p 52).

This cultural shift is being resisted. Monographs like Piketty's, notwithstanding their radical critics, provide in accessible language incredible resources for people concerned with the violence that current trends inflict upon so many people.[3] Similarly accessible books such as *The Spirit Level* demonstrate how harmful these trends can be, to privileged and unprivileged alike (Wilkinson & Pickett 2010).

These insights just serve to underline how dangerous celebrity humanitarianism can be. It is using privilege to combat privilege. Key critics of post-democracy, such as Crouch, may insist that elite strategies have to be part of the repertoire of political engagements that NGOs and social movements adopt. But we need to be aware of how risky this is, and how poorly it can serve long term goals.[4]

However, as the chapters of this volume have made so clear (and I hope this epilogue too), before we abandon this means of effecting change, let us properly understand what its politics are, and what its affordances might be. This is the major contribution offered here in this collection. And it stems from the empirical (and often ethnographic) approach that underpins this work. For using privilege to combat privilege may sound like a contradiction, and may reinforce the very categories it seeks to destabilize, but *how* it might do so demands thought and investigation. After all, it is only through careful ethnography of, for example, the conditions under which labor relations are reproduced that we can understand how contradictions and domination are maintained.[5] Likewise any attempt to challenge and explore the possibilities of celebrity humanitarianism requires a similarly empirically well-grounded approach. This means exploring more effectively how it alters the politics, and relations in South *and* North. It means both understanding the systems and the personalities at work. The surprises that crop up when doing so may not all be pleasant, but our prescriptions will not be harmed by better diagnoses.

But perhaps most importantly understanding the actually existing politics of celebrity humanitarianism, in all its diversity, actually creates more room for the normative agendas which can place such high demands upon it. For exploring the actually existing politics allows us to consider what the concrete consequences of these diverse interventions are. It allows us to consider what sort of world is being constituted by celebrity humanitarianism. And doing this, if we become dissatisfied with the results, it is easier to imagine alternatives which eschew such politics altogether.

Notes

1 This story is recounted by the journalist, Anne McFarren, in a LSE podcast in 2009, http://www.lse.ac.uk/newsAndMedia/videoAndAudio/channels/publicLecturesAndEvents/player.aspx?id=85 [accessed on October 8, 2014]. Ann's response to the advisors' challenge was that the story had already broken, and anyway this was something that should have been sorted out between UNICEF and Lange before the trip went ahead. Despite this episode (which is hard to unearth in media coverage of her trip) Lange went on to appear for UNICEF in Russia some years later (which is much easier to find).
2 Cox. pers. comm. January 8, 2013.
3 http://davidharvey.org/2014/05/afterthoughts-pikettys-capital/ [accessed on October 14, 2014].
4 See Crompton and Darnton and Kirk for a similar concern about what celebrity campaigning may do to long-term public values (Crompton 2010; Darnton & Kirk 2011).
5 I am thinking here of Paul Willis' classic work *Learning to Labour* (Willis 1977).

References

Agamben, G. 1998. *Homo Sacer: Sovereign Power and Bare Life*. Stanford, CA: Stanford University Press.
Brockington, D. 2014a. *Celebrity Advocacy and International Development*. London: Routledge.
Brockington, D. 2014b. The production and construction of celebrity advocacy in international development. *Third World Quarterly*, 35 (1), 88–108.
Chouliaraki, L. 2013. *The Ironic Spectator. Solidarity in the Age of Post-humanitarianism*. Cambridge: Polity.
Cox, B. 2011. *Campaigning for International Justice. Learning Lessons (1991–2011). Where Next (2011–2015)?* Save the Children UK and the Bill and Melinda Gates Foundation.
Crompton, T. 2010. *Common Cause: The Case for Working with our Cultural Values*. Godalming: WWF, UK.
Crouch, C. 2004. *Post-Democracy*. Cambridge: Polity.
Darnton, A. & M. Kirk. 2011. *Finding Frames: New Ways to Engage the UK Public in Global Poverty*. London: BOND.
Kapoor, I. 2013. *Celebrity Humanitarianism: The Ideology of Global Charity*. London: Routledge.
Pateman, C. 1970. *Participation and Democratic Theory*. Cambridge: Cambridge University Press.
Pateman, C. 2012. Participatory Theory Revisted. *Perspectives on Politics*, 10 (1) 7–19.
Piketty, T. 2014. *Capital in the Twenty-First Century*. Cambridge, MA: Harvard University Press.

Street, J. 2004. Celebrity politicians: popular culture and political representation. *British Journal of Politics and International Relations*, 6, 435–52.

Wheeler, M. 2013. *Celebrity Politics: Image and Identity in Contemporary Political Communications.* Cambridge: Polity.

Wilkinson, R. & K. Pickett. 2010. *The Spirit Level: Why Equality is Better for Everyone.* London: Penguin.

Willis, P. 1977. *Learning to Labour: How Working Class Kids get Working Class Jobs.* Farnborough: Saxon House.

Wolfe, T. 1970. *Radical Chic and Mau-Mauing: The Flak Catchers.* New York. Farrar, Straus & Giroux.

INDEX

Butt, L. 110
Bystrom, Kerry 93, 95

Cai Guoqing 119
Cameron, J. 53
Cammack, D. 50
capitalism: "Brand Aid" and reconciling
contradictions of capitalism and
inequality 92–3; distribution of benefits
of, inequality and 216; humane 77;
"iCare" 34
Cassim, Shahida 94
Catholic Church in Malawi 50; *see also*
Christianity
"Caught in Micro Debt" (documentary) 84
CBS News 167n61, 168n66
CCP in China: interventionist role in art
of hero production 117; membership
in, as prerequisite for positions of social
and political power 116; *see also* China,
celebrity philanthropy in
celebritization: depoliticization of global
inequalities and 53, 171; industrialization
of celebrity production process 197, 203;
process of, and its effects on participatory
democracy 14, 17–20, 134–5, 136
celebrity: cinematic, as "intimate stranger"
109; cultural specificity of 120,
170–1, 214; defining 8–9, 92, 106;
humanitarianism as driver of, in 19th
century 197; politicized 83; as proxy for
public involvement 213
celebrity activism: coevalness and 100–1;
institutionalized practice promoting
108; post-Katrina 156 (*see also* Katrina,
Hurricane, Penn's efforts to assist victims
of)
celebrity advocacy 6, 18; academic interest
in 30–1; as anathema to democracy 135;
bottom-up view of 134–5; elite politics
and 3, 6, 8, 15, 18, 31, 43, 44, 48–9, 60,
136; increase in 106; rationale behind
134; *see also* celebrity humanitarianism;
specific celebrities
celebrity apparatus 7, 8
celebrity colonialism 92–3, 190
celebrity cosmopolitan aesthetic 28, 29,
33–6, 44
celebrity humanitarianism: apolitical
response conjured by 42; broader

contradictions in 43; centrality of
assessing, across contexts 150; changes
in humanitarianism caused by celebrity
involvement 4; contemporary
scholarship on 3, 5–7, 53–4; crafting of
celebrity authenticity as key concern
53, 54; critiques of, as critiques of
humanitarianism in all its forms 192–3;
dependence on spectacle and politics
of pity 40, 190, 213; depoliticizing
effects of 53–4, 171; diversity of
Southern politics of 20, 214; dynamics
of power within and across North
and South 10–11; Ebola crisis and 1,
2, 3, 21n1–7; everyday geopolitics of
30–3, 44; gendered 30, 32; growth of
30, 106–7; historical roots of 13, 205,
206; importance of understanding
4–5; literature review on 6–7, 133–6;
mandate provided by 213; of 19th
century 192, 197–8, 205 (*see also*
colonialism, celebrity humanitarianism
and); politics of 3, 5–6, 20, 210–18;
post-colonial critique of 59, 60, 190;
structural readings of 149; tensions
between structure (system) and agency
(personality) at work in 210–11, 214–15;
see also Affleck, Ben, in the Democratic
Republic of Congo; Jolie, Angelina,
geopolitics of work in Burmese refugee
camps; Madonna in Malawi; Ndaba,
Sophie; Penn, Sean, humanitarian work
of; Pu Cunxin; Yunus, Muhammad
Celebrity Politics (Wheeler) 7
Celebrity Studies (journal) 5
Cell C (mobile phone network), Ndaba as
brand ambassador for 95
Chambliss, Saxby 147n29
Chapulapula, T. 66n10
charity 11, 30; ECI as public 140, 141
Chavez, Hugo 155
Chengdu shangbao 110
Chen Jiu 110
China, celebrity philanthropy in 17,
106–27; "AIDS hero" and cultivation
of Pu Cunxin 108–9, 113–16, 120–1;
CCP membership and 116; celebrity
health activism and cultivation of HIV
knowledge 109–13, 120; heroism,
civility, and philanthropic acts 116–19